W9-ADS-219

Thirteen for Christ

THIRTEEN for CHRIST

EDITED BY
Melville Harcourt

SHEED AND WARD
New York

© SHEED AND WARD, INC., 1963

LIBRARY OF CONGRESS CATALOG CARD NUMBER 63–8544

"Dorothy Day," by Dwight Macdonald, is condensed from the Profile "The Foolish Things of the World," in *The New Yorker,* October 4 and October 11, 1952.

MANUFACTURED IN THE UNITED STATES OF AMERICA

This Book

is

Affectionately Dedicated

to

Powel Mills Dawley

Priest and Doctor

John answered him, saying: Master, we saw one casting out devils in thy name, who followeth not us: and we forbade him. But Jesus said: Do not forbid him. For there is no man that doth a miracle in my name and can soon speak ill of me. For he that is not against you is for you. For whosoever shall give you to drink a cup of water in my name, because you belong to Christ: amen I say to you, he shall not lose his reward.

—Mark ix, 37–40.

Contents

Preface

The world of fantasy holds many a lesson for the practical-minded. When Alice climbed through the drawing-room mirror into the Looking-glass house it was to find herself in a land of inverse perspective; everything was the wrong way round, and each attempt to reach the distant hill at the end of the garden path failed to bring it nearer. It was only when Alice, thoroughly disgusted, strode off in the opposite direction that she approached the hill. And this, more or less, parallels the psychological experience of modern man.

In a world of decayed traditions and spurious values, a world whose problems seem too large for ordinary folk, men are turning to the State for fulfillment, in terms of personal security, and with the hope, maybe, of rediscovering their fellow men on a basis of organized comity. Alas, the hope is all too often illusory. They discover that bureaucracy is more efficient than humane, and that personal emotions, being stubbornly unclassifiable, hold slight interest for the civic statistician; their awakening is not softened by the knowledge that the State is not omniscient after all, though frequently omnipresent, and that as a man is superior to his garden tools, so he is greater than the institutions he ingeniously creates yet stupidly mishandles. Hence, the wisest of our race turn elsewhere for a solution to their problems. The Christian, with his heritage of personal redemption, turns to the individual who, curiously enough perhaps, brings him eventually to a richer and more replete fellowship—in short, he both loses and finds himself in the historic corpus of the Faith.

It can be argued today that each man—despite John Donne—is no longer an island to himself, but a cog in the machine of State which functions for the material benefit of the mass but for the spiritual enrichment of very few. The individual, often in spite of himself, identifies his destiny with that of the State. And what, we may ask, is the destiny of the modern State shorn of God and, in large measure, stripped of the traditional moralities? On the highest level it is breeding, feeding, and reading with, of course, their myriad ramifications. Men may subdue continents, bridle the incalculable energy of the winds and seas, conquer the entire planet, aye, and worlds beyond, but what does it all mean in the end if a man's soul, in the eyes of the State, is of less value than a conveyor belt and certainly less significant than some astronaut's multi-million-dollar capsule? Far better to be a superannuated horse with a chance of an occasional trip into the clover field, or even a cow who, if given to silly thoughts, knows she is of some use to man's economy on the baby level at least.

Those of us who enjoyed the twilight of man's innocence—say, from 1890 to the First World War—are distinctly uncomfortable in an age which has catapulted the ordinary person's mind and emotions into a global orbit. What happens in Peking today, for instance, may very well alter the whole structure of our private lives tomorrow, and a decision from Moscow is often awaited as anxiously as one from Washington; in other words, the world has become a great backyard in which an international game of hopscotch keeps us hopping through each other's lives. But the game, controlled by puissant yet anonymous umpires, has not brought us any closer together. We find that instead of meeting the stranger on grounds of humanity we meet him on terms of politics; we find that society becomes more and more complex, and increasingly you and I are forced into pigeonholes that negate individuality. We are being taught, in a hundred and one subtle ways, that modern man is the master and measure of all things—"Glory to man in the highest, for man is the master of things," sang Swinburne. It sounds splendid, but is it really true? Hardly. We are obviously the victims of our own ingenuities. World causes buffet us from side to side, competing for each man's petty allegiance, and the State looms larger and larger while the individual grows smaller and smaller. What, then, is to be done? Many things perhaps, but one step in the direction of sanity and equanimity is to rediscover the individual and relate him —true, it seems a bit difficult when you look in the mirror or at the fellow next door—to a purpose that soars above time and circumstance and derives its meaning from the Source of Creation. If the Christian religion cannot provide an answer to our dilemma, what can? And what does Christianity say? As a first step, examine yourself!—but also seek to understand yourself through knowing others, because no man, avers St. Paul, lives or dies for himself alone.

Most of us are curious about people; hence the undying popularity of storytelling which, for the most part, deals not with scenes and ideas but with human beings, their loves and hates, their ambitions and triumphs and disappointments. "I have a smack of Hamlet myself, if I may say so," said Coleridge with fine perception; indeed, every character in literature is but the projection of our vices or virtues, and the irresolution of Hamlet is balanced by the brusque virility of Hotspur. Whoever said, "When you see a good man, emulate him: when you see a bad man, examine yourself" had the secret of spiritual success. It is by scrutinizing the lives of others ("To know a man well, were to know himself," says Hamlet) that we gradually learn the delicate art of living with ourselves and with our neighbors.

The thirteen people in this book have one thing in common— devotion to our Blessed Lord. Whatever their particular milieu, each of them has exercised his talents in such a way as to contribute to the continuity of Christian thought and action in an age of conflicting ideologies. No doubt the arcana of T. S. Eliot's thought and metrical arrangements are a little beyond John Doe, and perhaps, as Lawrence Durrell suggests, the poet has chosen grayness rather than light; but none can gainsay his brilliant comprehension of the socio-religious problems of our time nor how unerringly he sees to the heart of the matter with the observation, "What we are seeking is not a program for a party, but a way of life for a people." Albert Schweitzer's Reverence for Life, even though the terms be modified, is a salutary reminder that brotherhood which is less than universal is meaningless. And the witness of Trevor Huddleston in hate-torn Africa (from which he was expelled to return, ironically enough, as a bishop), the consecrated impudence of Tubby Clayton dragooning generals and night watchmen, peers and taxi drivers into the service of Christ, the plangent voice of Martin Luther King converting the race-ridden emotions of the South into reasonableness—all are shining episodes in the long history of Christian courage.

If the future of our world is to be resolved in the realm of the spirit rather than in the area of material progress, then these men, in their several ways, will serve to illuminate the verities, personal and universal, that ensure the endurance of a civilization which, in the past at least, claimed to be erected on the conscious ideals of the New Testament. The personalities selected for this book are sufficiently various, we think, to reveal the many-sided character of Christianity and its relevance to the needs and urgings of contemporary life. Eliot, it is true, may differ as much from Pasternak as Pope Pius XII differs from Eliot, but they have this in common— they are basically men of faith who, each in his particular way, sees human destiny as a drama conforming to certain timeless and classic rules. Thus Ronald Knox, Dorothy Day, and the like, are skilled and dedicated performers in a drama that has become deeply meaningful to the average man of our time.

Every man has dirt on his hands and gold in his heart, each man is part Judas and part Peter, but yet *men* (as the personalities in this book eloquently emphasize) are all that we have to convey God's message of love and hope to mankind. When a man is old enough to do wrong, he should be old enough to do right also—

therein lies the key to Calvary. Therein, too, lies the essential dignity of man which, ignoring the pressures of life and the menaces of evil things, can define real success in those words of Robert Louis Stevenson: "That man is a success who has lived well, laughed often, loved much . . . who has filled his niche and accomplished his task . . . who leaves the world better than he found it, whether by an improved poppy, a perfect poem, or a rescued soul . . . who looked for the best in others and gave the best he had; his memory is a benediction." It is the standard by which we present this gallery of thirteen modern Christians.

M. H.

New York
MCMLXII

Thirteen for Christ

1

T. S. Eliot

BY PETER KIRK

PETER KIRK *is a son of the former Bishop of Oxford, England, and Member of Parliament for Gravesend, the youngest member to enter Parliament in the 1955 General Election. He was President of the Union at Oxford, and subsequently diplomatic correspondent for the London* Sunday Times *and Foreign Editor of the* Sunday Chronicle. *He speaks regularly over the B.B.C.*

"It is fitting," said Asquith as he left the funeral of Andrew Bonar Law, "that we should bury the Unknown Prime Minister next to the Unknown Soldier." When, in the fullness of time, Thomas Stearns Eliot dies, and if, as seems likely, he too is buried in Westminster Abbey, yet another Great Unknown will be added to the two who are already there—the Unknown Poet. For although he is freely acknowledged to be the greatest contemporary poet in the English language, a man who has had a vast influence on a whole Anglo-American school of poets and playwrights; although such of his doings as the press can get hold of—and he is careful to see that they are not very many—regularly make news, or at least gossip of the kind which now passes for news; although his second marriage to a lady much younger than himself who had been his secretary caused something of a sensation; and although, indeed, he is one of the few playwrights whose plays can fill a theater sight unseen, he remains in himself a most elusive man, and this too, no doubt, is by design.

The average well-informed man, if asked to say what he knows about Eliot, would be in something of a quandary. Of his poetry, unless he was an Eliot fan, he would probably remember very little. "This is the way the World ends, not with a bang but a whimper," almost certainly; the lines are world-famous. The famous and incomprehensible (to the modern generation) couplet from *Prufrock,*

5

> I grow old . . . I grow old. . . .
> I shall wear the bottoms of my trousers rolled[1]

might also strike a chord if only, for the English at any rate, because they have been guyed in review after review on the London
stage for years. Others might recall the sudden irrelevance of Mrs.
Porter and her daughter, about whose origins, as Mr. Clive Bell
has recalled, even Mr. Eliot himself was hazy.

Probing deeper, it would undoubtedly be possible to find the man
who recalls Eliot as the author of about the most devastating short
description of his fellow countrymen which has ever been penned.
"The decent Godless folk," he called us, and no one really resented
it, even though, as an example of uncomfortable truth, it comes a
little near the bone. And this would lead you to the fact that there
is one of Eliot's works which is known to everyone not only by its
title but also by its theme—*Murder in the Cathedral,* the play which
was something of a sensation in the 1930's, and has inspired other
writers, some of them as gifted as Eliot, to tackle the Becket theme.
About his private life, however, little would be forthcoming. Most
people are aware that he once worked in a bank, and is now a director of a publishing house, most know that he is a devout member
of the Church of England—though few realize that he is a convert
to that Church. And some even know that, in his politics, he is
something of an austere Conservative—a British Conservative, of
course, not the American variety; for although his American origins
are not forgotten, they seem to have become suffused with the essential Englishness of the man.

And in all this, the secret of Eliot and his anonymity becomes apparent. Unlike nearly all poets, he is an ordinary man. He did not
starve in a garret like Chatterton; he took a job. He did not die interestingly and young like Keats, or raise the flag of revolution like

---

[1] From *The Complete Poems and Plays of T. S. Eliot* (New York, Harcourt, Brace & World, Inc., 1952). This and the quotations from the same
book which follow are reprinted with the permission of Harcourt, Brace &
World, Inc.

Shelley. He lived a perfectly normal conventional life, midway through which he obtained the highest decoration which his country now affords to those engaged in the arts. The only other great poet with whom he might be compared because of his mode of life was Tennyson; but here the comparison stops short both because of the limited nature of his output, compared with the voluble Victorian, and also because of the revolutionary nature of both style and content. But he is distinguished from other poets also by his deep devotion to the Christian faith, and, in that connection, by his choice somewhat late in life of the Church of England as the means of expressing it. Both this decision, and the decision to become a British citizen, came at about the same time, and were in themselves significant of the man behind the poet.

This is not the place for a long analysis of Eliot the poet, or for a detailed account of his career. It may, however, be convenient to recall how he became the national monument which he now is on both sides of the Atlantic. He comes from Missouri, and though it is sometimes difficult to discern it, he himself is certain that the great river by which he played as a boy, with its overtones not only of the pioneering West, but also of the children's classics of Mark Twain, has had a decisive effect on his own outlook on life. Certainly, the immense spaciousness of his vision, and the calmness with which he has from time to time reviewed our contemporary scene, could both be explained in the terms of the wide flood rolling onwards through the vast prairies to the sea. But all that was many years ago, in the closing years of the last century. The poet has travelled very far since then.

His steps took him first to Harvard, where, from 1906 to 1909 as a student, and for the next twelve months as a graduate student, he soaked himself in literature and began to write poetry. It could not be said that the poems which he wrote in those days made much of a sensation, or indeed, rank among his best work. The first two "Preludes," the "Conversation Galante," and the "Portrait of a

Lady," are all lesser works. Eliot was no "marvellous boy," and it
was not until he was displaced from his native country that the vin-
tage Eliot began to appear. This displacement began the following
year, when he spent nine months studying at the Sorbonne, followed by six weeks in Munich, and it was in the Bavarian capital
that he finished his first major work, *The Love Song of J. Alfred
Prufrock*.

Mr. Hugh Kenner, in what is the major analysis of Eliot's poetic
work, *The Invisible Poet,* traces the origin of this absurd name to a
firm of furniture wholesalers in St. Louis at the turn of the century,
Prufrock-Littau. This would seem to be the only explanation,
though Eliot himself cannot now remember from where the name
came. Mr. Kenner has also pointed out that of Prufrock himself,
although his fame is world-wide, we really know virtually nothing at
all. He remains a voice, a splendid voice uttering sentiments at
times obscure, at others farcical, which have gripped the imagination of millions of people more and more strongly in the fifty years
that have intervened since he first made his appearance on the
world scene. And yet, important as Prufrock's voice undoubtedly
is, his name is probably even more so, for this name alone conjures
up the vision of the man in a way which his laments do not. It is the
first example, in fact, of Eliot's genius with words that makes him
so great a poet. The combination of the strange Germanic name
with the prosaic initial and even more prosaic Christian name—
what, I wonder, did that "J" stand for?—that makes us see precisely the sort of man he is even before we have ever read the
poem. Prufrock, in fact, is a vital figure in the development of
English poetry, even if he never existed, even in Eliot's mind. This
may have partly accounted for the success that attended the poem.
But success did not bring wealth, and the poet was soon back at
Harvard to spend a further three years as a graduate student.

Prufrock was finally published in June 1915, in the American
magazine *Poetry;* but in the intervening years, Eliot's whole life had
been completely changed, as were the lives of so many others, by

the First World War. He had set out for Europe in the summer of
1914 with apparently no thought in his head other than a certain
amount of research combined with a holiday, and then a return for
more work at Harvard, which he was coming to regard as his spiritual home. Certainly, he seems to have had no suspicion that, except for occasional visits, he had now left his native land for ever.
Equipped with a travelling fellowship, he went to Marburg University, and had hardly arrived before the war broke out. At the end of
August 1914, he made his way to Great Britain, and there he has
stayed ever since. He still moved first of all in academic circles,
studying for a year at Merton College, Oxford, but his marriage to
an English lady, Miss Vivien Haigh-Wood, seems to have been the
decisive factor in determining his choice of country. It also turned
his thoughts to the need for obtaining some secure employment, for
he had no money of his own. And this is where Eliot the bank clerk
first appears on the scene.

Actually, the work in Lloyd's Bank was only the last of a series
of temporary jobs which were all that a wartime Britain could offer
an alien. He was from time to time a schoolmaster, a lecturer, and,
above all, a book reviewer. He seems to have written little poetry,
certainly not much which has been published, though it may be that
there is still much to be found from this period which will eventually
come to light. His first book, *Prufrock and Other Observations,* was
published in 1917, and followed by another book of *Poems* two
years later. But all this was merely the preliminary to the work
which will always remain his poetic masterpiece, and by which, outside the plays, he is chiefly known.

The Waste Land was inspired, as its title implies, by the devasta-
tion of Europe at the end of the First World War. First published
in 1922—the only poem, so far as is known, which has ever been
published for the first time with copious notes by the author, notes
which have themselves been more widely studied for clues than the
poem itself—it is an extraordinary combination of reflections on the
terror of the times, coupled with a very large number of straight

cribs from other poets through the centuries, and from all languages. There have been many to reproach Eliot for this plagiarism; as Mr. Kenner has pointed out, they thereby miss the whole point of the poem, for what Eliot was doing was to distill out of the wisdom and imagery of poets through the ages some sort of hopeful message for the people of his generation, battered and lost by the most terrible war this planet had so far known.

It is certainly not an easy poem, nor do the notes make it very much easier. Many of them seem to have been designed as a joke; others were pure padding, as the poem was an awkward length to publish in book form. A lot of the poem reflects the hopelessness and wastefulness of the generation which wanted to do only one thing—to forget the horrors through which they had been, and have a good time. Eliot is not prepared to let them forget. In poetry of at times almost unearthly beauty, at times of horrifying frankness, he recalls them to a sense of their duty in the times that lie ahead. He sees only too clearly the misery which war brings, and the mockery of pretending that anybody can be doing God's will by fighting such a war, a theme which he is to develop at a critical time later on. Eliot is no pacifist; he had in fact volunteered for service with the United States Navy in the First World War, and had been turned down on health grounds. But he has an abiding hatred of the violence of society, which first comes out in this poem and which was to reach its finest expression in the great Christian message embodied in *Murder in the Cathedral.*

This theme recurs again, and even more forcefully, in his next poem, *The Hollow Men.* This poem has never attained the same popularity, nor had the same effect, as *The Waste Land,* possibly because it is in some sense a sequel, and sequels seldom have the electrifying effect of the original. It contains Eliot's most famous line, one which more than any other reflects the true Christian contempt for the pomps and vanities of this wicked world: "This is the way the World ends, not with a bang but a whimper." It is a reference to Guy Fawkes, the seventeenth-century English Roman

Catholic who tried rather clumsily to blow up King, Lords, and Commons and only succeeded in getting himself executed in the most painful way. His exploit is commemorated every November 5th with gigantic bonfires and firework displays all over Britain by children who now have long since forgotten what it was all about.

Throughout this period Eliot continued to work at Lloyd's Bank, to review books, and to edit a small magazine with a strictly limited circulation. In 1925, however, he accepted an offer from the newly formed publishing house of Faber & Gwyer (now Faber & Faber) to join the business, and there he has remained, sharing in the increasing prosperity of the firm, ever since. (If the complete writings of T. S. Eliot are ever published, they should undoubtedly include his blurbs for a vast number of books written by authors far inferior in literary knowledge and style to the blurbwriter himself. There is a certain irony in the thought that Eliot was freed to write his poetry by feeding, parasite-like, on the literary blood of others much less gifted.)

This job gave him for the first time settled employment and an adequate income. It was to be followed by another step of even greater significance. For some years now, he had been rationalizing a somewhat haphazard Christianity into a definite creed. A major step along the way was the study he undertook of the life and work of Lancelot Andrewes, the great seventeenth-century Anglican divine, whose magnificent prose style was to have a marked effect on his work. But much more than the prose style, the life of the bishop himself seems to have been the final copestone on a decision which had long been at the back of his mind. In 1927 he was received into the Church of England.

The comprehension of Anglicanism, that vast sweep of Christian thought, a tradition born out of a revolution but clinging passionately to what had gone before, was perfectly suited to the quiet but determined mentality of Eliot. He has always been something of a traditionalist—despite the revolutionary nature of his poetic style

—as his leaning on his poetic forebears in *The Waste Land* clearly showed. It is therefore hardly surprising that he should have turned not only to the Anglican Church, but to the moderately High Church within it. Not that he has ever been factious in his religion; he has a distaste for controversy which was to show itself very forcefully in political terms later on. The great crisis of Anglicanism which began just as he joined the Church with the rejection of the Prayer Book by the House of Commons, by the votes of those who were not only not Anglican themselves but were, in many cases, bitterly opposed to the Established Church, brought no great protest from him. No one could call Eliot a militant churchman; he does not seek to convert others, only to live his own life by the principles of the faith in which he so devoutly believes. In this, he has managed to acquire a serenity which breathes through all his work from now on. Some might even maintain, and not without justice, that this serenity too often takes the form of a detachment from the world which at times amounts almost to abandonment.

The two specifically religious poems, *Journey of the Magi* and *Ash Wednesday,* which followed immediately on his conversion to the Church of England, show better than anything else he ever wrote his sense of nearness to and living with a God which pervades every sense and thing.

> Suffer us not to mock ourselves with falsehood
> Teach us to care and not to care
> Teach us to sit still
> Even among these rocks,
> Our peace in His will
> And even among these rocks
> Sister, mother
> And spirit of the river, spirit of the sea,
> Suffer me not to be separated
>
> And let my cry come unto Thee.

The five quiet words "Our peace in His will" are a statement of a real, quiet faith, an abandonment not *from* the world but *to* God which must be attained by God's quiet men. Eliot is not one of the angry men; he is the contemplative, expressing his contemplation in poetry as Christian and, in many ways, as mysterious as that of St. John of the Cross. There is, it is true, little of the agony of *The Dark Night of the Soul,* though this can freely be found in *The Waste Land;* there is only the quiet realization that "underneath are the everlasting arms." In *Ash Wednesday,* with all its curious overtones of the search for the Holy Grail contrasting vividly with the sense that the poet himself has already found his Grail, the sheer joy of Christianity comes through with startling clarity and effect.

With the exception of the *Four Quartets,* which were to follow during the Second World War, and one or two minor works, *Ash Wednesday* is the last pure poem that Eliot has written. His activity now turned to drama, with a play which had an effect at the time it was first produced which has lasted to this day. *Murder in the Cathedral* can be considered on a number of different levels. First, it can be regarded as what it outwardly is—a play specially written for a religious drama group to commemorate the most exciting event that the Cathedral Church of Christ at Canterbury, the Mother Church of the Anglican Communion, has seen in its long history. In this respect, it has an importance far beyond that of just another religious play. A devout British actor, Martin Browne, had for some time had the idea of trying to revive the ancient connection between the Church and the stage which had to a large extent been lost with the end of the Middle Ages and the development of the secular stage. It is sometimes forgotten that, up to the Tudor period, plays in Britain were performed only in church, and were exclusively concerned with religious topics. Though Shakespeare was not the first secular dramatist, it was not the least of his enormous achievements in every field connected with the drama that he wrote entirely for an audience emancipated from the absolute Church control over the stage. The fact that the stage in England had merely changed one master for another, the Crown (a dominance still enforced by the fact that the Queen's Chamberlain has the right to censor all plays produced in Britain), could not mask the fact that drama as a whole had acquired a much greater freedom, which Shakespeare was the first to exploit.

But there were still many who resented the passing of the old "mystery" plays, which came with the passage of time and the arrival of the Puritans to be regarded as subversive and idolatrous. For three centuries they were not performed at all, and then Browne and his company of Christian actors revived one of the "mystery" cycles—the York Mysteries—in the 1930's. The experiment was a great success; the York Mysteries are now performed at York every year, and other mystery cycles have been revived with a deep religious insight, culminating in the adventurous but highly successful decision of the actor-manager Bernard Miles to stage the greater part of the Wakefield cycle—the longest and most complete which has been handed down to us—at the Mermaid Theatre in London in 1961.

This revival was, however, a little artificial. All that was being done was to take what was originally primitive folklore and adapt it to twentieth-century conditions. Something was bound to be lost in the process, all the more so when the plays were staged in a theater and not in a church as was originally intended. It is to Browne's eternal credit that he conceived the idea of trying to produce twentieth-century religious drama of a specifically contemporary kind, with a relevance to the very difficult world in which both actors and audiences lived; and also, not only with a definite feeling of Christianity—for there had of course been dramatists before who had written plays from a specifically Christian standpoint—but with a close connection with the Church, God's outward expression on earth, which had been the cradle of the British theater. It is also to his credit that he chose Eliot as the man who should carry out this plan.

Murder in the Cathedral, then, was the first of the new religious plays, designed not only to be acted by Christians as a contribution to Christian thought and living but to be performed in churches. The Church of England, which has always had a much closer connection with the stage than other denominations in Great Britain, welcomed this development as a way in which the lapsed people, Eliot's "decent Godless folk," could be reminded of the fact that everything stems from God, and must be offered to God as part of our service to him. Since *Murder in the Cathedral* the trend has broadened very greatly; there have been a large number of such plays, many of them by poets almost as eminent as Eliot himself, and this too has stimulated an interest in the earlier, less sophisticated plays which these new ones succeeded. Not all of them, of course, looked back to the Middle Ages, as Eliot did, for their inspiration. Christopher Fry's *A Sleep of Prisoners,* one of the most moving and telling of them all, was a strictly contemporary story with a strictly contemporary moral, but it was to Eliot's work that all his successors owed their inspiration.

On another level, *Murder in the Cathedral* is another stage in the study of one of the most fascinating characters in British history. Thomas Becket, as Jean Anouilh has recently shown, and as many other writers both within England and outside have done before, can never be fully understood, even considered within the context of his own time. He is the classic example of the man reluctantly compelled to undertake a task which he does not want, who comes to identify himself with that task, so that eventually he dies for it. The question that is bound to arise in any study of this extraordinary character is whether he was in fact a Christian at all, or whether, having been forced by the King to become the head of the Church, he did not merely identify himself with the Church—for purely personal reasons—in a way which eventually led him to die for it. His martyrdom, in fact, according to this theory, was only the result of a devotion to power politics, and the Stuart monarchs were quite right when they regarded him merely as an ambitious politician, and ordered his festival to be struck from the Book of Common Prayer.

Eliot clearly did not regard Becket in this way, and by confining his play to the last three days of the Archbishop's life, made it inevitable that he would be considered only as the saint he was subsequently recognized to be. At the same time, he was not prepared to swallow the Becket legend whole, and this is where the third level of the play comes in. For in addition to being a retelling, in beautiful poetry, of this terrible story, it is also a study in human pride, the pride which in fact brought two men to destruction. One of the protagonists, King Henry II, never appears in the play at all, but his presence can always be felt there, with the realization that Becket himself is never quite sure why he is adopting the attitude which he does in a matter in which there was clearly a certain amount of justice on both sides. But it is much more than pride in the Church as an institution which is Becket's danger; it is also pride in himself as a man. This is clearly brought out in the scene with the four tempters. These characters were originally intended by Eliot to be acted by the same men who play the four murdering knights, and therefore to give point to a scene which otherwise jars a little where the knights, after they have murdered Becket, engage in a rather futile discussion with themselves and the audience as to why Becket was killed, and eventually reach the conclusion that the only verdict which the coroner can possibly return is one of suicide while the balance of his mind was disturbed. In fact, these parts are usually played by different actors, or if by the same actors, without the point being made that they are meant to be the same, so that the audience tends to assume merely that the company is a little short of personnel.

The significance of the temptation scene, however, lies not so much in this doubling of the roles, or the absence of it, as in the offer of the fourth tempter. The other three have merely offered the normal things, to which any aspiring St. Antony would inevitably be accustomed; the fourth offers something much more subtle—martyrdom.

> Think, Thomas, think of enemies dismayed,
> Creeping in penance, frightened of a shade;
> Think of the pilgrims, standing in line
> Before the glittering jewelled shrine,
> From generation to generation
> Bending the knee in supplication.

As Kenner points out, the appalling proposition put to Becket in this passage is one which he and the audience know cannot in any event be avoided, as it was, in fact, exactly what happened. Eliot is here posing a problem which runs through a lot of his work; if a man knows that the consequences of his acts, which are at that stage in any case unavoidable, will nevertheless be of a nature corrupting to him either in his own eyes or those of other people, what is he supposed to do? If Becket, realizing that the temptation to martyrdom lies heavy within him, tries to avoid the temptation by avoiding martyrdom, he will inevitably fall into one of the other temptations. There seems, in fact, to be no way out for him.

Eliot, of course, would find deliberate incitement to martyrdom more abhorrent to his idea of Christian behavior than almost any other sin. It could hardly fit in with the policy of abandoning oneself to God that he himself favors, and yet he realizes, as does Becket, that only in such an abandonment lies safety, even if it does mean that the unwished-for martyrdom will come. But the martyr must be quite firm with himself. Just as is "Our peace in His will," so

> The last temptation is the greatest treason:
> To do the right deed for the wrong reason.

Becket must make it clear, and does, that the last thing he desires is martyrdom, but that, if it is God's will, he must accept it, and that he will in any event do nothing to avoid it, while making no attempt to seek it. In Becket, in fact, we see something of the forerunner of Luther's "Here I stand, I can do no other"; he is coming perilously close to the Calvinist's predestination. And yet even this is not a fair summary of Eliot's thinking in this strange passage. Becket *can* choose, he can even choose Christian martyrdom, but if he does so, he ceases in fact to be a Christian. For the Christian, the choice will always be offered, but it will be a choice with only one answer, even if the answer itself contains or appears to contain danger, not for the body, for that matters little, but for the soul. It is a hard doctrine, for it means too that the Christian will often, if not always, be in great difficulty in deciding what God's way is for him; but, nevertheless, his will be the blame if he chooses wrongly, or even if he chooses rightly for the wrong reason. Furthermore, the choice to be a Christian in the first place does not end the matter; it merely complicates things further, for it leads to a whole series of further choices, which would not arise if the first choice had never been made in the first place, and the man had chosen to remain right outside the Christian fold, as Becket in fact could have done.

It is a matter of some wonder why, in view of the success both material and spiritual which attended *Murder in the Cathedral,* Eliot has never again tried his hand at this particular type of drama but has left its later development to others. It may be, of course, that he never found another theme in this field which so perfectly fitted his philosophy, but it would seem more likely that he felt that he had, in this play, stated all that he wished to state on the subject, and that he was going to leave it at that. With the exception of *The Hollow Men,* which, to a certain extent, restates some of the basic ideas of *The Waste Land,* he has always been very averse to repetition, a distaste no doubt arising from the extreme economy of language which has been a hallmark of his work from the first.

Whatever the reason may be, although Eliot continued to write plays, they were not religious drama. *The Family Reunion* was the first of these, written in the year the Second World War broke out, followed after the war by *The Cocktail Party, The Confidential Clerk,* and *The Elder Statesman.* All these plays had one strange thing in common; so far from being specifically Christian, they were basically derived from a pagan culture, all of them being based on the great Greek dramatists, though transplanted in terms of English upper-class life. Yet this too is understandable; there is a lot of the Stoic in Eliot. But the fact that they seem to be rooted in something which is often alien to their setting has meant that none of them has attained great popularity, and indeed public interest in them seems to have diminished as each one succeeded the next, and it looked as though the poet had nothing new to say.

This is, of course, an unfair comment. *The Confidential Clerk,* at any rate, which is probably the best of them from every point of view, achieves the remarkable feat of teaching serious philosophy through often extremely funny comedy. Some of the comedy is, indeed, very broad, in an English tradition which at times seems to hark back to Wilde. But the last four plays have never had the success of *Murder in the Cathedral,* and *The Elder Statesman* was received by critics and press alike with the deference due, of course, to any work from that pen, but with the unspoken comment that really it was time that Eliot found a new track to branch off on.

These four plays bring Eliot's published work to an end so far; for he is, of course, very much with us still, and there is much still to be hoped for from him. His private life continues on its even course, broken only by the death of his first wife, in 1947, and his second marriage, to his secretary, Miss Valerie Fletcher, in 1957. He has managed to keep his private life private, in itself no mean achievement in the day of the gossip columnist, and he rarely figures in the press in any but a literary connection. There is one aspect of his public life, however, which has been extraordinarily neglected, and which is of vital importance to our consideration of Eliot as a Christian—that is, his attitude to the relationship of Christianity and politics.

The Spanish Civil War created the greatest upheaval in the British consciousness which has been seen for a very long time. For three years it dominated British public life; it divided friend from

friend, it split families, it caused the deaths of many young English-
men who went cheerfully off to fight in the International Brigade. It
may be that the *crise de conscience* which seized the country during
the crisis of November 1956 was intenser, but that lasted a bare
two weeks; this lasted for three years, and was the prelude to the
Second World War.

In no section of British public life was the emotional disturbance
greater than among the intellectuals. They felt in duty bound to
take sides, and many of them went to Spain to offer their services.
The vast majority, men like Orwell, Raymond Mortimer, Cyril Con-
nolly, poets, writers, and dramatists of all political persuasions,
sided with the Spanish Republican Government; a few, such as the
poet Roy Campbell or the novelist Evelyn Waugh, supported General Franco. But all of them declared themselves, all of them save
one—and that was Eliot. This refusal to commit himself caused a
great deal of comment at the time, as it was known that he was a
devout Christian, and it was felt that in a matter as tremendous as
this, a Christian must choose the path he is going to follow. Anyone who had studied *Murder in the Cathedral* carefully would have
seen that Eliot's idea of Christian choice was something a little different from this; he saw it as an intensely private matter, and one
too which was full of such convoluted byways that it was impossible to say definitely that here was a Christian path. (In any case,
he has always shown the greatest reluctance to take public stands
on issues of the day; it was a matter of considerable remark, for
example, that in 1961 he was prepared to lend his name to the
campaign for integrating Great Britain into the European Economic
Community.)

Very shortly after this, however, he had the opportunity to put
forward at some length his ideas on the Christian and politics in
three lectures, delivered in March 1939 at Corpus Christi College,
Cambridge, on the Boutwood Foundation, and these lectures were
published within a few weeks of the outbreak of the war later that
year under the title, *The Idea of a Christian Society*. Though this

little book—it is a matter of less than a hundred pages, including the inevitable Eliotic notes—has gone through several editions, it is curiously unknown. The theme that it states is not one which was popular at the time, when the air was full of the voices of politicians and parsons informing the world that we were fighting for Christianity against paganism, nor would it be overpopular now, when the same politicians and parsons are using the same phrases, having merely moved the pagans a little further East. Not that Eliot was prepared to condone in any way what Nazis or Communists are doing; he is merely pointing out that, whatever we are doing, and however right it may be—and it is astonishing how relevant the book still is to our times—we are not defending Christian society against paganism, because we are not living in a Christian society. (And here he is not concerned with the number of people who actually go to church, which seems to him to be irrelevant.)

The theme is stated with a characteristic bluntness, which in October 1939 must have seemed even more shocking than it does today.

To speak of ourselves as a Christian Society, in contrast to that of Germany or Russia, is an abuse of terms. We mean only that we have a society in which no one is penalized for the *formal profession* of Christianity; but we conceal from ourselves the unpleasant knowledge of the real values by which we live. We conceal from ourselves, moreover, the similarity of our society to those which we execrate; for we should have to admit, if we recognized the similarity, that the foreigners do better. I suspect that in our loathing of totalitarianism, there is infused a good deal of admiration for its efficiency.[2]

This is strong stuff; stronger is to come, when he considers the changes which we need on our side before we can call our society Christian.

[2] From *The Idea of a Christian Society*, copyright, 1940, by T. S. Eliot. This and the other excerpts from the same book which follow are reprinted by permission of Harcourt, Brace & World, Inc.

. . . my primary interest is a change in our social attitude, such a change only as could bring about anything worthy to be called a Christian Society. That such a change would compel changes in our organization of industry and commerce and financial credit, that it would facilitate, where it now impedes, the life of devotion for those who feel capable of it, I feel certain. But my point of departure is different from those of the sociologists and economists; though I depend upon them for enlightenment, and a test of my Christian Society would be that it should bring about such reforms as they propose; and though the kind of "change of spirit" which can testify for itself by nothing better than a new revivalistic vocabulary, is a danger against which we must be always on guard.

Here we are once again deep in an Eliot paradox. We must want social changes, yet if we want them too much, we are wrong to want them; we must want a Christian revival, too, but a mere Christian revival is "to do the right deed for the wrong reason," the same crime which he has already rejected in *Murder in the Cathedral*. By this time, the average reader must be wondering what on earth it is that Eliot does want, and whether we are not already so sunk in sin that we have no hope at all of getting it. But hope remains, for the remnants of Christianity in our society are not lost: ". . . a society has not ceased to be Christian until it has become positively something else. It is my contention that we have today a culture which is mainly negative, but which, so far as it is positive, is still Christian." This is damning with faint praise indeed, and must have sounded odd in the ears of those who were at that moment being assured that they were fighting for the True Faith against Antichrist.

Eliot then goes on to discuss the alternatives to the creation of a Christian society in our Western countries. He concludes that there are only two (for it is notable that he never at any stage seemed to consider the possibility of the Western countries either being converted to totalitarianism or being conquered by it). One is that Western liberalism might sink into an apathetic decline, rumbling gently on for a generation or so, but eventually becoming extinct—a forecast which some people might regard as having started to become horribly true—or that we might develop our own form of totalitarianism, slightly less vicious than that of the Nazis or the Communists, but none the less Antichrist for all that.

There is in fact nothing left, then, but eventual extinction or the Christian society. And here, his typically complicated mind immediately draws back; hitherto he has talked happily about the Christian society, but when it comes to positive definition, the awful choice begins to rear its head. Eliot puts forward three "working distinctions" as elements in the Christian society—the Christian state, the Christian community, and the community of Christians. By the first, he explains, he means "the Christian Society under the aspect of legislation, public administration, legal tradition, and form." He has some difficulty in describing precisely what he means by this. "I do not mean by a Christian State one in which the rulers are chosen because of their qualifications, still less their eminence, as Christians. A regiment of Saints is apt to be too uncomfortable to last." (Shades of Becket here?) "It is not primarily the Christianity of the statesmen that matters, but their being confined, by the temper and traditions of the people which they rule, to a Christian framework within which to realize their ambitions and advance the prosperity and prestige of their country." No man, in fact, can slough off his own personal responsibility to be a Christian on someone else; the Christian society demands Christianity from all of us.

So what about the ordinary man in such a society?

For the great mass of humanity . . . two conditions are required. The first is that, as their capacity for *thinking* about the objects of faith is small, their Christianity may be almost wholly realized in behavior. . . . The second is that while they should have some conception of how far their lives fall short of Christian ideals, their religious and social life should form for them a natural whole, so that the difficulty of behaving as Christians should not impose an intolerable strain.

From those to whom much is given, indeed, much shall be required, but quite a bit seems to be expected from those to whom little is given. And yet here the poet-philosopher is writing from his own experience. The difficulty of behaving as a Christian had never imposed an intolerable strain on Eliot, once he had taken the decisive step of being a Christian in the first place. And yet, as he makes plain, the type of behavior which he requires is not one which commands much conscious effort. "The religious life of the people would be largely a matter of behavior and conformity," and this is where the "community of Christians" comes in.

This phrase too is not redolent, according to Eliot, of easy interpretation. "These," he says, "will be the consciously and thoughtfully practising Christians, especially those of intellectual and spiritual superiority"—something indeed of the Conservative conception of an elite class. But this statement has been proved to be not far off the mark, especially in Eliot's own chosen Church, for the liturgical movement, which has been active above all in the Church of England, has been designed to achieve precisely this. Indeed, he goes on to define more precisely the group he has in mind. "My Community of Christians, then, . . . could hardly include the whole of the teaching body. On the other hand, it would include, besides many of the laity engaged in various occupations, many, but not all, of the clergy. . . . The Community of Christians . . . would contain both clergy and laity of superior intellectual and/or spiritual gifts. And it would include some of those who are ordinarily spoken of, not always with flattering intention, as 'intellectuals.'"

From this elite, the permeation of Christian values is to spread out both upwards, to the governing body, and downwards to the mass of people. Education plays a primary part here, and Eliot thinks little of the education which is at present available throughout the Western world. Yet, though this elite is to seize hold of education and the professions and arts above all, it cannot be regarded as a group, but as a "body of indefinite outline." But how is this body to be created, and how will it work? This leads inevitably to a consideration of the relations between Church and State, and he considers it, so far is he removed from the banks of the Mississippi, almost exclusively in English terms. For what Eliot has in mind is a "society [in which] the great majority of the sheep belong to one fold." This is to accept a strict discipline, but nevertheless the fact remains that for him the idea of a Christian society can only be realized in England through the Church of England, to which the vast majority of the people of the country owe at any rate a nominal allegiance. Here perhaps might be seen a weakness of the argument, especially for those who have been brought up to believe that an Established Church is, in itself, something immoral and anti-Christian. But Eliot is postulating no theocratic state; merely one in which the state will inevitably move within a Christian framework.

With the form which this state will take, Eliot is not concerned. "To identify any particular form of government with Christianity is a dangerous error: for it confounds the permanent with the transitory, the absolute with the contingent." Nor is he concerned with the way in which such a state might eventually be brought into existence; he is much more concerned to pose the problem than to prescribe the panacea. He even has some doubts whether it can ever be brought about, granted that human beings, who would have to have the responsibility for creating it, inevitably have human failings: ". . . we have to remember that the Kingdom of Christ on Earth will never be realized, and also that it is always being realized; we must remember that whatever reform or revolution we carry out, the result will always be a sordid travesty of what human society should be—though the world is never left wholly without glory."

He concludes this remarkable book with two typically Eliotic touches. First, a footnote written after the outbreak of war, to make it plain that the actual coming of war does not change his main thesis in any way; he is concerned with the eternal rather than with the transitory, which is what the war is. Second, a set of notes by someone identified only as "a distinguished theologian," which criticizes Eliot's argument, and which he prints without comment at all. Not that the criticism is very fundamental, but it is characteristic of Eliot that he will print the opposing argument without in any way trying to counter it.

The Idea of a Christian Society is, like so much of Eliot's work, very puzzling in parts. His lofty unconcern with detail must be infuriating for those who have always got to have their solutions cut and dried, and are never prepared to leave anything for anyone else —or even God—to work out. It is designed to provoke and stimulate thought rather than agreement, and in this it succeeds. It is something of an "ivory tower" type of work, typical of the man and of his faith; no one could call it proselytizing, for the arguments in it are put forward with the greatest diffidence, as if the author himself was a little surprised at the conclusions which he has reached. Yet, despite this, the theme of the book, and the arguments, are as immediate today, as they were when Eliot first put them forward twenty years ago, and it can be read as just as much of a contemporary work now as it was then. It is a great tragedy that, alongside the vast knowledge and scrutiny of his poetry which there has been throughout the world, this little, but vastly important, contribution to Christian philosophy is so little known.

Eliot the Christian stands as an example, rather than as a great teacher or prophet. A man of deep faith, he has no desire to ram this faith down other people's throats. In this reticence, it may be that he achieves more than the more active type of evangelist for whom he professes a thinly disguised distaste. For the example of the quiet Christian contemplative is one which, throughout the ages, has led many other men to Christ; happily, this one is still with us, to teach by example the immense peacefulness of a personal relationship with Christ.

2

Martin Luther King

BY JOHN HOWARD GRIFFIN

JOHN HOWARD GRIFFIN, *a Southerner who achieved remarkable success with his first book,* The Devil Rides Outside, *is a professional lecturer in history and music, with special emphasis on Gregorian Chant. During World War II he was blinded, but dramatically recovered his sight a few years later. He has contributed to various magazines, including* Sepia, *and his knowledge of the Southern Negro is profound: shortly after the publication of his second book,* Nuni, *in 1956, he disguised himself as a Negro and lived as such in the South for many months. The experience attracted national attention, through radio and television, but produced, more durably, the moving and perceptive best-seller,* Black Like Me.

Mrs. Rosa Parks, an attractive young seamstress, walked to a corner bus stop in downtown Montgomery, Alabama, on her way home from work. She was too tired to pay much attention to Christmas festoons that late afternoon of December 1, 1955.

Boarding the Cleveland Avenue bus, she took the first seat in the "Colored" section. Mrs. Parks was physically tired, but she was also tired in a deeper way, tired the way Southern Negroes get tired—tired of a lifetime of being discriminated against.

When the bus filled, the driver ordered the four Negroes who occupied the first row in the Colored section to give up their seats to white passengers. Since such demands were common in segregated communities, three of the Negroes immediately obeyed. Mrs. Parks hesitated. She saw that every seat was taken. If she complied, she would have to stand while a white male rested in the seat for which she had paid her fare. She felt the tiredness, the unbearable tawdriness of being forever second-class, and she quietly refused to move. The bus driver had her arrested. She was jailed on a charge of disobeying the city segregation ordinance.

Ordinarily, this would be an insignificant incident. Such sour notes occasionally disturbed the "wonderfully harmonious relations" southern whites claimed to enjoy with Negroes. Severe punishment usually righted the matter and discouraged others from making similar unharmonious mistakes.

But this time, no. The accumulated resentments of past slappings, cursings and unjust arrests had reached an explosive pitch in

the Negro community. Smoldering indignation flared into massive
protest over Mrs. Parks's arrest. The young seamstress had un-
knowingly touched off a revolution that was to catapult a local
minister, twenty-seven-year-old Martin Luther King, Jr., from obscurity to world prominence.

The Reverend Dr. King, recently out of Boston University, had
come to Montgomery to accept his first pastorate a little more than
a year before the arrest. His whole life appears, in retrospect, to
have been a preparation for the role he was to assume in Montgomery, and later in other areas. Dr. King, himself a Southerner,
had spent years pondering the philosophy of nonviolent resistance
as it related to his religious beliefs and to the problems of oppressed
minorities. Now he found himself in a locality that was engendering
a revolution. Conclusions he had reached in the calm of his meditations were to be tested in a laboratory of harshest reality—the
reality of man in crisis, man capable of behaving at the brute level.

King detests being given credit for the great social revolution that
held the world spellbound for the next year. He points out that he
did not start it, and once started certainly it was the product of co-
operative effort. But without his presence and his long preparation
to assume his leadership role, without his vision and his willingness to set an example of heroic charity, the story would have been
different. Nevertheless, Dr. King seldom acted without consulting
his colleagues in the ministry and other leaders of the Negro community; and wherever we mention King in these pages, we intend
to imply also the actions and counsel of his colleagues.

The Reverend Dr. King's task was gigantically difficult in two
principal areas.

First he had to inspire and persuade his fellow Negro citizens to
channel their outrage and their energies of revolt away from violence toward an absolute Christ Idea of behavior—behavior that
appeared hopelessly idealistic under the circumstances. They must
do battle to gain for themselves and their children rights of which
they were being defrauded under the "System."

This System—a complex of Jim Crow laws and traditions—says in effect that a Negro should pay taxes and defend his country from its enemies, but that he should *not* vote, have equal education, equal protection under the law, equal employment opportunities, equal housing; and that he should *not* have access to public eating places, lavatories, hotels, concert halls, libraries or most hospitals.

In Montgomery, the Negro community had reached a point where the System's inequities were no longer bearable. "Actually," Dr. King explained, "no one can understand the action of Mrs. Parks unless he realizes that eventually the cup of endurance runs over and the human personality cries out, 'I can take it no longer.' "[1]

Martin Luther King's first problem, then, was to inspire his people not only to persevere in their battle for freedom but to limit themselves to a single weapon—the weapon of Love: to return love for hate; to embrace a truth strange to modern ears but which the Negroes' life had uniquely prepared them to understand—that unearned suffering is redemptive.

He asked fifty thousand people to do that rare thing—to make themselves subservient to an ideal (the Christ Ideal) in the face of opponents who made ideals subservient to their prejudices.

The Reverend Dr. King's second problem was to place the Christ Ideal in firm opposition to segregationists who were persuaded that they themselves acted from the noblest Christian motives and who felt it wholly within the framework of Christianity to smear, terrorize, kill or do anything else to protect the traditional Southern Christian System from anyone who sought to alter it. Jacques Maritain has brilliantly summed up the religiosity of racists:

God is invoked, but . . . He is invoked against *the God of the spirit, of intelligence and love—excluding and hating this God. What an extraordinary spiritual phenomenon this is: People believe in God and*

[1] Martin Luther King, Jr., *Stride Toward Freedom* (New York, Harper, 1958), p. 44. This and the quotations from the same book which follow are reprinted with the permission of Harper & Row, Publishers, Inc.

yet do not know God. The idea of God is affirmed, and at the same time disfigured and perverted. . . . [This] is not less anti-Christian than is atheism.

Maritain concludes that this general paganization has resulted in man's placing his hope in force alone and in the efficacy of hate, "whereas a political ideal of brotherly love alone can direct the work of authentic social regeneration: and it follows that to prepare a new age of the world, *martyrs to the love of neighbor may first be necessary.*"[2]

The rarity of Martin Luther King's experience lies in the fact that he not only arrived at essentially the same philosophical conclusions but that he was given the opportunity to demonstrate them in his actions, in his willingness to love and to die not only for the good of the Negro, but for the good of all men.

This is some of the background of a revolution that was to show the world man bombing and beating his neighbors on the one hand and man praying for and confounding his opposition with love on the other hand.

The principal figure in this drama, Martin Luther King, Jr., was born in Atlanta, Georgia, and spent much of his life there. His father, whom Louis Lomax calls one of the most imposing men he has ever met in his life, was the pastor of the Ebenezer Baptist Church in Atlanta. The elder King bitterly resented and resisted the indignities of segregation. As a sharecropper's son he had met all the brutalities of discrimination at first hand and had begun to strike back at an early age. "I don't care how long I have to live with this system," he said, "I will never accept it."

Martin recalls riding with his father one day when the older man drove past a stop sign. A policeman pulled up to the car and said, "All right, boy, pull over and let me see your licence."

"I'm no boy," the Reverend King replied indignantly. Then,

[2] Jacques Maritain, *Scholasticism and Politics* (Garden City, Doubleday, Image Books), pp. 23, 29.

pointing to Martin, he said: "This is a boy. I'm a man and until you call me one, I will not listen to you."[3]

As pastor of the Ebenezer Baptist Church in Atlanta, where he presided over a large congregation, the elder King had great influence in the community and, as Martin observes, "perhaps won the grudging respect of the whites." In any event, the fearless and outspoken father was never attacked physically, a fact that filled Martin and his brother and sister with wonder as they grew older. Martin's mother, an educated and cultivated woman, herself the daughter of a minister, helped provide a warm and secure home in which she and her husband did everything in their power to minimize the crippling effects of discrimination on their children.

Some have contended that Martin Luther King, Jr., growing up in relative comfort and security, never knew the deep, bruising resentments that were the lot of most Negroes; and that his doctrine of love came with a certain facility and was not, in fact, a triumph over hate. But no one not totally insensitive could escape the essential ravages of the System. By the time he had reached his early teens he had been marked to his depths by these bruising resentments.

"I had grown up abhorring not only segregation, but also the oppressive and barbarous acts that grew out of it," he wrote. "I had passed spots where Negroes had been savagely lynched and had watched the Ku Klux Klan in its rides at night. I had seen police brutality with my own eyes and watched Negroes receive the most tragic injustice in the courts. All of these things had done something to my growing personality. I had come perilously close to resenting all white people."[4]

This was young King's state of mind when he entered Atlanta's famed Morehouse College in 1944. A strongly athletic, physically robust, life-loving youth, he evidenced no obvious vocation for the ministry, but his concern for racial and economic justice was already

[3] King, *op. cit.,* p. 20.
[4] *Ibid.,* p. 90.

substantial. Under the stimulus of such thinkers as Dr. Benjamin Mays and Dr. Samuel Williams it became far more profound. At Morehouse, he read for the first time Thoreau's *Essay on Civil Disobedience.* "Fascinated by the idea of refusing to co-operate with an evil system, I was so deeply moved that I reread the work several times. This was my first intellectual contact with the theory of non-violent resistance."[5]

By 1948 his vocation had crystallized. At Crozer Theological Seminary, he began a serious intellectual quest "for a method to eliminate social evil." In addition to his regular studies, he spent a great deal of time reading the works of social philosophers. Soon he had reached the conviction that "any religion which professes to be concerned about the souls of men and is not concerned about the social and economic conditions that scar the soul, is a spiritually moribund religion only waiting for the day to be buried."[6]

The young seminarian absorbed the social and ethical theories of the principal thinkers, from Plato and Aristotle down to Rousseau, Hobbes, Bentham, Mill and Locke.

During this period he began to despair of the power of love to solve social problems. The precepts of Christianity were not for the market place, could not compete against the evil means Christians themselves were willing to employ in order to win their battles.

Then one Sunday afternoon he heard a sermon by Dr. Mordecai Johnson, President of Howard University, who had just returned from a trip to India. Dr. Johnson's talk on the life and teachings of Mahatma Gandhi exercised an immediate and profound influence on King.

As the seminarian delved deeper into the philosophy of Gandhi, his skepticism concerning the power of love gradually diminished, "and I came to see for the first time its potency in the area of social reform. Prior to reading Gandhi, I had about concluded that the

[5] *Ibid.,* p. 91.
[6] *Ibid.,* p. 91.

ethics of Jesus were only effective in individual relationships. The
'turn the other cheek' philosophy and the 'love your enemies' philosophy were only valid, I felt, when individuals were in conflict
with other individuals; when racial groups and nations were in conflict a more realistic approach seemed necessary. But after reading
Gandhi, I saw how utterly mistaken I was."[7] In the Gandhian
emphasis on love and nonviolence, King perceived the method of
social reform that he had sought so long.

During the years that followed, King began to develop his syn-
thesis; to apply the Gandhian principle to the elemental problems of
the segregated Negro. True pacificism, he felt, was not nonresist-
ance to evil, but nonviolent resistance to evil. "Gandhi resisted evil
with as much vigor and power as the violent resister, but he resisted
with love instead of hate."[8]

The crucial point, with King, lay in his growing conviction that
"it is better to be the recipient of violence than the inflicter of it,
since the latter only multiplies the existence of violence and bitterness in the universe, while the former may develop a sense of shame
in the opponent and thereby bring about a transformation and
change of heart."[9]

The love ethic of Christ, the Gandhian method and philosophy
for applying that love ethic, the Sermon on the Mount, a firmly established hierarchy of values—all of these elements anchored in a
realistic knowledge of man that countered false optimism, evolved
through King's years of graduate study at Boston University into
the philosophy that was to play such a positive role in the Negro
revolt. A brief summary of the principal points of this philosophy
reveals that:

Nonviolent resistance is not "passive resistance"—it does resist.

It does not seek to defeat or humiliate the opponent, but to win
his friendship and understanding. The effects of nonviolence lie in

[7] *Ibid.*, pp. 96, 97.
[8] *Ibid.*, p. 98.
[9] *Ibid.*, p. 99.

the creation of a harmonious community, while the effects of violence lie in bitterness.

It attacks forces of evil rather than persons who happen to be doing the evil. "We are out to defeat injustice and not white persons who may be unjust," King told the people of Montgomery.

The nonviolent resister must be willing to accept suffering without retaliation. "Rivers of blood may have to flow before we gain our freedom," Gandhi had said, "but it must be our blood." If going to jail is necessary, the nonviolent resister enters it "as a bridegroom enters the bride's chamber."[10]

Nonviolent resistance avoids not only physical violence but also "internal violence of the spirit." As King often said: "The nonviolent resister not only refuses to shoot his opponent, but he also refuses to hate him." And again: "Love, *agape,* is the only cement that can hold this broken community together. When I am commanded to love, I am commanded to restore community, to resist injustice and to meet the needs of my brothers."

Dr. King's "love-*agape*" is disinterested love. He makes it clear that he is not referring to some sentimental or affectionate emotion. "It would be nonsense to urge men to love their oppressors in an affectionate sense. Love, in this connection means understanding, redemptive good will. . . . It is a love in which the individual seeks not his own good but the good of his neighbor."[11]

In 1954, after twenty-one years of uninterrupted schooling, Dr. King ended his formal training. He had created a positive social philosophy but it remained an intellectual accomplishment, untested; and he had no plans to put it to the test.

Dr. King had offers of two churches in the East, and three colleges had extended invitations to attractive posts. While he was considering these offers—whether to move into pastoral work or into education—he received a letter from the officers of the Dexter Ave-

10 *Ibid.,* p. 103.
11 *Ibid.,* p. 104.

nue Baptist Church of Montgomery expressing an interest in him. This interest soon culminated in a firm offer of the pastorate.

Dr. King considered the available possibilities. Though he had a real love for the South, he loathed the idea of returning to live under its segregated System.

Too, he had recently married and had to consider his wife in this decision. He had met and courted the beautiful and gifted Coretta Scott while she attended the New England Conservatory of Music in Boston. But Coretta was also from the South, from Marion, Alabama. They discussed the matter at great length. A serious musical career for Coretta would certainly be easier to pursue in some northern city. But Coretta was a brave and dedicated woman who was to prove herself extraordinary in the future turbulence. They reluctantly decided that their greatest service could be rendered in the South; that they had a moral obligation to return—"at least for a few years."

Dr. and Mrs. King were well established in the community when Mrs. Parks was arrested for refusing to give up her seat on the Montgomery bus to a white man.

Early the next morning, Friday, December 2, 1955, E. D. Nixon, an outstanding civic leader, telephoned Dr. King.

"We have taken this type of thing too long already," Nixon said. "I feel that the time has come to boycott the buses. Only through a boycott can we make it clear to the white folks that we will not accept this type of treatment any longer."[12]

A meeting of Negro ministers and other community leaders was called for that evening in Dr. King's church. Plans for the boycott were laid. Dr. King noted a strong atmosphere of unanimity and enthusiasm rarely typical of such gatherings.

During the week-end, every effort was made to get into contact with as many Negro citizens as possible. Preachers announced the message: "We can no longer lend our co-operation to an evil sys-

[12] *Ibid.*, p. 45.

tem." Mimeographed leaflets were distributed throughout the community. The news spread.

On Sunday evening, at home with their two-week-old daughter, the Kings discussed the prospects of success. Would the people have the courage to follow through? Would they fear reprisals? Would they act, or would they, as so often in the past, fall back into apathy, fearing that the System was too firmly entrenched?

They agreed that if they could get 60 per cent co-operation, the protest would be a success.

The Kings awoke earlier than usual Monday morning, December 5. They were fully dressed by 5:30. The hours stretched ahead. Would the boycott be successful? What would happen at Mrs. Parks's trial, scheduled for later in the morning?

A bus stop only a few feet from the Kings' house made it convenient for them to watch the opening stages of the drama from their front window. The first bus would pass at 6 A.M.

Dr. King was in the kitchen drinking a cup of coffee when he heard Coretta call, "Martin, Martin, come quickly!"

He hurried into the living room and joined Coretta at the front window.

"Darling, it's empty," Coretta said.

The South Jackson line, which ran past their house, usually carried more Negro passengers than any other in Montgomery. The first bus was always filled with domestic workers going to their jobs. A second bus passed—empty. A third, empty of all but two white passengers.

"Instead of the 60 per cent co-operation we had hoped for," Dr. King wrote, "it was becoming apparent that we had reached almost 100 per cent. A miracle had taken place. The once dormant and quiescent Negro community was now fully awake."[13]

A strange scene for the Old South city: buses drove about empty, with motorcycle police as escorts; Negroes walked or hitched rides

[13] *Ibid.,* p. 54.

to work. Unconventional transportation was seen—men riding mules to work, horse-drawn buggies. The sidewalks were crowded with laborers—many of them elderly people, "trudging patiently to their jobs, sometimes miles away." The atmosphere turned festive. They began to cheer the empty buses. Children sang out: "No riders today," whenever a bus passed.

Events moved rapidly that day. Mrs. Parks was found guilty of disobeying a city segregation ordinance. She appealed the case.

At an afternoon meeting of Negro community leaders, the Montgomery Improvement Association (MIA) was founded to guide and direct the protest. Dr. King, to his astonishment, was elected president. The MIA board included ministers of all denominations, schoolteachers, businessmen and lawyers. These realists wondered if the Negro community could sustain its fortitude and enthusiasm under such hardships; whether they should allow the boycott to continue, with the risk that it might "fizzle out" after a few days, or discontinue it while they were victorious.

They finally decided to let the mass meeting—which was only an hour off—be their guide. If the meeting were well-attended, they would continue. If enthusiasm appeared lacking, they would call the protest off and use its victorious tones to bargain for better treatment.

Dr. King tried to find a few moments of quiet to prepare his talk for the rally. This speech would be of crucial importance. It needed to be militant enough to keep the people aroused and yet moderate enough to keep their fervor within controllable and Christian bounds. He knew that many Negroes were victims of a bitterness that could easily turn to violence.

When Dr. King approached the Holt Street Church, where the rally was to be held, he saw cars lined up on each side of the street for blocks. A crowd of thousands had gathered.

The opening hymn was "Onward, Christian Soldiers." Dr. King says, "When that mammoth audience stood to sing, the voices outside swelling the chorus in the church, there was a mighty ring like the glad echo of heaven itself."[14]

When prayers and scripture readings were over, Dr. King was introduced. Television cameras began to shoot from all sides. The crowd grew silent.

After telling the story of what had happened to Mrs. Parks, he spoke of the long history of abuses that Negro citizens had experienced on the city buses, of which they were the chief patrons. And then this Ph.D. plunged into the heart of his talk in the eloquent language and rhythms of his people:

"But there comes a time that people get tired. We are here this evening to say to those who have mistreated us so long that we are tired—tired of being segregated and humiliated; tired of being kicked about by the brutal feet of oppression. Tired. Do you hear me when I said TIRED? Now we have no alternative but to protest. For many years we have shown amazing patience. We have sometimes given our white brothers the feeling that we like the way we are being treated. But we come here tonight to be saved from the patience that makes us patient with anything less than freedom and justice."

Dr. King then spoke briefly about the legal and moral justification for their actions. He compared their protest to methods used by the Klan and the White Citizens Councils, showing that "their methods lead to violence and lawlessness. But in our protest there will be no cross burnings. No white person will be taken from his home by a hooded Negro mob and brutally murdered. There will be no threats and intimidation."

He concluded with the cautions, urging the people not to force anyone to refrain from riding the buses. "Our method will be that of persuasion, not coercion. . . . Love must be our regulating ideal. Once again we must hear the words of Jesus echoing across the centuries: 'Love your enemies, bless them that curse you and pray

[14] *Ibid.*, p. 61.

for them that despitefully use you.' If we fail to do this our protest will end up as a meaningless drama on the stage of history, and its memory will be shrouded with the ugly garments of shame."

The audience responded with shouts of enthusiasm. After a moment, Dr. King quieted them and made his closing statement:

"If you will protest courageously, and yet with dignity and Christian love, when the history books are written in future generations, the historians will have to pause and say, 'There lived a great people—a black people—who injected new meaning and dignity into the veins of civilization.' This is our challenge and our overwhelming responsibility."[15]

Dr. King described that historic evening as "indescribably moving." As he drove away, he told himself that the victory was already won, no matter what struggles lay ahead. "The real victory was in the mass meeting, where thousands of black people stood revealed with a new sense of dignity and destiny. . . . That night we were starting a movement whose echoes would ring in the ears of people of every nation; a movement that would astound the oppressor, and bring new hope to the oppressed. That night was Montgomery's moment in history."[16]

That night also was Martin Luther King's moment. In effect, everyone there realized that he was calmly making himself the target for the racists' fury—fury that implied not only physical violence but also the more cunning and devastating techniques of character assassination.

But he did not stand alone. Others, notably the Reverend Ralph Abernathy, stood beside him at all times. And the people? They persevered in a crusade that lasted until victory was won a year later. Under the leadership of Martin Luther King and his colleagues, they discovered the invincible weapon of nonviolence and were transformed from a cowed and resentful people to a united,

[15] *Ibid.*, p. 61. Cf. Louis Lomax, *The Negro Revolt* (New York, Harper, 1962).
[16] King, *op. cit.*, pp. 64–70.

hymn-singing, fearless community. They walked for freedom, day after day, month after month. One elderly woman summed up the whole spirit of the movement. Asked if she were tired, she said: "My feets is tired, but my soul is at rest."[17]

With rare exceptions, the white community, including the police and the civic officials, indulged in their customary obstructionist tactics. Unconcerned about clearing themselves with history, they carried on a program of harassment and reprisals against the Negroes. But most of their strategy backfired, because the Negro had changed. He was no longer afraid. He no longer considered it a disgrace to go to jail. He accepted blows, curses, stares of hate as marks of honor. The white community was bewildered by this drastic, inexplicable change, and the racist elements grew more outraged. But everything they did was countered by the singing, laughing, praying Negro.

Typical of this change is an incident involving the Ku Klux Klan. This hardy group, clad in their white sheets, decided to stop the "foolishness" by marching through the Negro section. Always before, when the Klan had marched, the Negroes had cleared the streets and remained invisible. But this time they rushed out of their houses, lined the sidewalks, chattered, waved and cheered as they would at any parade. A sinister demonstration was turned into a festivity. The Klan made no more marches.

The deep irony of the situation did not escape the world. As the months passed and the white community sought in every legal and illegal way to suppress the Negro, as the bombings and beatings increased, the world was given the spectacle of a self-styled "superior race" behaving in a manner far inferior to the behavior of the so-called "inferior race."

The world's eyes focused on Martin Luther King, Jr. This young man had committed himself and his people to Christlike behavior. No matter what they did to him, he had to prove himself exemplary or the whole structure would crash. And yet King himself has never

[17] *Ibid.,* p. 10.

hidden his humanity, his human fears and weakness; he has never played the saint, never indulged in angelism, never assumed the ascetic role. He is a young, healthy family man, deeply in love with his wife and children, deeply fearful for their safety.

Dr. King keeps his intimate spiritual life to himself. He will not discuss it. But his actions have spoken eloquently, and because they have, his philosophy has spread and nonviolence has become the weapon by which the American Negro is gaining his freedom.

What were these actions? Perhaps a single one typifies King's heroism. After months of constant harassment, telephoned threats, assaults, when every day his friends wondered if he would live until the night, Dr. King had somehow managed to survive with a ragged set of nerves. One day a reliable white friend told him that plans were being made to assassinate him. At a mass meeting shortly afterward, King told the people: "If one day you find me sprawled out dead, I do not want you to retaliate with a single act of violence."[18]

He went into a depression of fear, fear of his own inadequacy before the task. "It seemed that all of my fears had come down on me at once. I had reached the saturation point," he said.

That night he reached a point of personal crisis and cried out in desperation to God: "I am here taking a stand for what I believe is right. But now I am afraid. The people are looking to me for leadership, and if I stand before them without strength and courage, they too will falter. I am at the end of my powers. I have nothing left. I have come to the point where I can't face it alone."[19]

The admission calmed him. Three nights later, he went to a mass meeting at the First Baptist Church. A member of his congregation, Mrs. Mary Lucy Williams, came to the parsonage to sit with Coretta and the baby.

The sound of the explosion at his home was heard many blocks away, and word of the bombing reached the meeting almost in-

[18] *Ibid.,* p. 133.
[19] *Ibid.,* p. 134.

stantly. Noting the agitation among some of his colleagues and their worried looks cast in his direction, Dr. King guessed that the disturbance concerned him. He called Reverend Abernathy and asked what was wrong.

"Your house has been bombed."

Dr. King controlled himself and asked about his wife and baby.

"We're checking on that now."

Dr. King managed to hide his agony. He interrupted the collection and told the audience what had happened. He urged each person to go straight home and asked them all to adhere strictly to their philosophy of nonviolence, no matter what might be the result of the bombing.

Rushing home, he saw hundreds of people with angry faces in front of his house. Many were armed. "The policemen were trying, in their usual rough manner, to clear the streets, but they were ignored by the crowd. One Negro was saying to a policeman, who was attempting to push him aside, 'I ain't gonna move nowhere. That's the trouble now; you white folks is always pushin' us around. Now you got your thirty-eight and I got mine; so let's battle it out.'" Violence was in the air.

Dr. King ran into the house and dashed toward the bedroom, where he saw his wife and child uninjured. "I drew my first full breath in many minutes." He learned that when Coretta and Mrs. Williams had heard the bomb land on the porch, they had run for the back of the house. If they had gone to the porch to investigate, they would surely have been killed.

His wife's composure, her lack of bitterness, steadied Dr. King. He returned to the front of the house to try to calm the crowd. There, he found the Mayor and the Police Commissioner, both of whom expressed their regrets. One of King's colleagues spoke up to them.

"You may express your regrets, but you must face the fact that your public statements created the atmosphere for this bombing. This is the end result of your 'get-tough' policy."

The crowd grew and began to get out of hand. Dr. King stepped up and asked for order. He assured them that his wife and baby were all right. "If you have weapons, take them home; if you do not have them, please do not seek to get them. We must meet violence with nonviolence. . . . We must love our white brothers, no matter what they do to us. We must make them know that we love them. Jesus still cries out in words that echo across the centuries: 'Love your enemies; bless them that curse you; pray for them that despitefully use you.' This is what we must live by. Remember, if I am stopped, this movement will not stop, because God is with the movement. Go home with this glowing faith and this radiant assurance."

When he finished there were shouts of "Amen" and "God bless you." And again: "We are with you all the way, Reverend."

Martin Luther King looked out over the throng and saw tears on many faces.[20]

Through physical attacks, jailings, framed-up assaults on his character, Dr. King has continued to lead and inspire not only "his people" but men all over the world. As Louis Lomax remarked, he is like a St. Paul, going from place to place inspiring his people to nonviolent resistance against injustice and then returning to suffer with them.[21] In the market place of harshest reality he proved his thesis: that the Christ Ideal is not only a valid way, but in the case of the American Negro in Montgomery, Alabama, was the *only* way to insure victory: that the highest idealism is the ultimate practicality.

[20] *Ibid.*, pp. 136–138.
[21] Lomax, *op. cit.*, p. 92.

3

Pope Pius XII

BY HENRI DANIEL-ROPS

TRANSLATED BY DOM P. FARINA, O.S.B.

HENRI DANIEL-ROPS, *university professor, officer of the Legion of Honor, member of the French Academy, has long been regarded as one of Europe's most distinguished men of letters. His main interest is religion, on which he has written brilliantly and informatively in a variety of journals and books: among the latter the best-known are,* The People of the Bible, Jesus and His Times, Cathedral and Crusade. *He has been honored by both Church and State, at home and abroad.*

The first Encyclical of Pius XII, "*Summi Pontificatus,*" dated October 22, 1939, was in itself a program of work. Beginning with a reference to Christ the King, placed definitely on a supernatural level, it drew from recent history a lesson which was to inspire his whole pontificate.

"The anxiety of the present," he wrote, "is such a vindication of Christian values that it could not be more impressive. From a gigantic whirlpool of error and anti-Christian hate have derived fruits so bitter that they are by themselves a clearer condemnation of irreligion than any doctrinal refutation." By straying from the Gospel, Pius pointed out, men have lost their way and find themselves poised on the brink of an abyss. Only by retracing their steps can they find salvation. Only Christ can supply the answer to the questions that vex them, and set their fears at rest.

The world, at the beginning of that ghastly Fall of 1938, was about to taste these "bitter fruits." On September 1, at dawn, the German army began its *blitzkrieg* toward Warsaw. It did, indeed, prove to be a lightning campaign. Britain and France both accepted the challenge, first with an ultimatum and then with a declaration of war. Poland, caught between Germany and Russia, collapsed within one short month and disappeared once more from the map. The rest of the warring nations settled down to a conflict that one could foresee would be long, difficult and frightfully sanguinary. The Pope had long seen the war approaching, almost as an inescapable doom. He had done all he could, nonetheless, to prevent it. His encyclical referred to these efforts. He had left no path unexplored "to spare Christendom and humanity at large the horrors of a world conflagration."

To world-wide prayers for peace, he had added a definite and unflagging diplomatic activity. Even as late as August 21, Pius XII had fruitlessly invited the five Great Powers to a conference, to be attended also by the United States and the Vatican, at which all disputes might be peacefully discussed and settled.

Fruitless efforts, indeed, and the Pope, with all the detailed information available to him, had no illusions about them. Yet it was necessary that the world should hear his voice once more, before bomb blasts might drown it forever.

To the very last he exerted what influence he could on the Italian Government by repeated appeals and a final message broadcast on August 22.

When at six o'clock on the morning of September 1 his Cardinal Secretary came to announce that Germany had invaded Poland, Pius XII, losing for once his habitual calm, sought his private chapel and there, kneeling a long time in prayer, gave free vent to his grief.

Could he, the common Father of all, take sides in the conflict? "We shall not," he declared in November 1939, "without being asked, engage in purely temporal or territorial controversies." While he remained ever ready to act as an intermediary, he did not wish the Church to become entangled in the conflict.

There were many reasons for this attitude. His vast knowledge of diplomacy reminded him that all the political initiatives taken by Pope Benedict XV in the previous world war had ended in failure. He realized, too, that by issuing condemnations he would expose to savage reprisals millions of Catholics living under the iron rule of Hitler and his accomplices. Lastly, the entry of Russia into the war on June 22, 1941, had created an extremely complex and ambiguous situation, since, whatever the outcome of the war, victory would be with either one or the other of the powers against which the Church had aligned herself.

The Pope's neutrality was, however, anything but indifference. The Nazi attack on Poland, bringing about, as it did, the destruction of an ancient Christian nation, aroused in him an indignation which he voiced on several occasions. When, for instance, Herr Ribbentrop, Hitler's Foreign Minister, came in 1940 to assure him of an early German victory, Pius XII replied with a detailed list of the crimes committed in Poland by the invading armies.

When, on May 10, 1940, Belgium, Holland and Luxembourg were overrun by Hitler's hordes and the Pope sent the sovereigns of the three countries a message of sympathy, a high Fascist dignitary remonstrated with him against what he termed "taking sides" in the conflict. The Pope's undaunted reply was, "We are not afraid to go, ourselves, to a concentration camp!"

Thus, before brute force, even at the height of its seeming triumph, Pius XII, without abandoning his unavoidable neutrality, stood up as the champion of the weak and the victims of oppression.

The entry of Italy into the war placed the Vatican in a very difficult position indeed. Its tiny territory, surrounded on all sides by belligerent Italy, found itself cut off from the rest of the world, except for such communications as the radio or the goodwill of the Italian Government permitted. Provisions soon grew scarce. Members of the diplomatic corps of the Allied Nations who had sought refuge in the Vatican increased the difficulty.

More delicate still was the problem of maintaining a strict neutrality in order to avoid possible retaliations. Steps had promptly to be taken to this effect. The official organ of the Holy See, the *Osservatore Romano,* was directed not to publish any official war bulletins. Bishops of all the countries at war, as well as those in invaded territories, were given detailed instructions on what their attitude should be: co-operation with civil authorities so far as the law of God permitted; moral assistance to combatants and civilians;

charitable work among war victims, whatever their country of origin.

Such prudent reserve did not however exclude, on occasion, a decisive attitude. The Pope's Christmas messages, remaining as they did on the plane of Christian principles, might possibly be interpreted with reference to either warring faction. But when clear-cut condemnations were issued, it was very clear to whom they applied. The whole world knew whom the Pope had in mind when he denounced anti-Jewish persecutions, the savage oppression of some occupied countries, inhuman modes of warfare, and in a special manner, the indiscriminate bombing of civilian populations.

It would be superfluous to set forth in detail the work of Pius XII in the field of Christian charity during the war; it would also be impossible, because much of it is unknown, and likely to remain so, since true charity works without blaring of trumpets. A few main efforts, however, may be recalled.

The Vatican Bureau of Information, which had functioned in the first World War, was reopened in 1939 and its activities greatly expanded. Under the direction of Monsignor Evreinoff, more than one hundred and fifty priests and religious worked full-time at the transmission of parcels and letters to persons who had no other means of keeping in contact with their dear ones. Vatican Radio, broadcasting in many languages, helped immensely in making inquiries and bringing about reunions. As many as two thousand requests for information were received in a single day.

Material help was sent to every place where a need was known to exist and whenever wartime restrictions permitted: to prisoner-of-war camps, bombed cities, undernourished children in France, Belgium, Greece, Yugoslavia, Ethiopia and the Malay peninsula. The Swiss Catholic Mission of Fribourg, working directly under Vatican direction, especially distinguished itself in this labor of love. Pius XII even sought permission to supervise the conditions prevailing in prisoner-of-war and concentration camps. His Delegate in Washington, Monsignor Cicognani, was thus able to inspect camps in the United States, and papal representatives inspected military camps in France, Germany, Japan, etc. They failed only to obtain access to Nazi concentration camps.

One of the most significant aspects of this charitable activity— significant because of the silent condemnation it involved—was the protection accorded to persecuted Jews. Pius XII openly urged all Catholics to shield them. He led the way by sheltering Signor Zolli, Rome's Chief Rabbi. This gesture so touched the Jewish dignitary that it was not long before he sought admission into the Church. At his baptism he chose for his name the Pope's own, Eugene. Another famous name among the Vatican "protégés" was Pietro Nenni, at that time the head of the Italian Marxist Party.

The Abbey of St. Paul in Rome had become so well known as a Jewish refuge that the Fascist police insisted on searching it. In France, the religious Communities of Notre Dame de Sion as well as Dominican convents throughout the country had become work-shops for the production of fictitious identity cards. Monsignor Feltin himself, then Archbishop of Bordeaux, secreted in his own home the Torah of the Synagogue.

Pius XII emerged from the War as the champion of moral values and the exponent of spiritual ideals. Everywhere in the world peo-ple were aware that out of the shipwreck in which the very founda-tions of civilization seemed to have foundered, there had emerged a man whom the horrors of gas-chambers had not frightened and the blasts of atom-bombs had not shaken: a white-robed old man who, during the conflict, had done nothing and said nothing except in the name of justice and love. The world emerged from the terrible or-deal even more unbalanced than it had been before. If mankind needed proof that war can never solve human problems, the proof was provided by this inhuman conflict. In it some forty million lives were lost, without one of the fundamental ills of mankind being any closer to its cure. True, the two totalitarian regimes that had caused the catastrophe were no more, but the excessive confidence which the Allies had placed in Russia had allowed her, directly or indi-

rectly, to clamp her authority upon three-fourths of Europe. At the
same time Communist propaganda, favored by the ills the war had
left in its wake, began to sow discontent and rebellion everywhere.
Countries in the Far East, such as China, Indonesia, Korea and
Indochina, were soon turned into battlefields which threatened,
each in turn, to spark off another general conflagration. Darkness
descended again upon the world, and with it a racking anxiety: an
anxiety made all the worse by newly discovered means of destruction; all the more hopeless because people still refused to face fundamental problems squarely.

In the midst of this darkness, all the clearer appeared the wisdom
of the Church. If, while the world threatens to crumble, it is necessary to save man from the deadly danger, it is still more necessary
to insist obstinately on the principles on which alone a new and
better order can be built, and to rear a generation that can build it.
These three main tasks are those which, with heroic perseverance,
the Church took upon herself during the post-war years (years, let
us observe, that have a strange analogy to the earliest Middle
Ages).

During this period, better than at any other time, people realized
the wisdom of Pius XI in renouncing for the Holy See all claims to
territorial possessions other than the juridical and, one might say,
symbolical. This policy, aiming at basing the Church's authority
only upon spiritual realities, was espoused by his successor, Pius
XII.

One of the first acts of Pius XII soon after the war—incidentally
one of the most important acts of his pontificate—showed this very
clearly. The Sacred College had been decimated by death and there
were thirty-six vacancies waiting to be filled. When the Consistory
was held in February 1946, of thirty new cardinals only four were
Italians. Thus ended an Italian majority that had continued un-
broken for four hundred years. Cardinals were chosen from regions
that had never had one before—Africa, Asia and Australia, Asia
being represented by a native Chinese cardinal.

The Pope's intention in this Consistory was obvious: he wished to see, in the highest Church assembly, "the greatest possible number of nations and races, so that it might worthily represent a living image of the universality of the Church."

On the international field the Church adopted the same spiritual and supra-national policy. The Pope's voice made itself heard on all questions wherein the moral interests of men were at stake. He denounced, for instance, the harsh treatment meted out to conquered nations; the excessively delayed release of war prisoners (1946); the enforced shifts of ethnic groups (Christmas 1947). One of his most moving messages was addressed to war prisoners all over the world on December 30, 1951. All this while, Papal committees such as the Catholic Assistance Services, the Refugee Organization, and the Emigration Commission served the interests of "displaced persons" who, in their hundreds of thousands, were tossed about the earth like the flotsam of a shipwreck.

Whether it was a question of world-wide organizations wherein nations sought, unsuccessfully, to settle their differences, or of proposals to weld Europe into one single federation, or, again, of attempts at unifying hearts and minds, Pius XII was found ever ready to co-operate.

There is one question, however, that calls for special elucidation because it might seem that on it the Church has committed herself more deeply than is her wont.

The doctrinal activities of the Holy See, these last one hundred years, have been chiefly directed towards the building up of a new world on Christian principles. This teaching, however, had not had, up to 1939, a visible influence on world politicians. Since 1945, however, Alcide de Gasperi, Konrad Adenauer, Robert Schuman, Georges Bidault, Maurice Schumann and several others have drawn upon themselves the attention of the world. There is no doubt that a strong link unites the religious persuasion of these leaders with the policy of international unification which they have pursued. This link is so real that some non-Christians have openly accused the

Church of trying to set up a "black-gowned International." Some have even permitted themselves to speak of a "Vatican Europe."

This accusation is entirely false. True enough, to quote Pius XII, "the Church cannot remain indifferent to the efforts of statesmen to bring about a unification of Europe"; yet we must not forget that the same Pope has also warned that, should such a dream eventually become a reality, it may be interpreted either as a work of pacification or of provocation, and he concluded that the unification of Europe makes sense only as a step to European and world peace. Neither he nor his accredited representatives have ever ventured to pronounce on the appropriateness, or otherwise, of the political and technical structure contemplated for an eventual United Europe.

This, after all, is all of a piece with Pius XII's general policy. After the 1946 Consistory, speaking of the "supra-national character" of the Church, reflected in the varied nationalities of the newly created cardinals, he observed that this quality did not depend on a "mathematical formula" but rather on a "mental outlook." The core of the matter does not lie in the proportionate number of black, yellow and white cardinals, but rather in training a new generation to think in terms of a "catholic," i.e. universal, Church. This Church is not directly concerned with the eventual success of some leaders of the Christian Democrats in constructing a United Europe. She *is* concerned with the formation of a truly world-size type of man, able to bring Christian principles to bear on all human problems.

Thus, in a world that is laboriously seeking rebirth, the recognition of Christian principles and the training of men ready to translate them into practice are, to the Church, tasks of much greater importance than engaging in politics. This explains why a career diplomat like Pius XII, trained by long experience to assess the efficiency of human endeavor at its proper value, should have been more restricted than was his predecessor in the political field. Although on exceptional occasions he took definite positions, it was only because essential principles were involved. Nothing was farther from his intention than to seek world peace in the turmoil of political and partisan strife.

The world at mid-century is divided into two camps, each of which represents a distinct philosophy. Both claim to represent the future of the world and to battle for its advent: Russia the one recognized leader of those who advocate a Communist way of life, the United States of America, in a somewhat less absolute manner, filling among capitalist democracies a role of symbolic guidance. Between these two giants, both claiming world-wide allegiance, has the Church made her choice? Must she make one?

Of the two philosophies of life, one is openly anti-Christian. On the emphatic assertion of its founders, Communism is militantly atheistic. Even when, in practice, this antagonism does not resort to persecution, its opposition to religion is not one bit less basic. On the ideological plane, which ought to be supremely important to a Christian, no compromise can ever be effected between Christianity and Communism.

This utter irreconcilability between Christianity and Communism was outspokenly emphasized in 1947 when Pius XII in his Christmas message denounced as "a traitor and deserter anyone who lends his material collaboration, his services, his resources, his vote to political parties which deny God, substitute violence for right and terrorism for freedom and render international peace impossible of attainment."

Finally, in July 1949, turning the denunciation into a disciplinary decree, the Holy Office struck with excommunication every form of co-operation with Communism, especially on the occasion of political elections. With this decree the Church made her position unmistakably clear and gave her final answer to Communism. Does this mean that she has finally aligned herself by the side of anti-Communist democracies? The question is too complex to permit a clear-cut answer.

The accusation *is* often made against the Church that she makes common cause with Western democracies, especially the United

States of America. Facts, however, do not support this accusation.

Naturally, the Church has no reason for taking a hostile attitude toward nations that respect her rights. When, for instance, Presidents of the United States, such as Truman or Eisenhower, declare that a lasting peace can be based only on Christian principles, the Pope cannot but agree. For this reason Pius XII's genuine friendship for Roosevelt was, to a large degree, extended to his successors.

Again, the dynamism of Catholics in the United States and the solidity of their institutions cannot but strengthen their influence in the Church. The creation of four American cardinals in the 1946 Consistory was a proof of this.

Nonetheless, understandably enough, the Vatican is reluctant to do anything that would suggest that she is "aligned" with the American Republic. When Mr. Myron Taylor, Mr. Roosevelt's "personal delegate," retired at the beginning of 1950 and a violent campaign prevented Mr. Truman from appointing a successor, the Pope did nothing to overcome the difficulty. In a letter to President Truman (June 10, 1950) he makes this clear: "The Holy See has refrained from bringing any pressure to bear upon the question of reestablishing diplomatic relations with the United States, and still refrains from doing so." Thus, the alleged subservience of the Vatican to American interests is merely a fiction of the mind.

Can it be maintained that the Pope has shown a preference for the system of the capitalist democracies?

Inasmuch as democracy claims to stand for the safeguarding of human rights, there is no doubt that Pius XII's sympathies have been with it. He clearly implied it in his Christmas message of 1945, the sixth of the war. "The scourge of war," he said, "would never have fallen upon the world if nations had not surrendered their right to supervise and control the activity of their political leaders." This statement, after all, involves a conception of democracy that rests on the noblest principles of the Christian religion and is pointed out as a basic truth in Western democracies. Democracy, according to Pius XII, is a system wherein "the dignity of man originates from the image of God in man; and the power of the State derives from the God-given rights of the people." It is, therefore, only insofar as democracies acknowledge these truths that they can expect the Church's approval and support.

As for the economic and social system which Western democracies seem to have made their own, there is no reason to suggest that the Church has given them her unqualified approval. In his message on the fifth anniversary of the outbreak of the war, in other words when the Allies were already faced with the task of building up a new world, Pius XII did not hesitate to say that "Christian morality cannot accept a social order that denies, on principle, or renders impossible and vain in practice, the natural right to private property, both as regards consumers' goods and in respect of the means of production." There followed a sentence that calls for deep thinking: "it is not the intention of the Church to give her unqualified support to the present state of things as if it were the expression of God's will."

On the racial question, the teaching of Pius XII is reflected in his frequent condemnations of racial prejudices, especially anti-Semitism, in his approval of President Truman's abolition of discrimination against Negroes in the American Armed Services and Government, and in his instruction to South African bishops to denounce their government's policy of segregation.

There has been, in fact, no occasion on which the Church has failed, through the voice of Pius XII, to remind Western democracies as well as the rest of the world that one cannot pose as the champion of Christian ideals unless he is ready, too, to live them out in practice.

The "politics" of Pius XII, therefore, consisted most of all in his fearless reminders to the mightiest nations of their human and Christian duties. Jacques Maritain speaks in a famous phrase of the "primacy of the Spirit." All the work of Pius XII is summed up in that phrase. Of that work, in some tangible manner, the super-

natural is the goal and the Spirit of God the driving force. To understand the nature of his "political" activity and of his work as a
whole, we must place it precisely where, in his own words, every
human action must be placed: "in the light of divine law and order,
and judge it according to God's own values and laws."

His "political" activity thus forms an integral part of his pontificate and cannot be separated from his role as defender and teacher
of Christianity.

He managed to keep the Church free from worldly politics because he wanted it accessible to every man, to the representatives of
every race. Deep in his thought was the conviction that the Christian—the light of the world—is commissioned by Christ to carry
with him the message of salvation only on condition that, firm in
his faith and ready to face all problems, he also have the charity to
soothe all sorrows and to deliver his message with the generous enthusiasm which the love of Christ inspires.

It is significant, for example, that during the pontificate of Pius
XII large sections of the Catholic clergy devoted themselves to the
demolition of that invisible but real barrier which former generations had built up between the priest and the worker. Significant,
too, that under him new formulae were tried in an effort to revive,
through corporate activities, the spiritual life of the masses. First in
France and then elsewhere, novel and daring forms of apostolate
among the workers were attempted. One such attempt, that of
priest-workers, after receiving initial encouragement, proved, from
all reports, to involve more danger for the priests' holiness than
hope for the reclaiming of souls. For this reason alone, Pius XII, in
January 1954, ordered the French hierarchy to discontinue this
form of apostolate and to essay other ways of spiritual regeneration.

This decision has often been criticized by people who have not
always been aware that some problems have world-wide implica-
tions and can be solved only in reference to their historical context.
But we should not forget that religious congregations such as La
Mission de France, The Missionary Brothers of the Countryside

and Les Petits Frères de Jésus, initiated a similar apostolate on the express order of the same Pontiff.

As author of the Liturgical Revival, that movement which has brought out the inner beauties of the life of the Church, Pius XII will go down to history as the Pope who has brought home to every man and every nation the spiritual reality of the Church.

This "primacy of the Spirit" is especially evident in his missionary work. Menaced or driven back on one side, the Church must make new conquests on another. The work of the missions, to which Pius XI had given such great impetus, received from his successor, too, the greatest care, all the more so as during his reign several missions were faced with grave dangers.

The institution of the hierarchy in China in 1946, and the erection of twenty archdioceses and seventy-nine dioceses just when a Communist regime was setting up its atheistic structure, was an act of courage and faith in the future of this young Christian community. He encouraged and lavished marks of fatherly affection upon missionaries in China, many of whom in Mao Tse-tung's persecution were to crown their work with the palm of martyrdom. But, again, determined to keep the Church on the plane of spiritual interests, he was careful to remind all that they should not confuse Christianity with nationalism.

The frequent choice of native bishops to minister to the vast missionary territories of Africa; the creation of an Indian cardinal; a missionary message to the Church in India; more significant still, the permission granted to Chinese Catholics, in December 1939, to "participate in ceremonies conducted before the image of Confucius or a tablet bearing his name"; the permission given to Western missionaries to wear, in India, the traditional robe of Hindu ascetics —all these and many more are marks of a far-sightedness which, in the midst of perils threatening again to plunge the world into the abyss, beholds the future of the Church from a world-wide point of view and with regard only to her spiritual interests. This broadmindedness is reflected also in his attitude towards the Eastern

Churches—not only those loyal to Rome, which are the object of his special care since they often share in the sufferings and persecutions of their Western brothers, but also towards all separated Christians, whom Catholics must regard as brothers in Christ. Thus, Pius XII ordered prayers for Christians in Russia without distinction of religious affiliation. Frequently he received in audience Protestants as well as Jews, and sanctioned the presence of Catholic priests as "observers" at the various congresses convened by the Reformed Churches.

If the Church would truly fulfill her mission on earth, she must show herself accessible and understanding not only towards men but also towards ideas. It is in this respect especially that we can gauge the depth of Pius XII's thought.

It is a demonstrable fact that mankind is today going through the process of a rebirth. The very bases of civilization, both moral and intellectual, are being called in question. If Catholics wish to avoid a non-Christian solution being given to these problems, they must themselves find an answer for them from within their own faith. One of the most remarkable aspects of Pius XII's activity consisted precisely in this effort to keep Catholics abreast of the times. His teaching deals with the most varied subjects: a teaching contained in such a great number of encyclicals, messages, allocutions and decrees, that it truly represents a "Summa" of contemporary problems and of the answers proposed for them by the Church.

It is not only a question of extraordinary occasions, as for instance when, in August 1950 with his Encyclical *Humani Generis,* he warned the faithful against certain modern theories which, based on imprudent generalizations and a wrong interpretation of new scientific data, posed a danger to the very foundations of the faith.

On ordinary as well as upon extraordinary occasions, vexing questions of fundamental importance were touched upon. Whether it be a line of conduct to be followed in particular cases of conscience, or the duties involved in the exercise of one's profession, or the attitude to be taken in matters of sacred art, so that the mean may be struck between routine mediocrity and banal audacity; whether his discourse be delivered to astronomers or gynaecologists, journalists or industrialists, there is a deep individual message for each person he addresses: a message so pertinent, so coherent that one might almost say it had been inspired.

An intense spiritual animation pulsates within his work. Of his twenty-three encyclicals, at least twelve have, as their principal aim, that of reminding men that the salvation of the world from the perils that surround it depends mainly on humble prayer. And he takes us by the hand, as it were, and leads us to the sources of living water in order to sustain in us the life of the Spirit.

His illuminating encyclical, *Divino Afflante,* published in 1943 in the thick of the war (designedly, perhaps), has given a fresh impetus to deeper biblical studies. The great liturgical movement he fostered, was, as we have seen, intended to nourish in the faithful this interior life of faith.

The Holy Year celebration in 1950 which brought to Rome some three million pilgrims was more than a manifestation of the extraordinary vitality of the Church and a proof of the Pope's personal prestige; it also gave him an opportunity to remind his spiritual children of the necessity of prayer and penance, and to reassert the universal brotherhood of men.

To give one last example, when, on November 1, 1950, Pius XII defined the dogma of Our Lady's Assumption, this definition (which some did not quite understand) was meant to remind us, once more, in a most beautiful and appealing form (a reminder contained even in the so often repeated and so little understood words of the Creed) that beyond the vicissitudes of this earthly life, man's suffering body is destined to rise to the glorious life of the Spirit.

Such was the man who stood at the head of the Church for almost twenty years. What his radiance had meant to the world, and how great his prestige had been, could be gauged on those days of mourning in October 1958 when his death plunged Christendom into deepest grief. A beautiful death, however, and all of a piece with his life, placing, as it were, the final seal upon it. A death in prayer and solitude. A Christian's death.

The world received it as a blow. The press of almost every nation had it splashed across the front pages. One could count on one's fingers the governments that were not officially represented at his funeral. Mankind knew that a great light had gone out. But from beyond the portals of death, the Church can hear his voice, teaching still.

In one of his most thought-provoking encyclicals, *Mystici Corporis* (June, 1943), Pius XII had written that to characterize "the Church of Christ, the Holy, Catholic, Apostolic and Roman Church, there is nothing more beautiful, more excellent and divine than the expression that calls her the Mystical Body of Jesus Christ."

What the work of Pius XII (a continuation and extension of the work of his predecessors) teaches us is that the Church would lose her meaning as well as her chances of success and her transcendent significance if, in her affirmations and denials, in her sorrows and hopes, she ceased effectively to be the Body of the Living Christ, abiding among men until the consummation of the world.

4

Paul Tillich

BY JOHN EDWIN SMITH

JOHN EDWIN SMITH *is a member of the faculty of Yale University, where he lectures in philosophy. His specialty is also a hobby, and he is much in demand as a public speaker and a contributor to learned publications, philosophical and theological. Among his published works are,* The Individual, The Religious Symbol and the Community; Beyond Realism and Idealism; *and* Royce's Social Infinite.

How shall we understand the powerful impact which Paul Tillich is having upon the American religious scene? Is it not surprising that a German theologian with a complex system of thought has come to be known and read by countless ministers and laymen across all denominations in American Protestantism? And is it not striking as well that his theology has engaged the attention of many who have little or no relationship with the Christian churches or organized religion? German thought has always been famous for its profundity and notorious for its obscurity, whereas the American intellectual climate has been marked by its practicality. Can these different tempers be related so that we can understand the phenomenon of Tillich in America and his ever widening influence upon Protestant thought?

The answers to these questions lie first of all with the man and his works, with the experience he has undergone and the manner in which he has related Christian faith to it. But there is also another side to the story; we must attend to those factors in modern life that have brought about the revival of concern for the questions of religion and the problems of theology. As the philosopher Hegel pointed out, events of historical moment always take place at an intersection, a crossroads where the demands of an age meet the career of a man who knows how to diagnose its problems and to prescribe needed correctives. Tillich's life and work upon the American scene represent such an intersection. We can understand both if we focus upon his main ideas and the problems to which they are a response.

Like countless others during those tragic years, Tillich came to America as a result of the Nazi tyranny. As a leader among those known as Religious Socialists—Christians committed to showing the bearing of Christian beliefs upon the organization of society and culture—Tillich saw the final impossibility of remaining with the Germany of Hitler. Born in 1886 in a village in the province of Brandenburg, Tillich was educated at a humanistic *gymnasium* and later became a theological student in the faculties of Berlin, Tübingen, and Halle. In 1912 he received his Doctor's degree in Philosophy at Breslau and became Licentiate in theology at Halle during the following year. His background thus prepared him for that dialogue between philosophy and theology which has determined the form of his thought ever since. In 1912 Tillich was ordained into the Evangelical Lutheran Church and two years later joined the German Army as a chaplain. After the war he began his teaching career at the University of Berlin.

In the years to come he was called to the University of Marburg, a place known to all devoted students of Protestantism's history, and then to Dresden. Tillich's call to the University of Frankfurt as Professor of Philosophy came in 1929; he remained until his dismissal in 1933, the year of Hitler's advent. In that same year he was brought to this country through the efforts of Reinhold Niebuhr and the interest of Professor Horace Friess at Columbia University. As he himself writes, "To begin life anew in the United States at forty-seven years of age and without even a minimum knowledge of the language was rather difficult." He met those difficulties with the courage about which he has written so vigorously. Union Theological Seminary called him to a chair in theology, where he continued teaching until his retirement a few years ago. He is at present University Professor at Harvard University.

Let us begin with the man and some of the basic religious interpretations he developed over the decades that have spanned two world wars and witnessed the deepest upheavals in Western civilization since the end of the Middle Ages. If we can come to some understanding of Tillich's central Christian convictions, we shall be in an advantageous position to comprehend their bearing upon the religious situation in which he has worked since coming to America. I believe we shall find that the time at which he appeared in America represents what he has called a *Kairos* or "right time" under the guidance of the divine Providence. We shall see that he has given us ideas of vital importance and we have given to him a new sense of the openness of things and the power of faith as risk accompanied by courage. Neither could have profited from the other were the time not "right."

Christianity has given birth to many types of theologians, and they have not all understood their office in the same way. Tillich has always viewed the task of the theologian as that of an *interpreter,* one who stands between two minds, or two ages, or two cultures, and attempts to bring them to mutual understanding. Applied to the special office of the Christian thinker, this means that the theologian starts out with the ancient and perennial gospel of a living God who has manifested his own nature in the figure of one called the Christ. Tillich has continually insisted that the theologian is always "under orders" to communicate in every age the classic and, in a sense, timeless doctrine. He must speak, however, to people who are very much in time and whose life continues amid the turmoils and upheavals of the ever changing present. The theologian's high office is to communicate the ancient gospel to the mind of the time in which he lives. At every period in the life of the Christian churches the office of interpreter has had to be filled anew. Augustine had to fill it for the fourth-century Christian and Thomas Aquinas for the thirteenth; Luther and Calvin performed the task in the sixteenth century. It can never be done once for all because history marches on and the man to whom we must speak marches along with it.

Tillich's conception of the theologian's task takes us to the very

heart of his thought. A formula which he expressed many years ago
runs as follows: Religion is the soul of culture, and culture is the
body of religion. In many writings, but especially in his recent book
of essays, *The Theology of Culture,* he has developed this theme.
Christianity is not the enemy of cultural life, holding itself aloof
from the city of earth and retreating into a special sphere of its own.
Christianity gives to cultural life an ultimate meaning, at the same
time standing over it as a judge. Culture from its side gives embodi-
ment to the religious concern. The theologian himself illustrates the
relationship. He must immerse himself in the culture of his time in
order to discover its religious roots, for no culture can preserve itself without them, or a substitute for them. Having done so, the
theologian must show the relation between the Christian message
and the problems surrounding human life. The theologian can relate his perennial Christian message to these problems because he
has participated in them himself and knows the idiom in which to
speak.

A major source of Tillich's power as a religious thinker and
writer is his ability to convince us that he knows what problems do
confront the man of the twentieth century who would call himself a
Christian. Like Kierkegaard, who tried to bring home to the modern man the costs of being a disciple in a world of science, technology and organization, Tillich communicates at once his deep
awareness of our predicament. He knows how infinitely strange the
traditional language of theology—sin, atonement, trinity, redemption—must sound in a world dominated by the mind of the physi-
cist and the will of the engineer. And instead of supposing that
Christian belief will communicate itself merely through the medium
of dogmatic preaching, he tries to show what its doctrines mean in
terms of current experience and language. Thus he speaks of estrangement as the inner meaning of sin, and of courage as the inner
meaning of faith; he speaks of ultimate concern as the experience
in which the presence of God becomes manifest and he speaks of
the New Being as the inner meaning of Christ, the One in whom

God makes plain his overcoming of the tragedy into which the world has fallen. It is not, as some critics have claimed, that Tillich abandons classical Christianity in favor of some private inventions; on the contrary, he is asking what its cardinal doctrines mean in terms of the experience of modern man. Knowing that when the average churchgoer hears the term "sin" he is likely to pass it off as a conventional piece of the preacher's rhetoric, Tillich tries to engage him by showing that his own life is separated from or estranged from a Divine foundation. He tries to point out that this separation comes about through our own rebelliousness, our refusal to accept from the divine Love a forgiveness which we cannot give to ourselves. Anyone who reads the sermon "You Are Accepted" in *The Shaking of the Foundations* will come to understand both forgiveness and sin at the same time; he will grasp the inner meaning of what traditional Christianity calls the grace of God. And he will, moreover, come to a realization of why it is so difficult for us to accept this gospel; so completely moralistic are we that we cannot abandon the idea that to be accepted by another we must first be acceptable in our own eyes. But the essence of the divine forgiveness that bridges the gap between ourselves and the Foundation of life is that there is One who accepts us even though we are imperfect, unjust, self-seeking—in short, unacceptable in the reckoning of those who know only the law.

We could continue through the whole of Tillich's thought, showing how the doctrines of God and of Christ, of the Spirit and of Providence, of Faith and of Atonement are all interpreted in a way which enters into the life, experience, and thought of the contemporary man. We need not carry out such an ambitious project; we need only to show how Tillich's conception of his task as a Christian theologian leads him into a dialogue with human culture and into profound sharing in the problems we all confront.

It is essential to his way of presenting Christianity that every Christian conviction be set in relation to the human problem or predicament which it is meant to resolve. He soon learned that no teaching is more empty and no preaching more futile than that which tries to provide answers to questions which no one is raising. He is also aware that no man can speak with power to the problems of another unless he makes it plain that they are his problems as well.

Important as a man's basic conception of his life work may be, we do not understand him fully until we have a grasp of the man behind the task. Four formative powers stand behind Tillich's life and activity as a Christian teacher. They have their foundation, as might be expected, in the earlier years of his life abroad, but they have been developed and nurtured during the period of his American experience.

First, there is the experiential and even mystical foundation of Tillich's faith. According to his own autobiographical commentary, he early experienced the meaning of the Holy as the Divine presence in the depth of human life. It is important that we take careful note of this fact, because the intricacy of Tillich's thought and language has often given rise to the mistaken impression that his interpretation of Christianity is too "abstract," whereas he has succeeded more than most in keeping theology in living interrelation with religion and the devotional life. He has variously described his approach to the religious relationship as mystical, aesthetic and even as romantic, but all point to a common feature: religious faith involves the individual person, and it means being grasped by the power of the Ultimate. Without first-hand experience, religion is merely conventional or ecclesiastical. From his idea that the Holy demands from us an unreserved response—"thou shalt love the Lord thy God with *all* thy heart"—Tillich developed his conception of religion as man's "ultimate concern." Religion is not in the first instance belief in spirits or even in God as a special being highest among all beings; religion is the concern which the individual has for his own ultimate purpose and destiny. When that final and fundamental concern is directed towards or fulfilled in what is really Ultimate, we have a relation established between the individual and

the Divine ground of all things. It is this view of God as the Ultimate Power which imparts to all of Tillich's writings, and especially
to the devotional ones, the sense of God as living and present. If
one reads such sermons as "Escape from God" and "The Experience of the Holy," one understands why Tillich is so impatient with
traditional images of God. For him God is the Ground of all created
things and that which is really Ultimate in everything. The truly
Divine is the Holy present in all creation both as its Sustainer and
Judge. Tillich's effectiveness as a preacher is explained chiefly
through his ability to convey to his congregation this sense of the
Divine omnipresence. It is difficult to overestimate the strength that
can come to a man when there first dawns upon him the possibility
that the God he has not found has been present to him all along,
even though he "knew it not." Many of Tillich's sermons bring a
vivid awareness of that possibility.

One very significant consequence is Tillich's understanding of the
sacramental element in the Christian tradition and his strong sense
of the importance of the world of nature as revealing the Divine
presence. In this regard, Tillich stands squarely in the Augustinian
tradition; the great company of those who adopt a meditative attitude toward nature as showing forth the divine beauty which is also
the beauty of holiness. This is the essence of the sacramental view;
the One who is Spirit and beyond all worlds is concerned to dis-
close himself through created things. One lifts eyes to the hills that the
hills may point beyond themselves to their Creator. One of the grave
dangers of Reformation Protestantism has been a tendency to un-
derstress the sacramental universe and to suppose that the dis-
closure of God is only through man and the written or spoken word.
Tillich's thought is of great interest to the Anglican tradition, for example, on this very count; it has ramifications as well for the whole
of Protestantism. The sacramental principle is deeply rooted in
Christianity, and neither humanism nor moralism should be allowed to obscure it.

Secondly, there is Tillich's profound sense of the broken character of all finite life, of evil and of tragedy. He adopted the concept of the demonic as a means of expressing the reality of the "dark side" of existence. Tillich's theology has always been realistic in the sense that it recognizes the living power of evil and its capacity to organize itself for destructive ends. At no period in his life has he been willing to gloss over those realities and powers that fight against the divine Love. He has not, moreover, been afraid to expose the limitations of human freedom. Time and again he has told us of the need to resist the tendency in American Protestantism to take the Kingdom by storm, as it were, and to suppose that everything can be accomplished through human will and good deeds. Like Reinhold Niebuhr, he has brought to American Protestantism a new sense of evil's force and of the possibilities for corruption which lie hidden in the best of intentions and the most dedicated of human wills.

Tillich seeks to take account of the demonic in every sphere of human life. This means that it must be considered in relation to religion itself. In the interpretation of Protestantism, Tillich has formulated what he calls the "Protestant Principle"—the idea that all human and finite realities, including religion and the churches, are subject to corruption and that in every acceptance of God there must be the acknowledgment of the Divine *judgment* as well as forgiveness. The church, consequently, stands under such judgment no less surely than any other institution or individual, and it becomes a matter of vital importance to anticipate the presence of the demonic through preserving some principle of self-criticism within the religious community. Tillich finds the basis for this principle in the Founder of Christianity himself. The Christ is the one who empties himself and who sacrifices his own will to God—"Why callest thou me good; only one is good, even God"; "Not my will but thine be done." For Tillich the distinguishing feature and also the great power of Protestantism rest in having the courage to keep alive a principle of self-criticism *within* religion and the churches. If God alone is the truly Ultimate, nothing finite and human can usurp his place; neither an individual, an institution, nor religion itself. The church militant is not so much the communion of saints as the community of sinners who hope to be saints.

Thirdly, there is Tillich's sense of the importance of history for religion and human life in general. Like Nietzsche, he not only lays emphasis upon the intimate connection between historical change and human culture, but points out the impossibility of understanding the meaning of our life without taking an active part in it. Thinking and performing are not two different tasks to be given out to two different kinds of men; both must be of concern to every man. In autobiographical remarks written in 1952 Tillich declared: "We are not scholars according to the pattern of our teachers at the end of the nineteenth century. We were forced into history in a way which made the analysis of history and of its contents most difficult." It would be dramatic indeed if we could say that Tillich acquired this concrete outlook on life and the role of the scholar from his experiences in America. He has indeed carried on vigorous social and political activity in our midst, but the sense of the scholar's responsibility and his need to achieve understanding through action were both well established at an earlier time. Tillich was and still is unusual in this respect; there are few among his German colleagues who can lay claim to having accepted greater responsibility for the achieving of social and political goods.

A concern for human history has always been at the center of the Judeo-Christian tradition. The God of the Old Testament was envisaged as a power manifesting his will through history; the later Christian conception of Providence is without meaning unless we can believe that history is the expression of a cosmic purpose. Tillich has not only taken these ideas seriously, but he has always seen Christianity as speaking to life caught in the midst of historical change. Two essays published together in *The Protestant Era,* "*Kairos*" and "Historical and Nonhistorical Conceptions of History: A Comparison," express his main ideas. Tillich seeks to recapture the essential meaning of the New Testament doctrine of "time fulfilled," the idea that there are certain crucial or "right" times in history at which the Divine becomes peculiarly manifest. Starting with a distinction proposed by the ancient philosophers between the uniform time measured by the movement of the sun and ordered through calendars and clocks, and special times such as seedtimes and harvest, the time of births and the time of deaths, Tillich interprets historical life under Providence as a series of "right" times (signified, as we have said, by the Greek word *Kairos*). Just as Christ is said to have appeared at the "appointed" time, the time called "providential" in the world's history, so God acts in the historical process. The special time has a quality all its own, and it obtains its special meaning from the place it has in a total providential plan. Just as not every time is the right time for sowing, but that time when everything is "just right," not every moment in history is a special time in which the power of God becomes peculiarly manifest. The activity of God in history is an activity which has its own time, the time of the *Kairos*. Although every moment of time is under the Providence of God, the special times are those at which the purpose of the entire process is revealed to us in a compelling way. The prophetic figures of the Old Testament from Moses to Daniel had each his "right" time and each interpreted the purpose of God for that time. The appearance of the Christ is for Christians the *Kairos* or special time at which the final nature of the Divine is made plain. God expresses his purpose for history through the happenings of history; it is for us to discern the signs of the times.

Tillich's interpretation of Providence is of great practical import because it drives us to live in the present. If all history stands under the judgment of God, we must see our own time in this light and seek to discover its religious significance. Our actions must be guided by our sense of the rightness of the time in which we live and the creative possibilities contained within it. Tillich applies this both to social and individual life. As the great men of faith have constantly reminded us, we often look for God in the wrong places.

We search everywhere but in the midst of our own *present* life and situation; we hawk after what is outside of ourselves in the expectation of something marvelous and dramatic and fail to look for the Divine in the depths of our own predicament. For Tillich *every* historical moment presents the person with the possibility of being turned toward God as the One who can overcome anxiety and fill the void of purposelessness. And indeed every moment holds out the possibility of rejecting God and of returning to the void or to occupation with the things of the world. Tillich asks only that we remain *open* to the Divine power. Being grasped by the love of God as it appears in the face of the Christ is an ever present possibility; it is one which comes more often in doubt and despair than in self-confidence and complacency. We cannot will to be grasped, nor can faith be attained through violent effort, but we can remain open to the possibility that now is our "right" time, the time when the response to God is made. The idea of the *Kairos,* then, is no mere piece of abstract theology interesting only to scholars; it touches the most important matter of all—the person's relation to God.

The fourth formative influence in Tillich's life and thought was his encounter with existential thinking. As a student Tillich became fascinated by the thought of the German philosopher Friedrich Schelling. Of special importance was Schelling's idea that all thinking should be directed to the *individual self* confronting the world and seeking to find a solution to the ancient problem of fate and freedom. Tillich had made this problem decisive for Christian thought. On the individual or personal side it means that thinking and the destiny of the thinker go hand in hand; on the social side it means that religious beliefs make a difference to the realities of social and political life. Unlike the orthodox Lutheran we so often associate wih German Protestantism, Tillich rejects a religious life lived in a private sphere untouched by technology, political upheaval and, in short, all the rigors of historical life. If faith is for the whole man and that man lives, as all must, in a perilous and changing world, then the stuff of politics and of art, of science and of society cannot be ignored. We must search constantly for the religious depth and meaning in these spheres of life; failure to do so means that faith evaporates into sentimentality and historical life is abandoned to demonic forces and to those who care nothing for the Divine depth of life.

A further consequence of the existential approach to religion is found in the importance it attaches to personal experience. Tillich has not only taken this consequence with fitting seriousness, he has also connected it with one of the most powerful movements in modern culture—psychoanalysis. Tillich has long been concerned with religion and mental health; he has often pointed out the connection between religious words for salvation which invariably mean "health" or "wholeness" and the idea of the healthy personality able to live an integral life and resist destructive tendencies. He has attacked the disparaging view of religion contained in orthodox Freudianism, while at the same time pointing up the positive resources to be found in psychoanalysis for the recovery of human life. For all of its emphasis upon the inner life, Protestant Christianity has often forgotten the psychological insights contained in the ancient theological tradition. As a result, moralistic distortions have crept in, reducing religion to a mere activism or moral fervor. More subtle problems concerning love and hatred, guilt and failure, forgiveness and self-rejection have been ignored, to the great impoverishment of Christian faith. Tillich has a large concern for bringing the properly religious questions back into the center of the picture; his aim is to see that the love that is so basic to the Christian outlook shall not be subordinated to a law of works and deeds.

Let us view these formative influences in Tillich's life and thought in relation to the Protestantism he has encountered in this country. In this way we can gain some answers to the questions with which our discussion began. First, his emphasis upon the personal element in religion has done much to revive a sense of the religious relationship as a living affair for the person, rather than an institutional affiliation. The idea of religion as the "ultimate concern" of the person has led many people who are otherwise indifferent to the things of religion to ponder anew the question of God in their own lives. American Protestantism has moved back and forth between the extremes of a sentimental piety and a social liberalism; there have been few attempts to hold a genuinely critical and well-grounded theology related to both personal and social life. Tillich has tried to show the intimate connections between theology and the religious life; he has been unwilling to accept a divorce between the two.

When we consider the optimism that has characterized American Protestantism in our century, Tillich's emphasis upon the reality of evil in man and the world takes on special significance. For all the stress laid upon sin and "hell fire" in the popular imagination of American Puritanism, a more comfortable and optimistic outlook has almost always gained the upper hand. In comparison, for example, with the dark and brooding tone of Continental Protestantism, our American belief in the possibility of transforming man and society through devoted effort has often appeared naive. Although, as Tillich has been the first to acknowledge, there is power in our daring to take religion seriously in historical life, we need the sobering influence of realism. Evil is not only a reality but it has the power of organizing itself and thus of offering a formidable resistance to all of the redemptive powers in which Christians believe. Tillich's idea of the demonic in human life and history can help us to achieve the needed corrective in outlook.

But there is another side to the story. Tillich is aware of the extent to which the communication of his idea of the demonic was made possible by the thinking of others. It was indeed crucial that Reinhold Niebuhr and others, joined together in what was then known as the Fellowship of Socialist Christians, should have been raising a prophetic voice against the easy optimism of American Christianity. In many powerful writings of his own, Niebuhr was recapturing the insights of the Augustinian tradition and leading us to a new understanding of what the corruption of human freedom could mean. Without in the least abandoning his concern for the social application of Christian principles, Niebuhr exposed the weaknesses of the older liberalism while showing the new relevance of the ancient doctrine of sin. Tillich added his voice to the cause through his theological and philosophical theory of the demonic. Tillich, moreover, profited from the close connection between thinking and acting to be found in our society. His own prophetic voice, however, would have been thinner and less comprehensible to us were it not for the preparatory work that preceded him. Tillich, it would appear, came into our midst at the "right" time; he added depth to a movement already under way, and we provided him with a further stimulus to relate his theology to historical problems.

We have already mentioned the resources brought to our own thinking by Tillich's emphasis upon history and the need to achieve human understanding through action and participation in historical life. We have also called attention to his doctrine of the *Kairos* and its role in directing us to the importance of the *present* time for individual and social life. But again the traffic has not been in only one direction; Tillich found in our life and thought a vital supplement to his own ideas. For, as he was quick to perceive, our own pragmatic philosophy and our practical temper reveal our concern to hold together both thought and action in one concrete situation. He has learned in his American experience that we have an enormous openness to ideas and courage in appealing to them as directive forces in our life.

Thus far we have focused upon an interplay of ideas, and we may find ourselves with the impression that Tillich the man has eluded us. We may feel that we have not yet explained the source of his power in the religious situation of our time. There are indeed further things to be said.

For all of the doubts we may have about its permanence or sincerity, a revival of interest in religious questions and concerns has been one of the striking developments of recent years. In a variety of ways and through different kinds of writing and activity, Tillich has spoken to that concern. He has also criticized it in incisive ways. He has done so, moreover, in a way which engages the type of person who is without ties to the historical churches no less than those who have been brought up within one of the Christian communions. His capacity to speak, as the Quaker tradition has expressed it, "to our condition" is the most important factor in his acceptance. Contrary to the impression often created by the complexity of his theological writings, his main message is directed to the individual and to his predicament in a precarious world. His conception of religion, of faith, of God and of overcoming estrangement in the self through the New Being or Christ, all point to experience of a personal sort. Enthusiastic response to his sermons and addresses (a radio address on the nature of man once brought so many requests for copies that a Connecticut station was forced to close its switchboard) testifies to his impact on the personal level. Those sincerely raising questions about themselves and their own purpose in life have been quick to grasp the relevance of his ideas. To enhance the impact, Tillich is able to lead his audience to feel that he understands the obstacles standing between them and what they must attempt to accomplish. His sense of how difficult it is to sustain faith when the skeptical forces of the modern age press in upon us enables him to establish community with those to whom he speaks. As one of Tillich's colleagues has put it, he can make the hearer feel that he speaks to him alone and even that he has stood in his place. For the communication of religious truth this is a powerful talent.

Tillich's most widely read work, *The Courage To Be,* delivered originally as the Terry Lecture at Yale University, furnishes us with a clear illustration of the points we have been making. That work and its enthusiastic reception sum up the meaning of Tillich's work for contemporary religious life. The main topics concerned are best suggested by the title of one section, "Anxiety, Religion and Medicine." Reinterpreting religious faith as the courage to continue life, not in the suppression of doubt and despair but in their courageous acceptance, Tillich tries to show how that confidence without which life is finally impossible is dependent upon a direct, personal relationship with God.

And indeed Tillich has done more than teach us about courage, he has embodied this courage in his own life, especially during the years of his American experience. Many Europeans, intellectuals and professional people chiefly, have failed in their efforts to make a settled home in America because of their unwillingness to participate in the ways of what they have assumed is a young, naive, and rude culture. Many have refused to risk themselves, with the result that they have remained outside and have failed to establish rapport with the spirit of American life. Tillich approached his life in America in a very different way. There is a spirit of genuine humility in the way in which he has tried to discover the inner motives of the American character with the aim of incorporating them in his own life and thus of deepening his understanding of ours. Many who have read his books or heard his lectures and sermons have come away with a sense that he understands our situation and has deep respect for it. This comes from the vigor with which Tillich has taken part in our pattern of life. His willingness to risk himself in the faith he describes as courage has given birth to an understanding which men without faith can never hope to achieve. And indeed had he not sought to understand us we would experience even greater difficulty than we do in understanding him. To dare to devote our present selves to something larger than we are in the hope and trust that we shall find our true selves in the end is the heart of religious faith. Tillich's life and thought furnish us with a vivid example of that faith in our time.

5

Trevor Huddleston

BY ALAN PATON

ALAN STEWART PATON *is probably South Africa's best-known author, and a writer of international reputation. His voice has the clear ring of sanity amid the race conflicts of his native land, which are vividly portrayed in his two most famous books,* Cry, the Beloved Country *and* Too Late the Phalarope. *He is the National Chairman of the South African Liberal Party and, as such, has strongly condemned the Government's policy of apartheid. An impartial study of the Union is to be found in his book,* Land and People of South Africa.

What is Trevor Huddleston like? He has a lean face of good color, dark hair turning gray, a spare athletic body, expressive hands. There is a kind of purity and vitality in his face, and this shines out through his eyes. His personality is warm not cold, winning not frightening. He gives the impression of youth, and this is because of his vitality. There is in him still a great deal of the boy burning to serve the world. But this boy is very much of a man. He knows what the world is like, he knows all the frailties of human nature.

I said that he had the appearance of one burning to serve the world. I could never describe Huddleston as a fanatic, but of course whether one sees a man as a fanatic or not depends largely on where one is looking from. This burning quality in him does not show in any fierceness in the eyes, or hollowness in the cheeks, or fever in the skin; it is, rather, the quality of a steady undiminishing flame, the light that so shines before men that they glorify their Father which is in heaven. Sometimes one is repelled by a burning quality because it speaks of strangeness and abnormality; not so with Huddleston. The ruddiness of his cheeks is that of spiritual health, not of fanaticism. He could well be called a dog of the Lord; wildness is not his attribute, but fidelity and courage.

One of the marks of any great priest of Huddleston's kind is that he has no fear of the world. He knows well what sin can do to the soul, but he does not draw back from sinners; or to put it positively, he likes them. Huddleston liked sinners of the earthy kind; he teased them and joked with them, but his deepest love he gave to those simple and devout souls who strove after holiness amidst the sordidness and carelessness of the city. He found it much harder to love those whose sins were of the spirit, the cruel and the arrogant, the makers of unjust laws. He argued that he had no right to be patient and forgiving towards them, and that Christ had not been so towards the Jews. This deep problem I leave on one side, never having found its solution for myself. But I shall record that Huddleston did not like our lawmakers very much.

He can flirt with the world on occasions, he can flash his eyes at it and tease it. He likes a good meal and good wine and good conversation. There seems in him to be an absence of all prudery and censoriousness. He likes rushing about from place to place, and being where things are on the move; I mean he likes it quite apart from any duty that he sees in it. He likes being alive; there is in him a strong, healthy, sensible tension between robust living and holy living. One is never conscious in him of deep and unhappy conflict (except on one occasion which I shall tell about). He has no lean and hungry look like Cassius; for though he hungers after righteousness, in a sense he is filled. I think it is true to say that although he hungers after righteousness in man's world, he is already certain of it in God's world, and that prevents him from falling into melancholy. In any case, as I have already said, he is alive and likes being alive, and therefore is no prey for melancholy. Of course he might deny all this, and say that my picture is too simple; I am merely writing it down as it appears to me.

This lively quality in him, his delight in living and doing, coupled with his hatred of injustice and in particular the injustice of racial discrimination, plus his courage and devotion to righteousness, brought him much into the public eye in South Africa. What is more, he was news all over the world. I think he liked it, but I do not think it was as simple as all that. I think also that he was prepared to step out into the limelight and the spotlight and the searchlight if that would advance his cause. But I think he quite liked it there; or at least he did not shrink from it. I might have thought of some other man that he was an exhibitionist, and that his exhibitionism was pushing him out into the light, not his devotion to righteousness. Many people have thought that about Huddleston, but it was the thinking of ignorance and hostility. Huddleston's love of justice, hatred of injustice, and love of man, all part of his love of God, are the main driving forces in his life; and if his actions bring him into the light, or if he goes into the light to let his actions be better seen, and if he quite enjoys it, and if he sometimes lets his enjoyment of it get him out there into the light a bit faster, and if he knows what a psychological moment is and uses it and enjoys it—then if all these things are there, that is the complexity that makes up the man. And what is more, it is a healthy, human, dedicated kind of complexity, mixed up with a lot of downright simplicity; for the simple love him. So do the sinners of the flesh love him; those whom he fights for love him; those who are searching love him; those who hunger after righteousness love him. Quite a lot of other people would love him, but his life judges them; and he himself judges them at times, sometimes in language that is fiercer than he. Some say outright, "You judge us, but we are right and we know what we are doing, and we reject your judgment altogether." Others say, "We believe in what you believe, but if we go about it as you do, we shall simply create implacable opposition; you are doing the right things in the wrong way."

What does Huddleston make of the perplexing question of how, in a country like South Africa, to move from the unjust position to the just? In the realm of religion and morality, his answer is unequivocal; he does not believe that Christianity is moderation in all things. He sees no compromise between just and unjust, right and wrong, false and true. For this reason he acquired in South Africa a reputation for extremism, for being foolish, unwise, immoderate, unstatesmanlike. Yet so long as he confined himself to the enunciation of the ideal, he continued to enjoy the support and admiration of many white South Africans.

But how does one *move* from the one position to the other? This
is a question of politics, is it not? Though he did not join any political party, he became more closely associated with what is called the
"Congress Movement," which has decided leanings towards what is
called the "left." He identified himself more and more with the
struggle of the African people to achieve freedom "in our lifetime."
He spoke at meetings where the police were present in force. He attended the famous "Congress of the People," one of the consequences of which gathering was the arrest of 156 people on charges
of high treason. By that time he had been recalled to England by
the Community of the Resurrection, but many of us believe that he
would have been arrested along with the others had he stayed. The
Congress of the People produced an idealist-socialist document
called the "Freedom Charter," which document set out the goals
but did not concern itself with the question of how to *move*. It is the
contention of the Government that the goals are so remote from
actuality, and appeal so little to the overwhelmingly white elector-
ate, that the move could only be made by means of revolution,
which if successful, would make South Africa a Communist country.

We may note in passing that Huddleston's association with the
Congresses alienated more and more of his white support. Even
some of his brothers began to feel that he was "making use" of the
Church. Here we come to a fundamental fact about him. He believed strongly in the actual identification of the Church with justice, in the prophetic duty of the Church to denounce injustice, in
the duty of the Church to show forth in her own body the true
fellowship of Christians triumphing over the barriers created by
men. He saw also, and with clarity, I think, that the Christian
Church in Africa stood at the crossroads, and that her archenemy
was not Islam or Communism, but a Christianity corrupted by possession and privilege. He wanted the Church to be a transforming,
not a conforming, body. I do not think that he, a faithful member
of the Community of the Resurrection, had any need to be taught
what was the true nature of the Church; but he saw her as a Church

in the world, eager to obey the commandments of her Lord, and to respond to his prayer that his disciples might be one. The arguments about language difference, culture difference, social difference—he understood them all; but his love was urgent, and rebelled against laws that would perpetuate these differences for ever, and would even dare to forbid men to make themselves known to their brothers, and would exercise over their lives a sovereignty that belonged only to God. Let us make no mistake about it, it was love that was urging him.

The witness that the Church seemed so unwilling to give, he would give. And so he associated himself with forces that respectable white people, and the Church too in general, feared or abhorred. He never really liked to discuss the question as to whether the Left was not "using" him; the possibility he would admit. But he resisted discussion on two grounds; the first was that he knew that fears and abhorrences can inhibit action that ought to be taken. The second was that for him, as for Chief Luthuli, South Africa was on fire, and he found it impossible to say to his fellow firefighter, "Where does your water come from, and what kind of bucket are you carrying it in?" How therefore could he be understood by those who, while believing that South Africa was in a sad position, did not believe she was on fire, and that all hands must come to her aid?

In any case, he did not like intellectual discussion of these problems; he lived largely through action, and by that I include his prayers. That is what endeared him to the people whose cause he fought. This course of action he never co-ordinated and planned ahead; the coherence and integrity of his cause came largely from his own character.

I shall now try to return to the present tense, because Huddleston is very much alive. But I shall first state one interesting thing about him which was the subject of much good-humored but quite serious teasing between us. Though he, living in South Africa, made the big leap (or had already made it before he came, it does not matter) and accepted all men as his brothers, yet in matters of religion he was anti-ecumenical, ridiculed ecumenical effort and gatherings, and regarded the Church of South India as a monstrosity. Nevertheless he and his Community prayed for reunion. I could not help thinking that his praying for reunion, and his ridicule for all attempts to achieve it, was in some respects not unlike the attitude of those whom he judged so severely, who acknowledged the brotherhood of man, and who either made it impossible to realize, or rejected as sentimentality any effort to move towards it. It is certainly fascinating to contemplate a person whose deepest joy is in association with his fellow creatures, so long as it is not in worship.

We used to poke fun at each other, he at my ecumenicity, I at his anti-ecumenicity. When I told him that his arguments reminded me of those for the continuance of apartheid, his color appeared to deepen, though I admit that might have been solely in my imagination, and the results of wishful thinking. The boy in him came out in these encounters; teasing was his main weapon, but he put heart and soul into it. He would compare his writings with mine, and pity me for never having written anything that had caused such a sensation as *Naught for Your Comfort*. He would write from England to tell me of fantastic but wholly imaginary offers for film rights, radio rights, TV rights. He would commiserate with me for never having been translated into Yoruba or Lozi, though he had not been translated into them either. Then he would invent clever names and addresses to be written on the backs of letters such as

Rev. N. O. Cullerbar,
Copse Watching,
Stillfree,
England

or

Miss Sedgie Nation,
"Piebaldings,"
Much Mixing

These exchanges he found completely relaxing, and when we were together he would laugh with a pure joy over the greatest absurdities. In fact, as soon as he knew I was preparing to deliver a shaft at him, his whole being would prepare for it, with a kind of inward anticipation, warm and human to see. When he was speaking in the Barbados on Monday night, and Alabama on Tuesday night, and New York on Wednesday night (which was the kind of absurd program his eagerness let him in for), and when he was quite exhausted, he could always rake up energy for one of these duels, and the lines of weariness and tension would disappear from his face. I personally never knew him to engage in any person-against-person contest except of this innocent kind, and I record here that never in all the years I knew him was I aware that he had any preoccupation with himself at all, a thing which I am normally quick to notice, nor any preoccupation with any other person, which frequently amounts to the same thing.

His sense of humor, however, once put me into a false position. He was speaking against apartheid at Westminster School and he wanted me to get up some time during the discussion, and put up a spirited defense of our rulers and their policies. I was very reluctant; I would have done it with zest when I was twenty, but at fifty-five I thought I would make a fool of myself, for quite frankly I would feel uncomfortable if an audience thought I was genuinely for apartheid, even though I was a perfect stranger to them all. However, he urged me to do it, and I did it in the end; I put on a medium show, and was a bit sour with him afterwards, which he thought just as funny as his original suggestion.

I am now hastening to the end of this lengthy "vignette," but of course I could go on much longer. I want to say something about his leaving South Africa. When he was recalled to England, it was said to be "for political reasons." So far as I know, the South African authorities had nothing to do in any direct sense with his recall. It is possible that his Order considered his recall to be wise lest he should come into conflict with the authorities. It is possible,

I think—though I do not know—that the Order might have thought that Huddleston was in some spiritual danger of becoming too involved in the affairs of the world, and perhaps was even in danger of becoming corrupted by the world's attention. Was he? I would not dare to express an opinion, for to me he seemed to be the perfect crusader; but I would not consider myself qualified to judge, because what he was doing satisfied my longing that the Church should in some way be more militant in the South African world. I never sensed any spiritual deterioration in him; his human love of action I understood, but I could not consider that reprehensible. Rebellion and obedience were perfectly combined in him. If it had not been so, his recall would have broken his heart. The fact that it did not is proof to me that Huddleston was not any kind of dog, but a dog of the Lord. When he was jerked in he growled and pulled, but he came in the end to the beloved Heel. Fidelity, not self-will, was what he lived by. And one cannot help noting that he is growling and pulling as much as ever.

Although Huddleston's recall from South Africa did not break his heart, it caused in him the deepest unhappiness and the most intense homesickness. There was a real conflict in him between his love for South Africa and his obedience to authority. The rumor went about that he would refuse to return. Such a thing would not have been possible. Behind what other Heel could such dog run? Beneath the longing, almost the despair, was the solid rock of the man and his obedience. And another thing that helped him too was that running about from Connecticut to Barbados, and the discovery of America, with all her tinsel and all her gold. Reinhold Niebuhr said of America, "I like this mess," and Huddleston liked it too; it helped to assuage his longing.

This is my picture of one of the most human of the saints.

6

Albert Schweitzer

BY GEORGE SEAVER

GEORGE SEAVER, *Anglican priest and scholar, is recognized to be the "classic biographer" of Albert Schweitzer. His biography of the great doctor is both penetrating and definitive; his writings have done much to stabilize the image of Schweitzer in the public mind. Among numerous other works, he is the author of* Scott of the Antarctic; Faith of Edward Wilson; The Story of an African Boy; The Magnet of the Cross.

Imagine yourself aboard a river steamer slowly making its way upstream through the mud flats of a tropical river in West Africa in the dry season of the year 1913. You are sliding along between the walls of a wide green tunnel with towering tree stems on either side, entwined with trailing creepers and arched with heavy branches: your roof is a long narrow strip of blazing sky, your floor is a brown, sluggish, watery mirror. Clumps of mangroves fill in the spaces between the tree trunks here and there, and thrust out their knotted roots into the oozy slime. Each new bend in the river is almost exactly like the last. If you shut your eyes for an hour and then opened them again, you would hardly perceive any difference from what you had seen before. For this is the edge of the primaeval forest and as such it has remained since the dawn of creation.

It would be difficult to conceive of a more elemental environment, or (for that matter) of more elemental fellow passengers. For they are all—with one exception—primitive Negroes. They have just finished their midday meal of porridge which is made of corn-meal called mealie-meal. The exception is a European, and he has been sharing the meal with them, for in his haste to get aboard he had forgotten to bring his own provisions. He is a man of powerful build, with a rugged, heavily lined face, deeply tanned, thick shock of dark hair, and kind, tired eyes. He is forty years of age. (But this is more than forty-five years ago; he is now eighty-five and he is still out there.) The reason he was in such a hurry to get on board is that he had been urgently summoned to give medical aid to the wife of a missionary friend nearly two hundred miles upstream.

He is evidently well known to all the Negroes; his presence among them is taken for granted. They call him Oganga—medicine man. But just now he is not concerned about them; he is sitting apart, his rolled-up shirt-sleeves displaying brawny arms wet with sweat, a pen in his hand and a notebook on his knee, in which he occasionally jots down brief, disconnected sentences, sometimes in German, sometimes in French; but for the most part he gazes straight before him engrossed in thought. And thus he has been sitting, with intervals snatched only for food or sleep, for the best part of three days. If you were to look over his shoulder at the scraps of writing on his knee, you would observe that it is extremely neat: the writing of a scholar who is also a scientist and a musician. For this man is world-famous as a specialist in four different branches of learning—philosophy, divinity, music, medicine—and to three of them he has made an original contribution. He is also a practical man, very much a man of his hands: builder, agriculturalist, organ repairer, as well as surgeon.

An Alsatian born and bred, an alumnus of the University of Strasbourg, and afterwards pursuing his studies in the Universities of Paris and Berlin, he is a product of Franco-German culture, but by every instinct of temperament and every direction of outlook he is cosmopolitan. Some of the churches in Alsace still retain a peculiarity which is unique in Christendom: they are Catholic-Protestant combined. The priest says Mass in the choir and the pastor says prayers and preaches in the nave at different times by mutual arrangement every Sunday. This practice, introduced by Louis XIV for the benefit of Catholics in districts where their own places of worship were too few, although in its origin due to the capricious edict of a king, is for Schweitzer something more than a curious historical phenomenon: it is the mark of a signal Christian grace—the grace of religious toleration; a symbol of the Church that is to be—a prophecy and an exhortation to a future of religious unity. And so the boy who was native to a Franco-German province, and within that province the child of a Catholic-Protestant church, has made of the man a unifying influence, political, religious, and in all other ways. It is his deep conviction that all philanthropic work, all work for the welfare of our fellow men which comes within the sphere of what we call Christian charity, should be international and interdenominational, free alike from patriotic sentiment and ecclesiastical partisanship; that in fact what the world needs, if it is to become truly Christian, is not less humanism but more.

When he was thirty years old he gave up all further prospects of a brilliant career in Europe in order to study medicine and qualify as a medical missionary to primitive man in the jungle swamps of French Equatorial Africa. He established his own hospital on the Ogowe River in Gabon at a place called Lambaréné, which Trader Horn and Mary Kingsley had made the center of their travels. He built, equipped, and maintained his hospital at his own expense. Where did he get the money to do this? He got it from the sale of his books and from his lectures and organ recitals. He would come back to Europe at intervals and tour the capitals and other cultural centers, delighting huge audiences with his rendering of the music of the great composers and especially of Bach. Partly by this means, and chiefly in later years by the help of admirers all over the free world, he still keeps his hospital going.

His departure has been called a breach with civilization, a flight from reality. But, as Pierre van Paassen has pointed out, it is the contrary that is true.

He did not formulate his plans. He did not say that he wanted to save souls or to bring joy and relief into the lives of the most underprivileged of human beings. He went away silently. But in his own mind was the feeling that he went out to do his part in atoning for the Western world's treatment of the natives of the most ruthlessly exploited continent in the world.[1]

[1] *That Day Alone* (New York, Dial, 1941).

The stimulus which drove him out of the cool, sequestered vale of life in order, as he put it to himself, "to try and live in the spirit of Jesus," may well strike us as a strange one; yet it demonstrates how deeply the recorded sayings—even the "hard sayings"—of the historical Jesus had woven themselves into the very fibers of his being. It is the parable of Dives and Lazarus. He saw himself, as one among a myriad heirs of all the ages, representative of centuries of civilization and culture—as Dives; he saw his brother man the primitive Negro, victim of want and woe, diseased and neglected, exploited and oppressed—as the poor man at his gate. Among so many ills in the world that call for curing, so many wrongs that call for redressing, he saw herein the need for a simple and immediate duty—a duty which he represented to himself as a debt of honor— as a white man to atone, if only in an infinitesimal degree, for all the wrongs that white men have inflicted on the black.

Africa is not for him an escape from life, nor is it even the goal of his life; it is the symbol of his life. His hospital in the jungle swamps has been called the visible expression in miniature of an ethical ideal. It is a cathedral of ideas realized in the sanctuary of sacrificial service which is Love in action. Without irony but in sober earnest it may be said that, so far from turning his back on civilization, he has gone out into the wilderness to find it.

Let us go back now to where we left him on the deck of the river steamer. He is thinking deeply—what about? Have you ever thought so hard about something that you could not stop thinking about it for three whole days? What is it, then, that he is thinking about? He is thinking of the age-old problem: What is the meaning of existence? Why are we here at all? It is a searching question—by far the most searching question to which anyone can address himself. In his search to find the answer to it—to discover what he calls the Basic Principle of the Moral—Schweitzer had ransacked the ages and spoiled the climes. He had left no stone unturned of philosophical inquiry, not only European but also Indian and Chinese. But he had sought in vain for any concrete formula which would satisfy him; all the systems of his predecessors when closely examined had seemed to him no more than types of ethical theory.

It is now towards late evening of the third day of his long river journey. The boat is making its way through a herd of hippopotamuses. This of course is by no means an unfamiliar spectacle in an African river, but the attention of the thinker is temporarily diverted from the scraps of paper on his knee to these huge beasts swimming in the water. Suddenly he rises, lays aside his papers, and stands up on the deck as if rivetted. A new thought, unforeseen and unsought, has flashed into his mind. It comes to him like a revelation; it is the goal of his quest. It expresses itself in a phrase of extreme simplicity: Reverence for Life. The phrase gave him the text and the title for a major treatise in philosophy in three volumes, only two of which he has as yet had time to complete: *The Decay and Restoration of Civilization; Civilization and Ethics;* and *The Civilized State.*

Other human lives have the same right to existence that I have. Their lives are, so to speak, an extension of the life that is in me. I ought to give them the same concern that I give to myself. I ought to feel a responsibility towards them. And this includes, though in a different way and in a lesser degree, all creatures great and small. For we inhabit the same universe. They too are the creatures of God's hand and the objects of His care.

To elaborate upon this thought. From the lowest to the highest forms of life there exists an inherent impulse, a purposive energy (whether conscious or unconscious), an imaginative force which is determined by ideals and strives to reach out towards the perfection with which it is endowed, to fulfill the purpose for which it was created. "From the crystal to the medusa, from the grass-blade to the flowering tree"—and so on up to all the multifarious forms of creaturely existence, in the sea, on land, in the air—lichen, fish, insect, reptile, bird, mammal—and to the crown of creation in human kind, we see this principle in ceaseless operation, this striving for perfection, for free activity, for a goal just beyond its reach; and it is the marvel and glory of creation. In man this striving becomes conscious. It expresses itself in the thought: I am life that wills-to-live in the midst of other life that wills-to-live. At first it is no more than a primary instinct for self-preservation and for self-assertion. Only in the man who is capable of sincere reflection and of conduct which is truly ethical does a contradiction to this urge of merely in-dividual self-assertion make its presence felt. He says to himself: I am not merely an individual isolated existence; my life is inesca-pably bound up with all the other manifestations of Being with which I am surrounded; the lives which I can touch and influence for good or ill are in some sense an extension of the life within me; I have a duty towards them; insofar as in me lies I must feel them as my own.

The man who says this to himself will feel that all life's experiences are his own; he will give them all the help that he possibly can, and will feel all the salvation and promotion of other life that he has been able to effect as the deepest happiness that can ever fall to his lot. Life will indeed become harder and more difficult for him in every respect than it would be if he continued to live only for himself; but at the same time it will be richer, more beautiful, and happier. It will become, instead of mere existence, a real and infinitely rewarding experience of life.

I am thrown indeed by Reverence for Life into an unrest such as the world does not know, but I obtain from it a blessedness which the world cannot give. I begin to learn the secret of spiritual self-expression. I win an unsuspected freedom from the various circum-stances of life. At moments in which I had expected to find myself overwhelmed, I find myself in an inexpressible and surprising happiness of freedom from the world, and I experience therein a clearing of my life-view.

The fundamental law of ethical behavior may therefore be expressed thus: *It is good* (*right*) *to maintain and enhance life; it is bad* (*wrong*) *to damage and destroy life.*

A man is truly ethical only when he obeys the inner constraint to help all life which he is able to succor, and when he goes out of his way to avoid injuring any living thing. To him all life as such is sacred. He shatters no ice crystal that sparkles in the sun, tears no leaf from its tree, breaks no flower, and is careful not to crush any insect as he walks. If he works by lamplight on a summer evening, he would prefer to shut the window and breathe stifling air rather than to see insect after insect fall on his table with singed and sinking wings.

To preserve, promote, and enhance life is thus to act within the sphere of the ethical; it is a free, constructive, and beneficent activity. But the circumstances of our lives are such that we are often compelled to destroy life in order to preserve other life which we deem to be of higher value. The act of destruction can never be felt by a human being as an ethical act; it can only be felt as a necessity within the realm of expedience. The conflict between the ethical and the expedient, between freedom and necessity, between spirit and nature, constitutes a perpetual tension in our lives as inhabitants of a world in which natural law does not correspond with spiritual law, and the world of fact is often incompatible with the world of values. It is for us to recognize the existence of this incompatibility, and to strive to reduce this tension, so far as in us lies, by realizing our debt to other lives which we sacrifice to our own.

In ethical conflicts such as this man can only arrive at subjective decision. There are no cut-and-dried rules. Each man must decide for himself alone, in each situation as it arises, whether and when it is necessary to destroy a life, which seems to him of lower value or of less importance in the scale, in order to protect or maintain a life of a higher order. . . . The farmer who has mown down a thousand blossoms in his meadow to feed his cows must be careful on his way home

not to strike off in thoughtless pastime the head of a single flower by
the roadside, for he thereby commits a wrong against life without being
under the pressure of necessity. Those who experiment with operations
or the use of drugs upon animals or inoculate them with diseases, so as
to be able to bring help to mankind with the results gained, must never
quiet any misgivings they feel with the general reflection that their
gruesome proceedings aim at a valuable result.

This, be it remembered, is the considered verdict of a man who,
as a surgeon and scientist, is in his own words "a mass-murderer of
bacteria"; and who, as a medical missionary in the pest-infested
swamps, carries on an unceasing war against termites, mosquitoes,
spiders, scorpions, snakes, leopards, and all the noxious vermin that
endanger human life—and none more vigorously, determinedly, and
deliberately than he; and yet who goes out of his way to lift a
parched earthworm from the dust and put it safely into grass, or
stoops to rescue a struggling insect from a puddle, and who prefers
to work in the stuffy atmosphere of a shuttered room rather than
let a moth flutter to its death around a lamp.

Concerning this aspect of Reverence for Life, Frank Kendon has
written with discernment:

It is not an arbitrary and willful definition; it is a mental attitude, it is
the opposite of ruthlessness, and of thoughtlessness. One can weed a
garden reverently, or ruthlessly. One can even kill a poisonous snake
reverently or ruthlessly, necessarily or unnecessarily. This principle
does not say: Be kind to your neighbor because this ensures the soli-
darity of society; it says: Be universally kind, whenever the choice
occurs. It does not say it is a sin to pluck a flower or kill a moth; it
says: Do not pluck flowers or kill moths without first greeting the divine principle in them.[2]

Once when a young volunteer in his hospital, newly arrived from
Europe, was about to crush a spider that had settled on his bare

[2] In *John O'London's Weekly,* January 1945.

arm, Dr. Schweitzer prevented him with the reminder: "Gently, Noel, gently. Remember that you are a guest in its country." The same courtesy should be observed by all human beings who are also guests among all the other denizens of the natural world and fellow inhabitants of the same mysterious universe.

What is the determining factor of this ethic of Reverence for Life, that which gives it its power and its inspiration? It is pity. "Ethics are pity . . . all life is suffering." Man can never be truly ethical as long as he regards himself and his fellows as, so to speak, the only pebbles on the beach of an eternal shore; as long as he maintains an attitude of aloof detachment from anything that lives; as long as he adopts the passive role of spectator, and not that of active participant, in the universal tragedy of life. For this would be to do his own soul an injury, to stifle himself, to deprive himself of the very breath of being. But once he accepts his kinship with, and responsibility for, all creatures great and small; once he realizes that they too are, each according to its kind, the concern of the same divine Creator; he experiences within himself an unburdening, a release, a sense that he has the right to his own place in the same universe. Each one of these other individual existences has its own contribution to the sum total of Reality. Not one of them therefore is to be despised. Each one of them indeed is to be reverenced. Each is unique, and of intrinsic value, because each is a vehicle of Life. And as man identifies himself with the experiences of other finite lives around him—creaturely as well as human, though of course the human are of infinitely greater value—he becomes increasingly aware of the presence of an all-encompassing Power— Infinite Being—Life everlasting. From his existence in the finite and the temporal he passes to an experience of the infinite and eternal, from Life to Love.

Even in his early boyhood Schweitzer was feeling out instinctively to this truth that he discovered in his manhood as a principle necessary to right thinking and put into practice as a principle necessary to right living. "As far back as I can remember," he tells us,

"I was saddened by the amount of misery I saw in the world around me." Human affliction was in itself a grim and saddening spectacle enough, but that the animal creation should also be tormented with such an excess of pain and cruelty was heart-rending. For example, the hook that tore the fish's mouth and dragged it from the water to gasp its life out on the hard ground; the old limping horse, tugged at in front and beaten from behind, to get it to the knacker's yard for butchery; thirsty, frightened cattle cramped together in a jolting railway truck; wild animals caged in a zoo, or tamed animals trained for a circus—the memory of such sights haunted him for weeks. It passed his childish comprehension that such things could be taken by his elders and betters as a matter of course; or why in his evening prayers he should be taught to pray for human beings only. So when his mother had heard him say his prayers before she kissed him good-night (this was when he was only eight years old) he used to add silently a prayer he made up for himself, for all living creatures. It went like this: "O heavenly Father, protect and bless all things that have breath, guard them from all evil, and let them sleep in peace." When he got older he was forced to realize of course, as we all are, that it is one of the dark and inscrutable laws of nature that all life preys on other life in order to maintain its own; and that even human beings who are endowed with moral and spiritual aspirations must also have recourse to this horrible expedient, and must often destroy other forms of life that endanger their own existence.

I too am subject to this necessity. In a thousand ways my existence stands in conflict with that of others. The necessity to destroy and injure life is imposed upon me. I get my food by destroying plants and animals. If I walk along an unfrequented path, my foot brings destruction and pain upon the tiny creatures which populate it. But whenever I injure life of any sort I must be quite clear whether it is necessary. Beyond the unavoidable I must never go, not even with what seems insignificant.

It is to be observed that there is no doctrine of *ahimsa* in this philosophy. Such a doctrine is (to use a modern word) unrealistic, and Schweitzer explicitly repudiates it. That doctrine is arbitrary and absolute, the ethic of Reverence for Life is subjective and discriminating. Destruction or injury to any form of life should never be inflicted thoughtlessly or needlessly, but always quickly and mercifully, reflectively and reverently.

But great as are the responsibilities of the ethical man to the rest of creation, they are small in comparison with those which Reverence for Life imposes upon him in respect to his fellow man. Here his responsibilities are so great and so unlimited as to be terrifying. "How much of my life, my possessions, my rights, my happiness, my time, and my rest, must I devote to others, and how much of them may I keep for myself?" Every human being endowed with his own special talents, health, wealth, knowledge or capacity, is like a costly piece of fixed capital; and the question he should ask himself is: How much interest do I yield in the form—not of self-giving—but of service to others? "Reverence for Life is an inexorable creditor!" For my life is not my own to do with as I list. It interpenetrates and is interpenetrated by all those other lives around me, whose life destinies my own life can reach and touch, whose welfare I can enhance and promote. "To everyone, in whatever state he finds himself, the ethic of Reverence for Life does this: it forces him ever and again to be concerned with the human destinies that are fulfilling their life-courses round him, and to give himself as a man to the man who needs a fellow man."

Even in his boyhood the question of the "right to happiness" was one, as he tells us, which caused him many a qualm of conscience, and which he could never bring himself to accept as a matter of course. His constant thought was this: "Whoever is spared personal pain must feel himself called to help in diminishing the pain of others." This was "the little cloud" that rose above the horizon of his otherwise sunny youth, and that grew "until it darkened the whole sky." How many boys—to say nothing of grown men—will pause to face the searching challenge of the apostle's question, "What hast thou that thou hast not received?" It would appear, however, that not this, but the saying of a yet more august authority, forced this question of the right to happiness upon young Schweitzer's conscience: "To whom much is given, of him shall much be required." And again: "He that loveth his life loseth it." Gifted as he was far beyond the ordinary, both in mind and body, and having early in youth attained a position of academic eminence and a worldly competence, he put to himself the question: "Have I the inward right to pluck all the fruit that my hand can reach?"

On the material level Reverence for Life requires of the ethical man that he should regard nothing as his own. The idea of the "rights" of private property, of exclusive possession, is an idea not to be thought of by him. He realizes his responsibility as a steward, not a possessor; as a trustee, not an owner. Similarly, in the matter of social "rights," he recognizes that he is a debtor, and knows only duties. Reverence for Life does not permit that he enter into competition with his fellow man, that he advance his own life at the cost of one who is weaker. It demands a renunciation which, judged by any worldly or self-regarding standards, would be considered quixotic.

At moments when I should like to enjoy myself, or to rest, Reverence for Life wakes within me reflection about misery that I see or suspect, and it does not allow me to drive away the uneasiness occasioned thereby. Just as the wave cannot exist for itself, but is ever part of the heaving surface of the ocean, so must I never live my life for myself, but always in the experience which is going on around me. It is an uncomfortable doctrine which the true ethic whispers in my ear. You are happy, it says; therefore you are called upon to give much. . . . You must show more than an average devotion of life to life. To the happy the voice of the true ethic is dangerous, if they venture to listen to it.

At the age of twenty-one, awaking one glorious spring morning at Whitsuntide to the sight of blossoms and the song of birds in his home at Günsbach, there came to him "the thought that I must not accept this happiness as a matter of course, but must give something in return for it." And then, pondering over the matter with calm deliberation, he decided that he was justified in developing his talents in learning and in music till he was thirty, but that thereafter he must devote himself entirely, as circumstances would dictate, to the direct service of humanity. During those years he acquired three doctorates, a professorship in the University of Strasbourg and a principalship in one of its Colleges, as well as the position of organist of the Paris Bach Society.

Just before his thirtieth birthday his eye was caught by an appeal in the Paris Missionary Society's magazine for volunteers to the Congo Mission in French Equatorial Africa. His decision was made at once, and his future life's course determined. Since then he has often been approached, as a man of independent thought and individual action, by people wishing to make a similar venture, but has only rarely felt justified in offering them immediate encouragement. He found himself often forced to recognize that the urge to do "something special"—to engage in some "extraordinary" form of serviceable activity—was born of a restless spirit: it might be the lure of religious romance, or dissatisfaction with duties that lay nearest; or it might be that practical considerations had not been fully weighed, or that physical constitution was unfitted to life in the tropics. His reflections on this matter are an illuminative and eloquent comment on the necessity for sobriety in forming an ethical judgment of the quality that Reverence for Life demands.

Only a person who can find a value in every sort of activity, and devote himself to each one with full consciousness of duty, has the inward right to take as his object some extraordinary activity instead of that which falls naturally to his lot. Only a person who feels his preference to be a matter of course, not something out of the ordinary, and who has no thought of heroism, but just recognizes a duty undertaken with sober enthusiasm, is capable of becoming a spiritual adventurer such as the world needs.

To this he adds another comment: "There are no heroes of action; only heroes of renunciation and suffering. Of such there are plenty. But few of them are known, and even these not to the crowd, but to the few."

He conceives the motive that prompted him to take his own line of extraordinary activity as nothing heroic indeed, but simply as the payment of a debt—a debt of honor. In moving words, in his book *On the Edge of the Primaeval Forest,* he exclaims against the long series of injustices and cruelties that the Negro races have suffered at the hands of Europeans—the "primitive" at the hands of the "civilized"—and concludes: "We and our civilization are really burdened with a great debt. We are not free to confer benefits on these men, or not, as we please; it is our duty. For every one who has scattered injury someone ought to go out to take help; and when we have done all that is in our power, we shall not have atoned for a thousandth part of our guilt."[3]

The ethic of Reverence for Life sees all life as one, its own life incorporate in the lives of others, the lives of others incorporate in its own. If it be objected that such an ethic is too idealistic, that human nature is not constituted like that, it is worth while to reflect for a moment on what can be achieved by education. Within our own times we have witnessed, with growing horror, the inoculation of the minds of whole populations with poison by means of the deliberate use of misdirected forms of education, resulting in wars which have left civilization in a state of collapse or paralysis. But if such insane enthusiasms can inspire the national soul with an ardor of selfless devotion, perverted however to destructive uses, what might not be achieved by education sanely directed to life-promoting purposes? What if not only in schools, but also by means

[3] New York, Macmillan.

of those two other most formative influences upon thought, radio and television, the ethic of Reverence for Life in all its multitudinous aspects were instilled both by precept and by the record of example? For what does it mean, after all? To put it at its lowest, it is simply the ethic of good manners, of inner courtesy and consideration, in a word, of civility—the habit of mind by which men can become truly civilized.

As long ago as 1922 Schweitzer foresaw the catastrophe which was threatening. He then affirmed that our vaunted civilization was in danger of collapse because we, as the units composing it and responsible for its continuance, had lost that civility which is the flower and fruit of Reverence for Life. "It is clear now to everyone," he then wrote, "that the suicide of civilization is in progress. What yet remains of it is no longer safe. It is still standing indeed, because it is not exposed to the destructive pressure that overwhelmed the rest, but like the rest it is built upon rubble, and the next landslide will very likely carry it away." Since then, the destructive pressure that overwhelmed the rest has overwhelmed it also: we have witnessed the decline of democracy and the rise of the collective state. Civilization presupposes free men who are self-controlled, but the modern world deprives them of personal freedom in action and even also in thought. Specialization in mass production and mass employment has robbed the worker of any joy in creative craftsmanship; organization has reduced him to chattel in human form. Mass suggestion in the form of propaganda has rendered him deaf to the voice of conscience and blunted his critical faculty; his spiritual life is stifled for lack of fresh air.

Schweitzer is an uncompromising foe of collectivism in any shape or form because it spells death to personality; and personality should above all else be held sacred and inviolate. "The final decision as to what the future of society shall be depends, not on how near to perfection its organization is, but upon the worth of its individual members. . . . Where the collective body works more strongly on the individual than the individual does upon it, the result is deterioration." The movement towards realization of the truly civilized state must be made from within and proceed outwards, not conversely. It would then become a living organism, not a mechanized organization. There is an irreconcilable difference between personal ethics and social ethics—which latter is a misnomer. Personal ethics spring spontaneously from the personal motives of disinterested altruism, and are intuitive: social ethics (as at present understood and practiced) are dictated by prudential considerations of social security, and are empirical. Personal ethics require of a man voluntary self-sacrifice in the promotion of the welfare of his fellows, personally and distributively; social ethics exact a contribution from the individuals who comprise the society, impersonally and collectively, for its own impersonal maintenance. It is an illusion to suppose that organized society can be personalized or even humanized: who was it who said that "a crowd cannot blush"? Social ethics should be more properly called legalism, the sanctions for which are to be found, not in persons, but in an abstract aggregate of groups. Personal ethics, on the contrary, derive from no regulations which are superimposed; their sanctions are to be found in the moral sense, in conscience.

But opposed as Schweitzer is to external constraint imposed on individuals by the collective will, he is equally opposed to the indiscipline of democratic regimes in which the "freedom of the individual" has degenerated into licence. Reverence for Life does indeed proclaim the truth that all men are of equal value, but not that all are of equal capacity—politically or in any other sense—nor that the majority are always in the right. "Everyone to count for one, and nobody for more than one"—this was Bentham's familiar version of the same fallacy of composition. According to this, it does not matter whether voters have been educated or not for the responsibility of voting, nor whether those whom they elect to govern have been trained or not for the responsibility of representing them. Character, education, experience, previous responsibility in positions of trust—these are factors left out of account in the universal suffrage. Equality of capacity in political affairs assumes that the art of government is one which, unlike all others, requires no special training but can be acquired by the light of nature. The result is inimical to the growth of personality; it represents a levelling down of ethical standards to that of the lowest common denominator.

But the ethic of Reverence for Life is concerned with the behavior of man, not as a unit in an organized group—whether political, industrial, or even religious—but as a person in relation to other persons. It is like yeast in a lump of dough, silently leavening society from within. Given the right relationship between persons, the true civilized state would spontaneously emerge and shape itself into the pattern of human fellowship.

Amid the babel of tongues that supervenes upon this period of humanity's most poignant distresses, the ethic of Reverence for Life, if heard and heeded in its gentle undertones, would prove a far more efficacious remedy for the whole world's pain than all the panaceas advocated in strident tones by the disunited politicians, or the theoretically minded sociologists, or even the divided churchmen; but whether it will be so heeded is a matter for doubt, since it would cost so much more in personal effort and personal sacrifice. Hard is the task indeed, but great is the hope. It is nothing less than to reawaken in men's minds reverence for truth, in scorn of propaganda; for humanity, not nationalism; for ideals, not for ideologies; for moral worth, and not material success. Drastic defects demand drastic remedies, and in this case the remedy would be so drastic as to occasion an almost total reversal of accepted standards, or, as another prophet of our times, Nikolai Berdyaev, has forcibly put it, "a radical change in the structure of human consciousness." Magnus Ratter has written thus of Schweitzer's life work in a brilliant metaphor: "As with a surgical needle he probes to find the vital artery of the African arm, that intravenous injection may cure the patient who would otherwise die of sleeping sickness, so he searches for the artery of European faith, that he may inject into the dying civilization a life-giving inspiration. The probing may be painful."

For Reverence for Life in its philosophic sense he has coined a new term: Ethical Mysticism. It is a telescopic term, combining serviceable activity in the world of sense, the plane of phenomena, with spiritual experience of Infinite Being. In it the two main streams of traditional ethical theory meet: the altruistic, which is directed outwardly and aims at the devotion of the self to others, and the intuitionist, which is directed inwardly and aims at self-perfection. The one is world- and life-affirming and regards the moral sense as an extension of an upward evolutionary trend in the natural order; the other is world- and life-denying, and, despairing of such concord of the natural with the supernatural, withdraws from outward activity in the world of sense and looks within itself for the lodestar of right conduct. The failure of the former is due to the fact that, lacking inspiration from within, its energies have been sidetracked from concrete personal service and have become dissipated in impersonal (that is, sociological) concerns. The failure of the latter is due to the fact that its aspirations have been directed to "an abstract notion of Being rather than to real Being within phenomena," and has resulted in the passive mysticism of resignation. The failure of these two kinds of ethics can only be retrieved, and their apparent dualism resolved, by deeper reflection upon the essential nature of them both. Self-devotion must look not only outwards (objectively and actively) to the world of sense, but also inwards for the hidden mainsprings of its activity. Self-perfection must look not only inwards (subjectively and passively) to the source of its being, but also outwards (actively and purposefully) to all the manifestations of Being in the world of sense. Thus only will man come "into his true relation to the Being that is within him and outside him."

A simple illustration may perhaps serve to clarify this point. A channel is open at both ends. If it gets blocked at one end, there is no intake; if at the other, no output. To be a channel of the divine life it is necessary that both ends should be kept open. As in breathing there must be inhalation and expiration to keep ourselves alive, so in the spiritual life there must be the same rhythm, the same interdependence. To love God with all one's heart, mind, soul and strength—this is indeed the first and great commandment, and without it spiritual life is impossible; but it is complementary to and interdependent upon the other, namely, to love one's neighbor as oneself.

"The essential element in Christianity as it was preached by Jesus and as it is comprehended in thought is this: that it is only through Love that we can attain to communion with God. All living knowledge of God rests upon this foundation: that we experience Him in our lives as Will-to-Love." And it is this which is the core of Schweitzer's ethical mysticism—the content of the true mystical experience.

There is an important aspect of this ethic which deserves emphasis. Reverence for Life—involving as it must in the reflective mind a sense of wondering regard in face of the mystery of animate creation, of all the manifestations of being that are unlike itself—engenders a yet profounder sense of awe and wonder and reverent regard towards self-conscious existences similar to its own. To some of these we feel ourselves attracted as if by a mutual affinity. Yet each one is to the other somewhat of a mystery. "None of us can truly assert that he really knows someone else, even if he has lived with him for years. Of that which constitutes our inner life we can impart even to those most intimate with us only fragments." It is wrong to seek with rude hands to unveil the soul of another fellow mortal, however dear.

For there is a modesty of the soul which we must recognize just as we do that of the body. The soul too has its clothing of which we must not deprive it, and no one has a right to say to another, "Because we belong to each other as we do, I have a right to know all your thoughts." Not even a mother may treat her child in that way. . . . It is only giving that stimulates. Impart as much as you can of your spiritual being to those who are on the road with you, and accept as something precious what comes back to you from them.

Reverence for Life is another name for the Will-to-Love; but love which seeks to be possessive is not worthy of the name. As one of our own poets has said: "Be ready to release as to receive. Deem those the nearest, soul to soul, between whose lips yet lingers reverence on a sigh."

When in 1905, as the result of nine years' deliberation culminating in a hidden fixed resolve, Schweitzer was about to embark on the adventure of Christian discipleship and acquainted his friends and kinsfolk with his decision, he found himself exposed to a hurricane of expostulations. Why had he not consulted them first? Why waste his talents thus? What was the motive that prompted such a quixotic enterprise, or the reason to explain it? "How much I suffered through so many people assuming the right to tear open all the doors and shutters of my inner self . . . and who tried to dig their fists into my heart!"

For nearly half a century since then he has toiled at his self-appointed task in the jungle swamps, for most of that time—save for brief visits to Europe—in obscurity. In 1949 came the offer of a lecture tour in America, when he emerged with reluctance into the limelight, and since then he has become the target of full-scale publicity. In 1952 the announcement of the award of the Nobel Peace Prize was made. The news reached him while he was engaged in cleaning out the pens of his pet antelopes. On hearing it he offered no remark but went on with his work. A few days later, however, when telegrams and letters began to pour in by the sackful, he was heard to murmur, "Well, if this is fame, I'd just as soon it was posthumous." But it was also for him the fulfilment of a long-cherished dream: he could now at long last, in the evening of his life, build his leper hospital on enduring foundations. Not till the following year could he find time to go to Oslo to receive the award.

Then the magnitude and enthusiasm of his reception, it was said, was equalled only by that accorded by the Norwegians to their own fellow countryman, Nansen. One remark that he made in his address deserves notice. "Only as the common peoples of the world, and the individual persons contained in it, foster within themselves the ideal of peace, will those at the helm of the world's destiny begin to conform to it. Only then will we see the beginnings of an effort made by every nation to repair, as far as possible, the wrongs which each has inflicted on the other."

In the following year he was awarded the honorary Order of Merit by the young Queen of England. It is an honor which only one other man of non-British nationality in our day has received— President Eisenhower. He was deeply touched by this, for he has never forgotten that England was the first country to support his mission in Africa, even before it had recovered from the shock of the First World War, and he has adopted the word *fairplay* as a favorite word in his vocabulary. I had the good fortune to meet him in London on the following day and received the impression of a most colorful and vigorous personality. His manner is exceedingly animated and alert; his utterances and gestures emphatic and decided. But his eyes are his most expressive feature. When he is silent they are lowered and half closed, but when in conversation their expression varies with his mood: brooding or twinkling or kindling or quizzical—but always friendly. His voice is low, mellow, and musical—a tenor—the pitch varying with his mood; he has a silvery, tinkling laugh. One receives the impression of tremendous vitality, yet he can relax at will into an attitude of complete repose. Then the mobile features, alight with vivacity a moment before, become set with the gravity of an old coin. For four uninterrupted hours on that day and the day following he received—as his custom is when he returns to civilization—a host of unknown visitors in an apparently unending queue who had come from far and near to seek his counsel or to question his opinion without premeditating upon any and every kind of topic: a concentrated brain trust, as it were. By far the majority of this host of interviewers were ordinary folk; only some few were persons of eminence. Among the latter on the first day came Ralph Vaughan Williams to request his interpretation of a passage in a fugue of Bach; and Bertrand Russell to talk of the prohibition of atomic bomb tests and of their mutual friend Einstein. He rose from his chair to escort these distinguished men to the door with due courtesy, but he allowed to them no longer an interview than to the humblest of his visitors, to each one of whom he gave his undivided and respectful attention, and gave himself to them without reserve. It was a moving experience to witness, and one felt that one had oneself been in the presence of, and had had the privilege of conversing with, a modern disciple of Christ.

During recent years he has spoken out in broadcasts, and wielded his pen in pamphlets translated into many languages, in appeals to the conscience of mankind to put an end to atomic bomb tests. Severely scientific in its approach, his treatment of the subject is a technical summary of the meteorological effects of such experiments on animal and vegetable life, with the warning that they will not make their devastating presence felt for many years. Naturally this has been contested by government-sponsored scientists, but acclaimed as true by the free scientists throughout the world. It was the last request of his friend Einstein that he should lead this campaign. His appeal is addressed, just as his Peace Prize address was, to the conscience of individuals. "When public opinion has been created," he says, "then the statesmen may reach an agreement to stop these experiments."

Elsewhere I have ventured the opinion that Schweitzer is probably the most gifted genius of our age, as well as its most prophetic thinker. What manner of man is he? Temperamentally, he is possessed of a nature unruffled and serene, free from the conflict of strong passions, in harmony with the moral order: evidently a "once-born" type. Certain it is that he has never undergone the experience of conversion, but has grown up in the Christian faith as in his natural rightful environment. Nevertheless, this has been gained at the cost of constant inner discipline and steady self-control. In every sense of the word he is a big man. His lack of all self-consciousness; his freedom from inhibitions; his enthusiasm, forcefulness, and directness of address; his quickness of apprehension, his feeling for essentials and impatience with irrelevances; his versatility and the amazing many-sidedness of his interests and pursuits—these are qualities that might be disconcerting to duller wits, were they not tempered with an innate humility, a disarming shyness, and a ready sympathy that invites confidence. Sanity and soundness—all that can be expressed by the word wholesomeness—are the hallmarks of his own vigorous personality. It is difficult to say which is the strongest characteristic, sobriety or zest. Emotionally, the dominant sentiments that have motivated his conduct all through his life may be said to be these two: gratitude and compassion.

Toil and hardship and isolation have not dulled the edge of his alert, adventurous mind or dimmed his vision of the One Ideal or quenched the ardor of his quest for all that is good and beautiful and true. Scholar, thinker, musician, physician, citizen of the world, he is one of those of whom it may be said with truth that "age cannot wither them, neither the years condemn." At the end of a sketch of his life and thought, written as long ago as 1933, he mentions the many anxieties, troubles, and sorrows that had even then fallen to his lot, and the heavy burden of responsibility that had been laid upon him without a break for years; and then proceeds, in moving and noble words, to enumerate his many blessings: the fact that he had been allowed to work so long in the service of mercy; his many friends and helpers; the gift of a robust constitution and equable temperament and capacity for conserving energy; and finally the fact that he can recognize whatever happiness that comes to him as a thing for which some thank-offering is due.

One last comment. It is his unalterable conviction, which he has put to the test and proved upon his pulses, that it is only by obeying the commandment of Jesus, "Follow Me," that we shall ever truly begin to know him or to enter into his fellowship. Only as we strive to participate, each of us in his or her infinitesimally small degree, in the work of the world's redemption which is still in progress— only so shall we ever come to know him as our Redeemer. Only by the daring adventure of "following Jesus in the way" shall we ever come to recognize him for what he really is. The memorable words with which he ended his *Quest of the Historical Jesus,* penned as they were in his untried youth, may yet stand as the most fitting ending to any account of him and his whole life's work:

He comes to us as One unknown, without a name, as of old by the lakeside he came to those men who knew him not. He speaks to us the same word, Follow thou me; and sets us to the tasks which he has to fulfill for our time. He commands. And to those who obey him, whether they be wise or simple, learned or unlearned, he will reveal himself in the peace, the toils, the conflicts, and the sufferings which they will pass through in his fellowship, till as an inexpressible mystery they shall come to learn in their own experience Who He Is.[4]

[4] New York, Macmillan.

7

Tubby Clayton

BY MELVILLE HARCOURT

MELVILLE HARCOURT *has served as a priest in the Episcopal Church of the United States for some years. He is the author of several books, one of which, concerned with a* cause célèbre, *was primarily responsible for legal reforms. His full-length biography of Tubby Clayton was published in London and this country in 1953. He is at present Rector of the Diocesan Church of St. Ann, Bishop's Vicar, and Canon Pastor in the Diocese of Long Island, New York.*

On the Fourteenth Sunday after Trinity in the year 1954, I stood at the altar of All Hallows, Barking-by-the-Tower, London, and celebrated Holy Communion according to the American Rite. All around, seen and sensed, were the tragic evidences of the recent war and the implements of workmen busy with the task of reconstruction. But neither time nor human contrivance, I thought, could erase from the minds of many kneeling before that altar the dreadful memory of the night when a bomb, plainly meant for the Tower of London, crashed into the east vestry, which disappeared in a moment, or the later occasion when German planes streaking across the sky left behind them a trail of incendiaries that completely gutted the ancient church.

For well over a thousand years All Hallows had stood on that spot. Through the generations the old church had seen the fields that once embraced it transformed into the dwellings of prosperous merchants and then, sadly, into tenements and gloomy warehouses that stifled the freedom and gaiety of the children of East London. In 1922, however, a wonderful thing happened in the life of the Hill. There came to All Hallows a new vicar, Tubby Clayton, with the Gospel on his lips and a world movement, Toc H, in his hands, and Tower Hill became the focal point of an international brotherhood drawing its inspiration from Jesus Christ and its dynamism from the dedicated energy of one man. Soon the Hill, in truly scriptural fashion, began to throng with all sorts of people, men of divers tongues and races, each trying to realize the ideal of Christian brotherhood as preached by this jolly, portly parson who, among many other things, had begun to dream of a remodelled Tower Hill on which beauty and Cockney laughter would eventually replace ugliness and the harsh sounds of industry. At the center would be All Hallows, ever reminding men that they are brothers touched with the dust of immortality. Then came, in the course of time, the dread nights of the early 'forties which razed All Hallows to the ground, but also, with the one stroke, much that had obscured the vision of beauty.

Thus it was that I stood at the altar of a new All Hallows, rising impressively from the ashes, while all around, beneath chisel and hammer, were emerging the actual outlines of the beauty envisaged by Tubby thirty years previously. It had all been made possible, Tubby told me, by brotherhood, a brotherhood that scorned local prejudices and national boundaries to recognize, instantly and generously, a fellow Christian's need. Certainly the vicar of All Hallows, and his "complicated series of friends" across the globe, can say with William Penn, who worshipped at the church and founded the State of Pennsylvania, "In making friends consider well first; and when you are fixed, be true; not wavering by reports, nor deserting in affliction; for that becomes not the good and virtuous."

Characteristically, Tubby, tenaciously loyal in friendship, has always blithely ignored the opening clause of William Penn's dictum; indeed, his entire ministry, not to mention his peculiar effectiveness as an individual, has been based upon the acceptance of a maxim less circumspect but rather more perceptive: "You win men by trusting them." In his personal diary is to be found a vast and curious miscellany drawn from every class and across practically every national boundary, and to him all of them—be they British proconsul or a Southern sharecropper, a Turkish pasha or a Masai tribesman, an American college boy or a London taxi driver—are "perfectly splendid fellows." It was this unusual capacity for affection that was marked by all ranks and quickly secured him a unique place in the dangerous economy of the Western Front in World War I. The man was instinct with humor and affection, he not merely loved his fellow men, he actually liked them, and the difference is both subtle and enormous. The letters he wrote home at the time are full of phrases such as these: ". . . the men are quite wonderful. One is always unearthing something splendid . . . jolly chaps of the very best type; they nearly brought the chapel floor down on Sunday with their numbers. . . . The Guards were not only admirable, they were actually lovable." He really meant every word of it and it did not occur to him that some might be rascals, or had motives that were questionable.

But if Tubby was uncritical of the troops, they themselves did not look upon it as a matter for censure; and while we may be inclined to regard such an attitude as a flaw, there is no escaping the fact that it was an advantage at the time. After all, it is not the critical manner that elicits confidence from others, but the suggestion of trust and understanding. "The mark of true sublimity in a man," it has been said, "is that he does not seek his own"—and no one has ever accused Tubby of seeking his own. Men sensed this unselfishness and rated it as the measure of his faith. His air of gaiety, his irrepressible humor, could not conceal the real purpose of his life which, quite frankly, was to bring men to God. If men sought other things, then he was not the dispenser. It was as simple as that.

It seems almost irreverent to suggest that the bearer of the distinctive sobriquet "Tubby" should actually possess another name, but official records reveal it as Philip Thomas Byard Clayton, often shortened to "P.B.C." He was born in Queensland, Australia, in December 1885, but the Claytons returned to their native England when he was a year old and he did not see the country again until after the First World War. His parents, a truly remarkable couple, had lost a substantial fortune in Queensland, but the father, though past forty, walked into the City of London and amassed another within twenty years; unusual, perhaps, but then the Claytons and

Sheppards (the father married his cousin) had been doing unusual things for several centuries, and often to the great benefit of the realm.

It was in the lower forms of Colet Court that Philip Clayton, cylindrical though miniature, first acquired the nickname "Tubby," and an inscrutable providence apparently decreed that the *embonpoint* and the nickname should remain conjoined forever. At his public school his gifts for phrase and friendship were already patent, and contemporary Paulines still recall, with a catch of the breath, the sight of this extraordinary schoolboy, circa sixteen, walking arm in arm with the awesome High Master of St. Paul's, F. W. Walker, as they chuckled their way down a corridor. And years later, on the eve of a world tour, we have A. A. Milne paying tribute to the same basic qualities that distinguished the schoolboy, "You have the best of gospels to preach. I see Toc H in your person, rolling round the world like an enormous snowball, getting, if I may say so, tubbier and tubbier with the new devotees it attracts to itself."

The schoolboy was unusually bright and the "tubbiness" exceptionally tough. Although his brother Hugh (later Sir Hugh Clayton, Governor of Bombay) had been Captain of the School, it was not long before young Tubby won respect in his own right. Among his endowments had been discovered, quite by accident, a most useful talent for swinging a right of such power that opponents three or four years his senior had been dropped in their tracks. This convincing accomplishment permitted him to address himself, without undue interference, to the mastery of the classics and the development of a smashing forehand at tennis, besides which he acquired a dilettantish whim for reading Spinoza and composing vers libre over tankards of ginger beer. It is hardly surprising that the holidays of such a lad were apt to be a little out of the ordinary. Accompanied by Cecil Rushton, with whom he had formed a sensitive and enduring friendship, the teen-age consorts—if not riding the North Sea in an old tramp steamer—would invade the Continent on expeditions whose planning owed more to Mandeville than to Baedeker. Each armed with five pounds and a scorn for the accepted routes, they travelled as far as their money would take them and then, bereft of funds but not the white magic of imagination, made their way home by ingenuities seldom learned in schoolrooms. Turnu-Severin . . . Lichtenstein . . . Scheveningen, and many besides, surrendered their fabled mysteries and gave Tubby his first acquaintance with a "motley medley of nationalities"—perhaps, too, they were really the basis of his oft-repeated remark, "There is more truth in legend than in fact."

The remark should be discounted when Tubby occasionally shows visitors to Tower Hill six large notebooks which, he declares, contain all that he ever learned at Oxford. It is one of the minor exaggerations he sometimes uses for dramatic effect or personal belittlement; in fact, he owed a great deal to personalities. It was Dr. John Stansfeld, dark-bearded and magnetic, who summoned him and some of Oxford's brightest and gayest to learn their first lessons in social consciousness amid the dreary streets and lives of London's Bermondsey district. And Henry Scott Holland, preaching a gospel of grand designs from the pulpit of St. Paul's Cathedral and in the common rooms of Oxford, caught the heart of Tubby, as he caught the hearts of many, with the beauty of truth. Tubby, like so many alert young men, had coquetted with agnosticism. He had even gone up to the University with the express object of proving Christianity demonstrably untrue, but, he afterwards confessed, the facts were too good and he ended up being converted. But that was not all. The influence of Stansfeld and Scott Holland turned his thoughts to Armitage Robinson, the remarkable Dean of Westminster, whose custom it was each year to take four young men of recognized brilliance (in law, politics, theology, and medicine) to read with him at the Abbey. It was a cathartic experience because the one-eyed Dean, a scholar and Alpinist of international reputation, was both sweet-natured and terrible-tempered. "A wind-blown personality," remarked a contemporary, "more fitted for the Helvetian altitudes than the interior of an Anglican church."

At the Abbey, where, incidentally, his researches earned him a fellowship in the Antiquarian Society at the age of twenty-three, he came within the orbit of the frail and saintly Richard Rackham, one of the founders of the Community of the Resurrection, Mirfield, and chief of the Dean's staff. Many notables came and went, among them Charles Gore and the painfully able Hensley Henson, but it was to Rackham that Tubby turned in his hour of spiritual crisis, and that skilled physician of the soul sent him to his knees in the Abbey to review his life searchingly. Writing of the experience years later, Tubby had this to say:

Today, when many forms of auricular confession are practiced in churches and in Harley Street, and some without all scientific safeguards, it is not easy to recapture the animosity with which Rackham knew I would receive his next suggestion. It was that I should go to a good priest and lay open my grief. This I refused to do; and went on fighting until I could fight no longer. He sent me to Father Trevelyan, then at Liddon House. And there one autumn night I left my past behind me.

His curacy at St. Mary's, Portsea, was in many ways an exercise in humility. There were fifty-six thousand souls in the parish and eighteen curates, whom he joined, the most junior of all. The fact that Magdalen had offered him an appointment on the strength of the ablest papers of a generation in his subject, and his research work at the Abbey had been officially recognized, mattered not at all—he was put in charge of housekeeping for the clergy and commanded to unravel the hopelessly entangled domestic accounts! It says much for his resourcefulness that he not only did the job extremely well—feeding his confreres with eupeptic ardor and, at the same time, straightening the accounts—but became a legend in the parish to boot.

The chunky figure, with the inevitable pipe and infectious geniality, was a familiar in practically every Portsea doorway, and his brisk enthusiasms, his cheerful disregard for time or place, had all sorts of people doing the most extraordinary things with the most extraordinary gusto. He had about him a quality of radiance which found immediate expression in the total unawareness of self and an untiring concern for the needs of others. He had, too, the rare talent of making people feel they mattered, really mattered, and that went for young peers as well as forgotten charwomen. Cyril Garbett, the vicar of Portsea and future Archbishop of York, gives a glimpse of the youthful Tubby working his incantations on the vicarage lawn:

I at once gave him [Tubby] charge of a large Bible Class and Club for boys between the ages of sixteen and twenty. A fortnight later, on a Sunday evening after church, I heard roars of laughter from the vicarage garden; on looking out of my window I saw Tubby surrounded by a great crowd of boys and young men, sitting on the grass or standing, while he was holding forth to them on a variety of subjects. From that time I had no doubt that he was superlatively good with lads and young men. Before long he knew individually every one of the lads who were in his Club and Bible Class, everything that concerned them was of interest to him, and in return they gave to him a loyalty and devotion which continued in a great many cases throughout their lives. . . . Throughout the war Tubby kept in touch with the parish, always coming to it for a few days on his leaves.

War means many things to the men and women involved, and the glorious and the inglorious are not always distinct. To some few it brings self-realization, an unexpected release from the commonplace; to others fear, heartbreak, the corroding bitterness of loss; to many mutilation or, more mercifully, death: to Tubby it brought the opportunity to serve human beings. It is doubtful whether he ever rationalized the political issues—that could be left to others, safely or otherwise—but his days and nights were tormented by the needs of others, men he had known, men he had loved. If Christ were to walk in Flanders, if His voice were to cheer, His hands to help and heal, then Tubby, and others like him, must be His agents of hope.

By the time he landed in France the war was already several months old, and the jingoism of the early days was giving way to the realization that the war was going to be long and diabolic, quite unlike all previous wars. The mobility of the old-time armies had congealed into the bone-rotting misery of trench warfare, and men were discovering that they had as much to fear from mud and boredom as from guns and poison gas. Although he could not have been aware of it at the outset, it was to be Tubby's singular task to acquaint men with the sanity of familiar things, and to lift their hearts above the paralyzing boredom that was more fearful than fear itself.

He was first stationed at No. 16 General Hospital, Le Tréport, and then sent, by special request, to work under his old friend Neville Talbot at Poperinghe, Belgium. Poperinghe, a town of approximately eleven thousand, was near enough to the front line to be readily accessible to the troops but not sufficiently important militarily to be mentioned on ordnance maps; its population varied according to the dictates of strategy or fortune, sometimes being not more than fifty souls, at others nearer a quarter of a million. But, empty or congested, the *estaminets* and souvenir shops on the great square and narrow gnarled streets went gaily on, often to the rataplan of distant cannon, occasionally to the shuddering blast of a large shell in a nearby garden. For four years Poperinghe was a halfway house to death for untold numbers, to others a blessed though temporary relief from the mud and blood and horror of the trenches; but for four years it never lost its sense of crisis and the emotional extravagances that go with it. To Tubby, ever a son of the market place and billeted in a "kind of Wild West log hut," the challenge was magnificent—"more in the style of a prehistoric peep at my old parish than anything else," he wrote—and he thereupon borrowed an elderly and asthmatical horse to explore his new responsibilities. He quickly recognized the urgency of acquiring a house, or some sort of headquarters through which the Church could be brought into more durable contact with all "those perfectly splendid fellows."

The acquisition of No. 16, a tall white house on the arching Rue de l'Hôpital, is a tale in itself, and not one that particularly favors the owner, M. Camerlynck. Be that as it may, No. 16 promptly changed its Flemish respectability for the lively bonhomie of a wartime hostel—run strictly on unconventional lines. It was to be known as Talbot House. This was intended to honor Neville Talbot, the senior chaplain, but he objected so strenuously that the name was adopted to commemorate his brother Gilbert, the youngest of the Bishop of Winchester's sons, who had been killed at Hooge on July 30, 1915. It was in such wise that Talbot House entered the world of reality.

It was a large edifice, liberally designed, and, in spite of certain damage to the upper structure, it still retained an elegance of line. A wide hall ran the length of the house from which could be seen the capacious drawing room and the smaller dining room whose windows opened to the flowers and trees of the garden; on the right of the hall was an office and kitchen. An ornate gold-and-white staircase climbed to the ample rooms on the first floor, above which were the servants' quarters and a huge nursery; finally there was the attic, used for storing fruit and vegetables and reached by an awkward companion-ladder. Tubby's fecund imagination instantly grasped the possibilities. The drawing room, he cheerfully proclaimed, would become the recreation room with some sort of refreshment bar, dry of course; the next floor the library, writing rooms, and the chaplain's room; and the floor above would become bedrooms to accommodate for a night or two fellows going on leave or passing through Pop'. But what of the chapel—the focal point of an establishment controlled by the Church? It was then that Tubby thought of the attic, the Upper Room he called it, and by an inspiration hardly less wonderful an old carpenter's bench, discovered in the garden, became the altar. The symbolism was to be deeply meaningful to the customers of Talbot House.

Over the years Tubby has often begged, and, whenever the cause demands, no one can be more irresistible. Men of high and low degree in all parts of the world have received, from time to time, letters that have made them suddenly aware that they owned a conscience, and not a very comfortable one at that. The letters are often gems of importunity in which begging is refined to a spiritual exercise. Few, however calloused, have resisted the appeals, and certainly not the dear old ladies whom, through friends or personal acquaintance, he tracked down to their various homes. By means of this private thaumaturgy the House was comfortably furnished within weeks; moreover, marvellous to relate, two pianos had been acquired in the Salient under circumstances most mysterious. "I handed over one to Bates," he records, "for a hut at Peselhoek— the worst one, of course. The other was very good indeed, and even in its old age, after three years of constant strumming, retained its tone. Moreover it had learnt things. If you so much as sat down before it in 1918, it played 'A Little Grey Home in the West' without further action on your part." It was not going to be the innkeeper's fault if his customers lacked song—they would have to look elsewhere if they wanted wine and women.

He was an innkeeper by official fiat, but surely an innkeeper unique in the world of his time. He ministered to the physical needs of his customers as good hostelers have done everywhere in every age, but *his* customers had either just escaped or were on the verge of death: he brought to them a verve, a brilliance of spirit which made them, suddenly, unexpectedly, aware of deep things and unfamiliar destinies. Looking at him in those Poperinghe days was much the same as looking at him in his Oxford days or thirty years later, plus or minus wrinkles and the grayness of age. There was always about him a curious immutability, derived from the spirit rather than the body, and this has tended to stabilize his image in the minds of his friends and the public.

He was about five feet five or six, and his rotundity, then as always, had a puckish, Churchillian line suggestive of considerable power and stamina, not flaccid but firm with the resilience of good muscle tone. It was the head that set him apart. Large and noble, it could have dignified a giant with its splendid sweep of brow beneath crisp brown hair; the eyes behind the horn-rimmed spectacles were those of a thinker, a dreamer, and the strong, almost ruthless line of the jaw was redeemed by a certain sweetness of mouth and the sensitive nostrils. It was a face that engendered confidence, a sense of trust; perhaps the face of a mystic committed to action. And the deep-timbred voice, with its repetitive mannerism, "My . . . my dear old boy, I . . . er . . . I . . . ," was as individual as the man himself. It was obvious to most, of course, that his gifts and record had equipped him superbly for the scholar's life, but the obsessive concentration, to the exclusion of every competing interest, would have been quite unendurable to one of his temperament; and his temperament, in all fairness, would have been catastrophic to any normal university which preferred tranquility to anarchy, however cheerful and right-minded. In any case, in Tubby's rationale faith and works are inseparable; and while he was quick to concede that if a faith were to endure the best minds of each age must collaborate in its formulation, yet, at the same time, he would impishly observe that without works there would be no real faith for people to believe in, not even the scholars. "There's a believin' side to religion," said the old Negro evangelist, "and a doin' side"—and Tubby wholeheartedly put the accent on doing.

It was the "doin'," robustious and mirth-provoking, with the undertone of deeper things, that gave to Talbot House its individual quality. Laughter was the prime commodity, and the well of its inspiration was amply supplied by Tubby's gnomic genius; throughout the house, in rooms and halls, appeared a variety of notices, pertinent and impertinent. Three of the notices were permanent fixtures and were familiar to every visitor. The first, in the form of a hand, pointed to the front door with the inscription: "To Pessimists —Emergency Exit." The second was over the Visitor's Book required to be signed by everyone; it read: "Please write your name and address in the Visitor's Book. Otherwise how can we forward your umbrella or trace our teaspoons?" And the third, with welcoming irony: "If you are accustomed to spit on the carpet at home, please spit here." The tone had been set, and the visitor prepared for the indiscretions of the Notice Board; these varied but were seldom inapposite:

STOP PRESS

A tiny draft of reinforcements in woolies—i.e., socks, etc.—has reached T. H. from the ever-generous Mrs. Fry of Bristol. Applications for the same should be made to the Chaplain. All queues prohibited by Sir A. Yapp. Allotment, one sock per battalion.

HOW TO FIND YOUR BEARINGS ON A DARK NIGHT WITHOUT A COMPASS
THIS IS AN OLD SCOUT'S TIP

Take a watch, not your own, tie a string to it, swing it round your head three times, and then let go, saying to the owner, "That's gone West." The points of the compass being thus established, you proceed rapidly in the safest direction. P.B.C.

EXCELSIOR!

The number of otherwise intelligent human beings who hang about the hall, reading silly notices, and catching well-deserved colds, is most distressing. An occasional straggler drags himself up the staircase, generally in futile search for the canteen, which confronts him in the garden.

> Otherwise oil and fuel upstairs waste their sweetness
> and the rooms and pictures their welcome.
>> Come Upstairs and Risk Meeting

THE CHAPLAIN

As Kipling so finely says:

> What shall they know of Talbot House
> Who only the ground floor know?

It was worth the struggle through the hall and up the crowded staircase to reach the Chaplain's door, above which was printed an arresting parody of Dante's inscription over the Gates of Hell, "All rank abandon, ye who enter here." The command, apparently, was taken quite literally because the congested, smoke-filled room held every conceivable rank, standing in groups, lolling in chairs, propped against the mantel, perched on the windowsills, as they chatted gaily and unselfconsciously or roared with laughter at the repartee and audacious sallies of the rubicund gnome presiding over tea at the fireplace. The atmosphere struck like an electric charge, and before a man could decide whether to stay or leave a huge red-faced brigadier or an Australian digger would haul him into the room; the next thing he knew was Tubby pumping his hand and introducing "Clapham Common" (if he came from those parts) to "Harrow Weald" or "Rose Bay, Sydney." It was wonderfully friendly and, somehow, reassuring to the stranger, especially a youngster fresh from home. The barriers were down and men met as men undivided by the artificial insignia of rank. The visitor soon caught the mood of uncritical friendship and the reason behind the most inflexible rule of the house, "Today's guest is tomorrow's host." It was a vivid practical illustration of Christian brotherhood which owed its impulse to an unusual man—but, unfortunately, the Tubbies of this world are as rare as genuine brotherhood. It was, indeed, to perpetuate this very spirit that Tubby, with inspired pertinacity, transplanted the ethos of the Old House, as it was affectionately called, to the shores of Britain and beyond, giving Talbot House its conspicuous Morse Code rendering, Toc H.

Let it not be imagined that The Reverend Philip Byard Clayton spent his entire time and talent amusing the soldiery in Talbot House. His parish, to use his own words, was that particular sector of the Salient where he regularly visited his beloved batteries far and near, bringing them something of the gay optimism of the Old House; to officers and men these visits were red-letter days, touched with solemnity, for he invariably brought "the Crown Jewels," as he called the sacred vessels for the Eucharist. It was on one such occasion that he earned a Military Cross for gallantry, and on another sat up all night with a weeping young lieutenant, much decorated for bravery, who, having reached the very limit of endurance, was certain he was going to die on the morrow. He followed a merciless routine, often working eighteen or twenty hours a day running the house, conducting services, dispatching a mountainous daily mail, counselling worried and desperate men, dashing to points hither and thither as he kept in constant touch with his "parishioners" along the Front. His sleeping all too frequently consisted of catnaps in library and hall chairs, but even his cyclonic energy could not take such beating, and every now and then he would collapse with a high fever. It was then that Dr. Browne and Pettifer, his batman, stepped in, and, dismissing his violent protests, forced him to bed with the dire threat of being invalided to England.

It has become habitual for those who have known Tubby and his works to write about him with an enthusiasm that sometimes appears exaggerated. In fairness it must be admitted that, like every strong character with a sense of mission, he has evoked devotion or resentment, but none has ever questioned the selflessness of his motives; during later years the means by which he achieved the ends may have appeared a little harsh, but they were never petty or selfish. And it was this cheerful abnegation of self under conditions that were often provoking, and frequently dangerous, that excited esteem and, very quickly, genuine devotion. Even if we accuse the sentimental of apotheosizing a popular figure whose tricks and fancies happened to catch the imagination of war-weary troops, it is not so easy to dismiss the tribute of a trained observer who worked beside him, shared his problems, and knew him intimately. Such a one was Captain Leonard Browne of the Royal Army Medical Corps, who had this to say:

It is wonderful how the childlike spirit appeals to men—or at any rate to the best of men. It seems to have the power of drawing out the very best that every man possesses. An infinite belief in human nature, especially the men of the B.E.F., enabled P.B.C. to get into the real "back-shop" of most men's minds. He was able to lift them out of the sordidness of their surroundings and set them on their feet again. . . . Talbot House was to the B.E.F. in the Salient what the House Beautiful was to the pilgrims in Bunyan's wonderful "Similitude of a Dream." From the House many a man, after resting for a while in the chamber which is called Peace, went on his way ready to fight victoriously against Apollyon, the Prince of the Powers of Darkness.

It was never forgotten by Tubby, and great numbers of his "customers," that the source of his power lay in the Upper Room. Among the few golden memories of many an old soldier is the sight of "the Padre," stooped and reverent, celebrating the Sacred Mysteries in his oddly intimate manner, while the Chapel creaked and groaned protestingly to the exploding shells in near-by gardens. It was not by chance that thousands of men climbed to the hop-loft where hung the Cross, any more than it was chance that led a young soldier-poet of the time to write as a prelude to his own death,

> And think, this heart, all evil shed away,
> A pulse in the eternal mind, no less
> Gives somewhere back the thoughts by England given.[1]

[1] From "The Soldier," by Rupert Brooke. Reprinted from *The Collected Poems of Rupert Brooke* by permission of Dodd, Mead & Company. Copyright, 1915, by Dodd, Mead & Company, Inc. Copyright, 1943, by Edward Marsh.

Cynics may scoff and say with Charles Hamilton Sorley (who was indignant but hardly old enough to be cynical), "He has clothed his attitude in fine words; but his is, nevertheless, the sentimental attitude." They can point to the thousands with their dirty songs and dreary minds, half-men and half-beasts, trained for murder but indifferent to decency, and they are right, but only half right. There were others, such as climbed to the Upper Room, whose thoughts could rise above their boots and bellies and feel, occasionally, a kinship with something fine. It was they who gave character to the chapel, it was they who would recognize the essential truth of Neville Talbot's words written in a foreword to one of Tubby's books after the War: "Talbot House . . . was open to all the world, was full of friendship, hominess, fun, music, games, laughter, books, pictures and discussion. And at the top, in the loft, obtruding upon no one, but dominating everything, was the Chapel—a veritable shrine, glowing with the beauty of holiness. Thus, above and below, the House was full of the glory of God."

From these men, and indeed the hundreds of thousands who visited Talbot House, came the first names for the Service Ordination Scheme, the scheme whereby men, be they temporary colonels or gentlemen rankers, expressed their desire to prepare for Holy Orders in a post-war world whose most imperative need would be moral leadership. Tubby, quite spontaneously, began to recruit men after reading an article in a Church paper, *The Challenge,* emphasizing the acute shortage of priests, and when the names at the house had reached five hundred—a truly astonishing effort for one man—the matter was reported to the Church authorities.

With commendable vision they accepted the offer and appointed the Archbishop of York to represent them in making the necessary arrangements for training the men, a formidable task by any measurement. Yet scarcely had the Armistice been signed than two schools for trainees were opened in France—one at Radingham for officers, the other at Le Touquet for the ranks. It was the latter that Tubby joined in December 1918 with a group of selected chaplains.

The school was lodged in the old Machine Gun School but, owing to the shortage of space, lectures were held on the wind-swept beach where the letters of the Greek alphabet were drawn with a stick in the sand. The students filed by, committing them to memory and, no matter how biting the wind, no man was dismissed until all had mastered the lesson; the laggard was not popular. The high-pressure technique got excellent results. In one of his books, *Plain Tales from Flanders,* Tubby has this to say:

Lectures were given of the most far-reaching character, some instructors being so learned that men rubbed their eyes, and others intellectual adventurers who skated precariously across the thin crust which covered their consummate ignorance. I was myself notorious for a series of three lectures embracing the history of the world. The first ranged from the Creation to the death of Julius Caesar; the second to the Reformation, and the third to the Armistice. My colleagues, however, were far better equipped, and included some far-sighted men of real capacity.

But the students of Le Touquet were anxious to have done with khaki and get on with the job of preparation. Demobilization played strange tricks with the national economy and Government promises, and it also confronted the Church with the problem of accommodating the men it had promised to train. It was the crucial test—had the Church the ability to redeem its pledge? On this occasion it responded impressively. In short, Tubby was instructed to secure quarters in England, and, accompanied by Leonard Browne, he swung round the kingdom in a fruitless search, going even to an American Army camp at Winchester. Suddenly, with real insight, he turned to the Home Secretary, and came up with a most surprising solution—Knutsford Prison.

The deserted Knutsford Prison was a vast, gloomy pile whose great walls had known only tragedy and human degradation. "We shall never forget the horror and disgust struck into us by the first sight of our new home," wrote F. R. Barry, later Bishop of Southwell; but Tubby was completely fascinated by it, his mind leapt to its possibilities, his buoyant spirit soared to the challenge of its massive ugliness. Knutsford, it must be remembered, was not a substitute for a university or a theological seminary but a place designed to "test vocation" and prepare men to enter such institutions. Some of the men had received first-class educations and others very little, but all had character, or otherwise they would not have been at Knutsford. It was at Knutsford that the concept of brotherhood acquired some reality at the sight of colonels and naval commanders hobnobbing as equals with buck privates and riflemen, and the students were more conscious each day of the leavening wonder of their faith. In four years Knutsford helped prepare for Holy Orders sixteen hundred men—many of them scattered across the globe today—and the Church expended nearly £500,000 on their training. The Bishop of Southwell truly wrote on the occasion of Tubby's sixtieth birthday, December 12, 1945:

. . . the days when we worked together at Knutsford in that prison School for Service Ordination Candidates, of which he was the true Father Founder, and to which he gave his genius and insight. Nobody looking back on that great time can say he was a particularly docile or cloistral inmate of the institution; but to him it owed a very great deal of what was best and characteristic in it, and the Old House at Poperinghe was always its background.

In his First Epistle to the Corinthians St. Paul refers to the diversity of gifts among men and how each is called upon to exercise his particular talent because it is "the same God which worketh all in all." Quite obviously, a distinguished theologian or historian is seldom to be found far from the world of libraries and scholarly opinion any more than a barn-storming evangelist is going to spend most of his time thumbing old manuscripts. Each must recognize his mission and try to fulfill it to the best of his ability. If his talents are varied, then clearly he must operate that which is best suited to realize God's purpose for men. Tubby, for instance, had the equipment of the scholar but also the talents of a first-class entrepreneur; the latter, allied to creative genius and a genuine love for men, destined him to play a significant role in the world of action. He was, it might be said, an activist by inclination and circumstance, though not entirely by mental bias; having acknowledged his role, he developed it to the full. And what is more, he did it with incomparable cheerfulness, a cheerfulness that sent sunshine and laughter darting through the corridors of men's hearts. It was no accident of taste that Max Beerbohm caricatured him so gaily and *Punch* featured him—he belonged, by nature, to their laughing company. One of his most characteristic remarks has always been, "If your religion makes you gloomy, you may have dyspepsia but you haven't got religion."

If the spirit of Talbot House was the background of Knutsford, it was the same spirit that took him periodically to London to meet old friends and explore the possibility of creating some sort of permanent fellowship. Ideals, he realized only too well, are not translated into action by the visionary who prefers the armchair to the battlefield, and he who estimates his losses before taking the field has already lost the battle. Losses there would be—he had the courage to take them—but the eventual gains would more than compensate, and, in the meantime, it would be best to cut all commitments and get on with the job. Nineteen pounds and an old typewriter were not much in the way of assets, but the courage was there and ingenuity most often offset the lack of money. Those were the days of such honored names in the early history of Toc H as The Challenge, Queen's Gate Gardens, Effingham House and No. 36 Red Lion Square—where, in the absence of a doorbell, a luggage label attached to a long piece of string was hung from the window. On it was written: "Rev. P. B. Clayton, once of Talbot House, Poperinghe." When the string was pulled, Tubby or his batman, Pettifer, rushed downstairs to greet old friends.

An executive committee had already been formed by 1920 and

the support secured of influential figures. It was unanimously agreed to call the new society by the signaller's diminutive for Talbot House, Toc H.

Its name [explained Tubby to the Royal Empire Society in 1931] is simply due to the old Army method of calling letters by symbolic syllables, which served to keep them quite distinct when men's lives hung upon the accuracy of a telephone message. During the War D was called Don, V was Vic, and T was Toc: with the result that troops, speaking in "signalese," instead of saying, "Let us go down to Talbot House in Poperinghe," said "Let's go down to Toc H in Pop."

It was a clever maneuver because, though the symbol was familiar to ex-servicemen, it was sufficiently odd to demand explanation for the inquiring layman. Here, of course, is not the place to give a detailed account of the genesis of Toc H in Britain, but it should be borne in mind that Toc H is inexplicable apart from Tubby, its founder and inspirer. And Tubby, in so many ways, cannot be fully understood without reference to Toc H, which he once graphically described as "a family in which life at its strongest is running errands for religion at its best." Sufficient to say that by 1922 the Movement, with its Four Points from the famous Main Resolution (To think fairly, to love widely, to witness humbly, to build bravely), had become a national organization which included some of the first names in the realm. Further, men like G. K. Chesterton (an old Pauline friend), A. A. Milne, his cousin Dick Sheppard, William Temple (the future Primate and a friend from Colet Court days) not only lent their names but gave much active support. In point of fact, the first large sum of money given to Toc H, £10,000 (about $50,000 at that time) to endow two chaplaincies, came through Dick Sheppard at St. Martin-in-the-Fields.

The mounting significance of Toc H, and its extension throughout the world in a variety of channels, served but to accelerate the Movement within the United Kingdom. Marks—that is, hostels, using an army term—and Branches sprang up in all parts of the country, each a nucleus of practical Christian enterprise. On the material side, by way of example, the evidence of the ledger books is conclusive. The balance of Toc H in the bank on December 31, 1920, was (in terms of American currency) about $100. Four years later the balance sheet showed receipts of $85,000 and total assets exceeding $290,000. Twenty-five years later the assets were well over $2,000,000 with twenty Marks and fifteen hundred Branches. But reverting to the twenties, we find that Toc H, having acquired an individual structure of its own, drew its inspiration from the spirits of the Elder Brethren (the men who had died in action) and its active strength from the loyalty and energy of younger members. Each formal meeting of House or Branch early conformed to an accepted pattern which is maintained, more or less, to the present day. Before the business or entertainment began, lights were lowered, and, as a signal for one minute's silence, the Lamp of Maintenance was lit, while the haunting "Words of Remembrance" (from Laurence Binyon's "For the Fallen") were spoken by the chairman:

> They shall grow not old, as we who are left grow old:
> Age shall not weary them, nor the years condemn.
> At the going down of the sun and in the morning
> We will remember them.[2]

An important feature of each meeting, at which, incidentally, a gasfitter might be the chairman and a lieutenant-general the secretary, was "jobmastery." The function of the "jobmaster" was to assign to members of the House or Branch such tasks as he saw fit to be discharged in the coming week or month. It might be reading to a blind person, tending to someone's garden, escorting an invalid to a football match (instead of playing in it), supervising young-

[2] Reprinted from *The Collected Poems of Laurence Binyon* with the permission of The Macmillan Company.

sters at play, or doing the shopping for a harassed mother. By such means a Toc H Branch or Group quickly identified itself with the everyday life of a community in which it found itself and proved to the carping that Christianity is really a Way of Life and not a rose-tinted theory manufactured by clerics and long-haired university dons.

Barclay Baron, who devoted his life and unusual gifts to Toc H, called 1922 "*Annus Mirabilis*"—"The Wonderful Year"—and it was certainly the most momentous in the history of Toc H, if not in the life of Tubby himself. It was the year Toc H was granted a royal charter of incorporation with the Prince of Wales as its patron, the first Birthday Festival was held in the Guildhall, and Tubby was appointed to the ancient and coveted living of All Hallows, Berkyngechirche.

Tubby has left no record of his emotions during that amazing first festival, but the sight must have brought a lump to his throat. Over two thousand people, including the representatives of nineteen great English schools, crowded that venerable place, and the company on the dais included the Prince of Wales in the Chair, the Archbishop of Canterbury, the Bishop of London, the Duke of Devonshire, his cousin the Earl of Cavan, Neville Talbot and his father, the saintly Bishop of Winchester, and the burgomasters of Poperinghe and Ypres—truly a contrast to the tattered glories of Talbot House and the optimistic penury of Red Lion Square. The lighting of "the Lamp"—a chaste and lovely replica of the Roman lamp used by the persecuted Christians in the catacombs—was officially initiated that night with the handing of the "Prince's Lamp" to His Royal Highness by "The Gen" (as Tubby's batman, Pettifer, was fondly known); thenceforth from its flame would be lighted the lamps of branches all over the world and, between festivals, it was to burn perpetually in All Hallows.

The induction to the ancient living had taken place earlier the same day. By terms of the appointment—it was in the gift of the Archbishop of Canterbury—All Hallows was to be primarily the

Guild Church of Toc H with its widening international commitments, but it would also enable the new Vicar, and by the same token the Church of England, to keep a finger on the pulse of commerce. It was an original conception on the part of the Archbishop, Randall Davidson, because it not only provided a central sanctuary desperately needed by the new and growing Movement, but supplied a focal point for religion in the heart of commercial London. "All Hallows thus achieved a double purpose," observed Tubby some years later, "being the parish church of city workers and also the gray shrine whence consecration quietly caught Toc H and made it live."

His love for the church and Tower Hill on which it stood was instant and irrevocable. Even in those days his mind's eye had swept clean the Hill which modern banality and greed had littered with tenements and warehouses, and beauty once more was returned to her rightful place. To him Tower Hill was not just the scene of a number of historical incidents—the execution of Laud, the Gordon Riots, the Dock Strike, and so on—it was a pageant, the name he chose for his book on the scheme for its beautification. Saxon serf and Norman conqueror had walked the streets around his church; Chaucer and Shakespeare had looked upon the eastern wall of All Hallows; Sir Francis Walsingham, Secretary of State to Elizabeth, and Robert Devereux, Earl of Essex, her ill-fated favorite, had been its parishioners; the sainted Bishop Lancelot Andrewes had been born within its purlieus; and Pepys had climbed its tower. The personality of the Hill absorbed him, it was a vivid cross section of the English character; and it must be freed of its monstrosities so that English character could again be truly formed on that scene. Most fortunately, Sir Charles Wakefield (later Lord Wakefield), a millionaire by personal achievement, caught Tubby's vision and, with generosity unqualified, helped largely to clothe it with reality. "The soul of London," stated Tubby, "dignity and freedom, were in his code the ultimate allegiance."

The skein of Toc H activities gradually ran to the far corners of the earth, and exotic names began to appear in the records on the Hill—Mendoza, Baiha Blanca, Valparaiso, El Paso, Manawatu, Woolongong. It was from West Africa that he brought back stories of the horrors of leprosy—which he first encountered in Kano—and the grievous need for money and skilled help. Before long he had the greatest in the land appealing to thousands from public platforms, and Toc H itself contributed over $400,000 and a succession of volunteers. From South Africa he brought reflection and advice:

The problem [the Color Question] cannot be solved by any abrupt impatience.

> "There is no workman, whoever he be,
> Who worketh both well and hastilie."

And God, greatest Workman, to Whom our universe is but a wayward flower, will scarcely bless the forcing of His hand. In Christ all faithful men are indeed already one. . . . Yet for the time we must content ourselves with pushing forward step by step along the road of understanding. To ignore animosities and divergences, differences of creed, and caste, and culture; to say that these things are not where they most plainly are, is to deny the evidence of our senses. . . . The main task of Toc H for the next few years is surely to provide the child races with a working example of European civilization, expressing Christianity in acts of tolerance and unselfishness which need no gift of tongues.

It became the practice of Toc H Members of Parliament—eventually numbering almost a third of the House of Commons—to invite him, whenever he returned from abroad, to their committee meetings to hear his views on situations overseas that might conceivably concern the Government, and there is no doubt that his opinions were thoughtfully pondered. It was on Tower Hill in 1932 that he received his first invitation from Admiral Sir W. W. Fisher, Commander-in-Chief of the Mediterranean Fleet, to be his guest aboard his flag ship, and thus began Tubby's, and *ipso facto* Toc

H's, close connection with the Royal Navy. Interestingly enough, through Sir John Cadman, the powerful head of the Anglo-Persian Oil Company, an indissoluble link had already been forged between Toc H and the British tanker fleet.

The practical-minded might well ask if the parish suffered through these constant trips abroad and throughout the country. Not at all, because by the terms of his appointment All Hallows was the Guild Church of an international movement which demanded frequent travel, and this was allowed for by Tubby's appointment of deputy vicars during his longer absences. Again, while tens of thousands of office workers thronged the parish during the week, it was left almost empty on Sundays, and this presented opportunities that were far greater than the problems. Whenever resident on the Hill, he regarded office visiting as a prime obligation. To watch him at work on such occasions was a joy to behold. Escorted by one of his curates and carrying in his arms Smuts—a tail-wagging cocker spaniel given to him by Lord Hugh Beresford —he would visit floor after floor without lessening for a moment the flow of raillery and common sense that kept everyone entranced, making them feel, for a while a least, human beings and not mere slaves to an automatic time clock. "Often," remarked John Graham, "I have taken instant dislike to some businessman and then, when we left the office, have been astounded at the insight of one who could say, 'Well, old boy, I think we've got a superb man there to deal with the whole problem of the tanker fleet'—or whatever it might be."

His instinct for the needs of others seldom erred. Shortly after his appointment to the living he shocked the ultra-conservatives, including some of the clergy, by throwing open the doors of All Hallows to office workers who had nowhere to eat their lunches except on the streets, often cold and rain-swept; and he continued his sanctuary until suitable quarters were found elsewhere. He believed that our Blessed Lord who had compassion on the hungering multitude would look tolerantly on a few paper bags in the nave. Partly with tongue in cheek, too, he brought bright young men down from the universities to preach the Gospel at noonday to strolling crowds on the Hill in opposition to the soapbox agnostics who for years had bellowed forth their impieties. Being younger and rather more attractive, they got the crowds—mostly women! It can hardly be said that he ever neglected All Hallows, which, standing empty and forlorn before his appointment, now daily welcomed hundreds of visitors from all parts of the globe, and whose amazing vicar, notwithstanding his travels and a myriad cares, managed to meet privately with some three thousand persons a year. By that wondrous telepathy that somehow circulates the most personal habits of the priest among his congregation, the daily routine of Tubby was soon common knowledge, and his hours, as the drayman who had seen him at 7 A.M. agreed with the "bobby" who had been speaking to him at 2 A.M., were "in'umin." There is no doubt that he had a capacity, possessed by few, to return from his frequent trips and resume a piece of work exactly where he had left off; he accepted no division between his work and that of Toc H—each was part of the over-all campaign to win men for Christ.

It has often been regretted that a life such as his precluded the fuller exercise of a conspicuous gift—his writing. Since early boyhood, not excepting his editorship of the *Isis* at Oxford, he had displayed a precocious mastery of language, at times miming and capering with words in a climate of pure nonsense, or, according to the mood, revealing the chiselled grace of the craftsman. But although through the years he has written numerous articles on social and religious topics for the press and magazines—often in trains on the backs of old envelopes—there has been no major, really significant work. True, several slender books have come from his pen—*Earthquake Love, Letters from Flanders, Tales of Talbot House, Pageant on Tower Hill*—and in them is to be found, by the highest critical consent, some of the best prose in the language. Nevertheless, his friends, mindful of the noble literary tradition of the Anglican clergy—Swift, Butler, Traherne, Donne, Kilvert, Newman, Inge, to name a few—have always regretted that the exactions of his work have prevented him from producing a magnum opus.

But if he failed to produce he certainly did not fail to absorb, and he has always walked in the realm of books as a native son; literature for him was related to life, it was a prelude to entry into the world, not an escape from it. Such books as he knew and valued portrayed men in all their moods, dissected their minds and emotions, and the knowledge thus acquired allowed him to move with a high degree of confidence in the shifting world of human values. It was all very simple, as he saw it. He was a parson, schooled to love and teach men, and anything that gave him the key to their hearts, even popular "thrillers," he avidly assimilated. "I can see him now," wrote John Graham, "as three of us sat in the back of a rickety car piled high with luggage driving up the Suez Canal from Cantara to Port Said, torn between the desire to read a thriller and a conviction that he ought to say Evensong. Evensong finally won the day, and included the singing of 'Abide with Me,' much to the edification of the Mohammedan driver."

In 1935 Tubby, who two years previously had been created a Companion of Honour and was shortly to be made a Chaplain to the King, had been removed from the Army Reserve. When, therefore, World War II was declared, the Army, insisting it was "a young man's show," refused to reappoint him to an Army chaplaincy—he was too old! The Royal Navy, less finical and fully aware of his record, immediately provided him with credentials to minister to naval personnel and fishermen in the North of Scotland, an area he knew well. Two years later, in 1941, he left there to join the tanker fleet, to which he owed deep allegiance in their most dangerous calling.

World War II brought him few gains but many losses. All Hallows had been destroyed, beyond all hope of architectural repair; and with its physical destruction a part of Tubby died too. Talbot House, Poperinghe (purchased by Lord Wakefield in 1929 as a perpetual shrine), was in the hands of the enemy. Dear friends, young and old, joined the Elder Brethren, and in their vanguard walked Charles Wakefield ("the Old Chief"), killed by a land mine in his garden, W. J. Musters ("Mus"), his first fellow-servant after the War ("thus Sergeant William Musters came Home"), and William Temple ("God must have had some very difficult task, and wanted Billy's help"). It was truly "winter among men," but outside, over the hill, Tubby knew with every fiber that there was a brighter day for which men should prepare. All Hallows had been destroyed, but by God's grace and human endeavor its more resplendent child would rise from the ashes to proclaim His Glory.

It was a very gallant thing for a man past sixty to set out to rebuild a shrine that had ennobled Christendom for over a thousand years. Jeremiahs there were aplenty, even friends with faint hearts, but he set his face to the New World, confident that America, far-seeing and generous, would not allow something precious and reclaimable to pass from the face of the earth. He had many friends in the United States, which he loved and respected, and to them in 1947 he put his case. No site in all the world, he claimed, should be nearer to American hearts than Tower Hill, for on that historic scene American freedom had actually been born and cosseted in the families of the Saltonstalls, the Penns, the Udalls, the Appletons, and the Washingtons, who lived within its boundaries. His listeners were not unmoved, and eventually contributed the first $40,000 to help restore the north aisle; their example brought similar gestures from the Dominions and from all over the world. When, therefore, I celebrated the Eucharist on Tower Hill in 1954 the sinews of beauty were already taking shape and the promise of splendor seemed fresh and vigorous. Today All Hallows stands a noble witness to one man's dauntless courage but, more veritably, the resurrected sanctuary of a millennium of unbroken piety.

It was typical of the man that in coming to ask he should also give. At a luncheon in New York he erupted the idea of the Winant Volunteers (named after John Winant, sometime American Ambassador to the Court of St. James's) casually, almost capriciously, the scheme whereby young Americans, paying their own way, were to work during their summer vacations among the poor children of East London and, eventually, the provinces. There is little doubt that the British Voluntary Overseas Service launched in the fifties and the Kennedy Peace Corps in the sixties have drawn inspiration, directly or indirectly, from the Winant Volunteers, a tried and successful scheme—General Eisenhower is the chief patron—to promote understanding between the peoples of different lands. The scheme is now reciprocal with the Clayton Volunteers (though in smaller numbers) coming to the United States, and is yet another example of Tubby's genius to catch the spirit of his time, a spirit that yearns for friendship, and turn it to Christian advantage.

Talbot House, it has been said, is the key to Tubby's life and All Hallows Church his one great love, but whatever the virtues of buildings or the sanctity of ancient shrines they have never been to him a substitute for the warm hearts of men. It is by men that worlds are reshaped, it is through men that heaven is reached. And clear through the dramatic pattern of his life can be seen an unvarying theme—the spirit of Talbot House which, at its best, has sought to serve men without seeking reward, save that of knowing it does Christ's will. And if, by God's grace, Tubby has mused, some small merit entitles him to enter the ghostly company of the Elder Brethren, he trusts he will march in a platoon of old friends —Temple, Baggallay, "Siddy," "Ludo," "Mus," "Sawbones," and so many others—for then there will be laughter, the laughter of souls set free.

8

Ronald Knox

BY ARNOLD LUNN

SIR ARNOLD LUNN, *the author of numerous books on modern thought and theology, is also a recognized authority on skiing. He has been called the "Father of Skiing in Britain," and has written extensively on the subject. However, he is probably better known as the author of such books as* The Revolt against Reason *and* Now I See, *and for his famous correspondence with Ronald Knox, published under the title,* Difficulties. *He was editor of the* Isis *at Oxford; he has been a literary collaborator with J. B. S. Haldane and C. E. M. Joad, and is a* Citoyen d'Honneur of Chamonix, France. *He was knighted in 1952.*

Ronald Knox, the youngest of a family of six, and the son of Edmund Arbuthnott Knox, later Bishop of Manchester, was born on February 17, 1888, and died on August 24, 1957.

His father was a stubborn Protestant who, as bishop, did his best to resist the encroachments of Anglo-Catholicism and who, on at least one point of Church history, cordially agreed with Catholics, for like them he was convinced that the Church of England was the creation of the sixteenth century. Among the doubtless legendary remarks attributed to Ronald Knox was his alleged explanation of his conversion: "I felt I had to have some religion and I couldn't stand Father's."

Ronald Knox was my contemporary at Balliol, the most brilliant undergraduate of my year. At Eton he had been captain of the School, and at Oxford he was president of the Union, a debating society which is the nursery of future Cabinet ministers, and editor of the *Isis,* the undergraduate weekly, a position in which I succeeded him. After taking his degree he took Orders as an Anglican, and was appointed chaplain at Trinity College, Oxford, Newman's College. Today there is a bust of the great Cardinal in the gardens of Trinity, and of Ronald Knox in the porch of the library. Knox soon became famous as an exponent of extreme Anglo-Catholic views, and still more famous as an ecclesiastical wit. A group of modernist dons were engaged in preparing a book to be called *Foundations.* Knox, who knew their views, anticipated their book by one of the most brilliant lampoons in the language, *Absolute and*

Abitofhell, a poem in the manner of Dryden. In 1917 Knox was received into the Church and described his conversion in *A Spiritual Aeneid,* a book from which, so Mr. Evelyn Waugh tells us, he "turned in disgust"[1] when he reread it many years later. This is understandable, for the book is valuable evidence of that transformation which began with his reception into the Church. In *A Spiritual Aeneid* he confesses to vanity as "one of the vices which I know to be in my nature," a confession for which he provides evidence in the book in question. In his youth he had been, as Mr. Waugh remarks, a "pot hunter" keenly interested in success, social and intellectual, and something of this remained. I do not agree with Mr. Waugh that his appointment as domestic prelate gave him no particular gratification. I remember being faintly surprised by the care with which he explained to me the differences between monsignori, in rank and dress, making it clear that he was one of the more exalted variety, but even in vanity there is often a streak of humility. If he had been more conscious of his position as a national figure, he would have realized that none of his friends would be impressed by these external dignities. What is certainly true is that with every year that passed he grew in holiness, and his interest declined in what Burke calls "the solemn plausibilities of the world."

Knox's *A Spiritual Aeneid* had an important, if indirect, influence on my conversion. The book irritated me so much that I determined to attack it, and decided that the most telling attack would be to write a book *Roman Converts,* which would contain a chapter dedicated to the demolition of Knox. My essay on Cardinal Manning was very appreciative, a rebuttal of Lytton Strachey's dishonest attack. The other converts discussed were Newman, Chesterton, Tyrrell, and Knox. Knox was an Etonian, Manning was at my old school, Harrow, but it was a coincidence that my essay on Manning

[1] *Monsignor Ronald Knox,* p. 109. Copyright ©1959, by Evelyn Waugh. This and the quotations from the same book which follow are reprinted by permission of Little, Brown and Co.

was by far the friendliest, a coincidence which provided Sir Shane Leslie, at that time editor of the *Dublin Review*, with an amusing title for the article in which he reviewed the book: "The Non-Harrovians." Chesterton wrote a genial article on Roman Converts in the *Dublin Review*, but Knox declined to reply to my book. "It's all very well for G. K. C. because he's 'arrived' but I can't do that kind of thing without being accused of self advertisement. Chesterton has only to refute an attack on Chestertonism; I shall have to refute an attack, not on Knoxianism, but on Knox."[2]

In my essay on Knox in my book *And Yet So New*, I wrote at some length about our personal relations and described how disarmed I had been by Knox's courteous and amusing letter, acknowledging a copy of *Roman Converts*. His friendly reaction encouraged me, a little later, to suggest that we should co-operate in a book of letters in which I would advance my objections to the claims of the Catholic Church and he would reply. Our letters were published under the title *Difficulties*.

Sir Arnold [writes Mr. Waugh] stated his case with great vigour. Ronald's replies are briefer and superficially slighter; often he does no more than delicately rearrange in a different order the materials which Sir Arnold throws to him, and so reconciles them with their apparent contradictions; he is always "away from his books" when answering and has to rely on an antiquated encyclopaedia, while Sir Arnold has all his authorities pat, but somehow the encyclopaedia suffices. There is a deceptive air of casualness about Ronald's handling of his case: some critics considered that Sir Arnold conceded more than he need have done, and that even so Ronald did not provide quite the conclusive answer which simpler minds expected. Ronald frankly admits that there are human oddities and logical puzzles which do not admit of a single, irrefutable explanation. He is plainly never the least disturbed in his own convictions. He simply admits that difficulties do exist and always will; that they are part of God's providence and that they never kept a man of good will from finding the faith. And that in fact was

[2] Waugh, *op. cit.*, p. 199.

the outcome. Sir Arnold was received into the Church by Ronald in July 1933, less than two years after the last letter was put in the post. . . .[3]

My only criticism of Mr. Waugh's brilliant biography of Ronald Knox is that he is not always just to the Hierarchy. On one particular point, the Hierarchy's alleged lack of gratitude for the £50,000 which Knox's translation of the Bible earned, and which he placed at their disposal, Mr. Waugh has handsomely admitted that he was misinformed; but his disclaimer will not catch up with his attack, particularly as the latter was quoted in *Time*. Again I do not think Mr. Waugh distinguishes as carefully as he should between Knox's tribulations which were due to subjective causes and those which might be deemed to be the fault of others. Knox was, no doubt, to quote from one of Mr. Waugh's letters, "a deeply unhappy man at most times." But authentic tragedy only entered his life during the First World War, which struck down one by one his friends, the most brilliant group that even Balliol has ever produced. In general, however, Knox was one of fortune's favorites. He was an immense success, social and intellectual, at Eton and Oxford. He did not have to wait long for national recognition. At every stage of his career he was the object of the affectionate solicitude of friends and, as we shall see, the Hierarchy, in the main, did their best—and a very good best—to adjust their views of what they wanted him to do to Knox's views of what he himself wanted to do.

After he was received into the Church Knox spent seven years at St. Edmund's, a college which consists of two distinct bodies under one president. There was the seminary for men preparing for the priesthood, and there was a school for boys of preparatory and public school age. The term "public school" conveys to Americans an idea the exact opposite of the facts. Public schools are really private schools where the upper classes receive an expensive education. The nearest equivalent of Eton or Harrow in America is,

[3] *Ibid.*, p. 263.

perhaps, Groton. The leading Catholic public schools, Downside and Ampleforth under Benedictine, and Stonyhurst and Beaumont under Jesuit control, rank socially with the leading Protestant schools. Cardinal Bourne was worried by the fact that the best Catholic schools were controlled by the Benedictines and Jesuits, who tended to recruit potential priests into their own ranks. He hoped, with Knox's help—Knox being ultimately destined to be headmaster—to transform St. Edmund's school into a public school which he and his successors would control, and which might eventually rival Downside or Stonyhurst. He was unduly sanguine. "One lady of an old Catholic family, after an interview with the cardinal, remarked in frank bewilderment: 'His Eminence seemed almost to be suggesting that *we* should send *our* boys to St. Edmund's.' "⁴

Instead of staying on at St. Edmund's, as the Cardinal wished, Knox accepted the chaplaincy to the Catholic undergraduates of Oxford. Later he left Oxford to have leisure for translating the Bible, and accepted the position of private chaplain at Aldenham, Lord Acton's seat. Lord Acton was the head of an old Catholic family, and his wife was the daughter of Lord Rayleigh, an eminent scientist and an agnostic. Her family were strongly anti-Catholic, and Lady Acton herself was at the time of her marriage entirely hostile to her husband's faith. One of Lord Acton's sisters had married Mr. Douglas Woodruff, the editor of *The Tablet,* and it was Mr. and Mrs. Woodruff who aroused Lady Acton's interest in the Church. It was on a Hellenic Traveller's Club cruise that she informed Ronald Knox that she had decided to become a Catholic.

"The miscellaneous tourists," writes Mr. Waugh, "whom Sir Arnold Lunn used to coax into the delusion of being enthusiasts for classical culture were disposed to think that the price of their tickets included the acquaintance of the savants whose lectures they attended and whose holidays they subsidized. There was resentment on board when Ronald spent his time exclusively with Lady Ac-

⁴ *Ibid.,* p. 175.

ton."[5] The friendship which ripened on this cruise was destined to prove of immense importance in Knox's life.

Meanwhile Cardinal Hinsley had offered Knox the presidency of the St. Edmund's Seminary, which if accepted would probably have led to a bishopric. In his longer letter begging to be excused, Knox wrote, *inter alia:*

> I cannot take the stern line, or impress people with my dignity. To be called by my Christian name by second-year undergraduates may be a gift, but it is not the gift needed if you are to be the Awful Presence in the background which the Presidency of a seminary demands. . . . I think I might easily be popular, but it is because I find it very hard to say No to people. . . . I feel that if I went to Old Hall the whole discipline of the place would be subtly relaxed.[6]

Thus for the second time Knox found himself unable to accept the plans for his future on which the Archbishop of Westminster set great store. Instead he was allowed to retire to Aldenham. There were, of course, some clerical criticisms. "Instead," writes Mr. Waugh, "of gratefully embracing the normal clerical preferments open to him, Ronald, it seemed, chose to sequester himself among patrician converts, whose habits of thought and devotion were strange to the generality of industrial parishes and whose way of life was assumed, quite wrongly as things turned out, to be more luxurious than that of the presbytery."[7]

"If I have made too much," writes Mr. Waugh, "of Ronald's tribulations it is because he hid them." But what, in fact, were these tribulations? Or rather to what degree were other people responsible for them? Knox was ultra-sensitive, and minor setbacks troubled him greatly. He felt intensely the rejection of his translation of *The Manual of Prayers* and was upset by the delays before

[5] *Ibid.,* p. 250.
[6] *Ibid.,* p. 266.
[7] *Ibid.,* pp. 270–271.

his translation of the New Testament was finally adopted by the English Hierarchy; but these tribulations were trivial in a life which was both sheltered and privileged. He had not to wait like Newman for belated recognition nor to contend like Newman with hostility in the highest ecclesiastical circles. At every stage of his career he received generous praise, and not only from laymen. Newman, to cite one example, was commissioned to translate the Bible, but at the last moment the scheme was vetoed. Knox's translation met with much criticism and is still disliked by many critics whose judgment deserves respect, but was in the end officially adopted by the Hierarchy of England and Wales.

"It is at least arguable," wrote Monsignor John Barton in *The Month* (December 1959), "that the note of suffering in his life is overstressed here" (i.e., in Mr. Waugh's biography). "He was unquestionably a great sufferer from dyspepsia, his mental sufferings, if at times acute, were not so persistent as those of his fellow-priests who have been made responsible for the interest and capital repayment of a heavy debt."

Knox was one of fortune's favorites not only in life but also in posthumous recognition, for no biographer could have been more successful than Mr. Waugh in protecting his personality and his achievements against the rust of time. Mr. Waugh, who writes better prose than any of his contemporaries, not only appreciates the deceptive simplicity of Knox's style but can convey his appreciation to the reader. Perhaps only those who have themselves tried to write biography will fully realize how much this book owes to the tact and discernment with which Mr. Waugh has selected the episodes, letters, and obiter dicta which inform with vibrant life this convincing portrait. One example of the delicate art which evokes not only Knox in a minor role but also the restrained irritation sometimes provoked by his foibles may be quoted. Mr. Waugh is describing an evening at Mells, Knox's last home, where he lived as private chaplain to Mrs. Raymond Asquith and where he died:

The evening was always devoted to recreation. There was often reading aloud. He devised a way of doing the crossword which some of
his friends found too laborious. He allowed himself to read only the
horizontal clues. When these were complete he filled in the perpendicu-
lars by guesswork, and only then verified them from their clues. Every
Christmas he composed a crossword which he copied out, not always
quite accurately, and sent to his friends; they were expected to send
him the solutions and held in disgrace if they neglected this duty. In
Lent he denied himself the crossword entirely. In the last years of his
life the American game "Scrabble" greatly took his fancy. He made a
copy in cardboard and paper of the first set which he saw. It was a
mitigation for his friends when he acquired a real set, but the intensity
with which he played and the solemn silence he demanded were especially trying to visitors who came to Mells in the hope of enjoying
their host's and hostess's conversation.[8]

Knox's range of pleasures was narrow. He seemed to be com-
paratively unmoved by the beauty of nature or of art. I remember
standing beside him as we sailed up Phaleron Bay. It was a perfect
morning, but Athens and the distant Acropolis evoked nothing but
a lackluster expression on his face. His happiest moment on this
Hellenic Cruise was when he got into his sleeping car at Venice for
the return journey. He was complacently insular. On his first visit
to Rome, as an undergraduate, he wrote complainingly about the
difficulty of buying *Punch* in Rome. It was not until he visited the
Actons in Rhodesia, at the age of sixty-five, that he travelled by
airplane, and it was then that he saw his first "talkie." He did not
applaud the march of progress. Indeed he regarded it as his duty to
erect "some kind of barrage against this revolting age." Among "the
things that make you glad to be going home" he noted of his return
journey, were

(i) The sight of the Nile and the reflection that this belongs to the
history of the world, whereas everything else you have seen in Africa
dates from Livingstone. (ii) The conversation of waiters in Rome;

[8] *Ibid.*, p. 318.

speech of which you can catch the inflections, and understand a few fragments. (iii) Getting into a *train* at Paddington; catching it at the last moment, while the guard keeps his flag unwaved, because the porter has not yet appeared with the luggage.[9]

He was happiest either in the society of the few intimate friends with whom he felt completely at ease, or with priests. No priest was more popular with the clergy, particularly as a giver of retreats. The tendency is for Catholics, born or converts, with Knox's kind of background, to join one of the Orders if they enter the priesthood, and for this, and other reasons, the secular clergy were proud of, and very attached to, Knox. His election to the "Old Brotherhood of the Secular Clergy," which has its roots in penal times, being founded in 1623, gave him as much pleasure as his election to an honorary Fellowship of Trinity, Oxford. Knox was not particularly happy at St. Edmund's or as chaplain to the Catholics at Oxford. His scrupulous sense of responsibility for the undergraduates entrusted to his care was a source of anxiety rather than of happiness. He was by nature a recluse, yet he was never alone at Oxford. Three undergraduates lived under the same roof.

Throughout all his years at the Old Palace Ronald suffered from qualms about his own fitness for the work . . . his intellectual sophistication in the face of adolescent problems, which kept boredom at a distance only by a continuous exercise of the will . . . he was by nature inclined to advert to his rare failures rather than to his numerous, manifest successes; but with due allowance for all this the consistent undertone of the document ["Chaplaincraft," a report which Knox compiled for his successor in the chaplaincy] is unmistakably that of a man driven by duty rather than joy.[10]

"There is only one sorrow," says a character in Léon Bloy's *La Femme Pauvre,* "the sorrow of not being a saint." It was perhaps

[9] *Ibid.,* p. 323.
[10] *Ibid.,* p. 237.

this sorrow rather than dyspepsia which explains that recurring melancholy in Knox's life. The most effective of the many letters which he contributed to our joint book *Difficulties,* and certainly the letter which I found the most persuasive, was his letter on sanctity. He was too diffident to recognize his own slow but unmistakable approach to holiness, for his humility which, as Mr. Waugh rightly observes, "was observed by all who met him," aggravated his own acute consciousness of the degree by which he fell short of sanctity. He would have been embarrassed to discover the impression he made on the girls as chaplain of the Assumption Convent, which was evacuated to Aldenham in the war. "Their clear young minds," writes Mr. Waugh, "recognized holiness and loved it. . . . A girl had occasion to go through the chapel one morning as he was making his thanksgiving; he knelt completely absorbed in prayer, and she later told a nun that passing between him and the altar was like 'cutting through the supernatural.' "[11] Dr. Flynn, the present Bishop of Lancaster, had been profoundly impressed by seeing Knox absorbed in prayer before the Blessed Sacrament. Years later, preaching on the love of God as an act of will which would not involve the emotions, he said, "Don't tell me that this is all that the love of God means. I have *seen* people in love with God."

Advance in the spiritual life is often, perhaps even normally, accompanied by a withdrawal of "consolations" in prayer, and Knox's melancholy may have been partly due to the fact that he could write: "In the great bulk of my prayers, vocal and mental all my life, I have not felt I was talking to God in his presence, but rather apostrophizing him in his absence." "To be dry in Lent," he wrote to a correspondent, "when our Lord fasted, to be feeling irreligious on Good Friday when our Lord suffered dereliction—all that is quite correct and liturgical. When you do 'get any kind of satisfaction out of one's prayers,' say 'I am such a feeble creature God has to give me sweetmeats.' " In *The Priestly Life* he develops this theme:

11 *Ibid.,* p. 281.

In an age like ours, so full of questionings and of false philosophies, the mind which is not comforted by any relish in the practice of religion is exposed, as on a bare nerve, to the chilling airs of doubt. It does not lose faith, but the clearness of its convictions is dimmed; it maintains itself by an effort, instead of basking in the sunshine of assured belief. That, too, the Saints have known; at the end of her life St. Theresa of Lisieux suffered, to the last, this obscuration of belief. God wanted her, in this as in other ways, to be the Saint of our age.[12]

In January 1957 Knox was operated on for an obstruction of the colon, and a malignant and incurable cancer was discovered. A few months later Lord Evans, physician to the Queen, and I were fellow guests of Captain Neil McEachern in the Villa Tarranto, Pallanza. The Prime Minister, Mr. Macmillan, had asked Lord Evans to come round and have a look at Knox, who was staying with him at 10 Downing Street. "Knox wanted to know," said Lord Evans, "how long I thought he'd live. His literary plans depended on my answer. He wondered whether it was worth while to start a new book. How long could I give him? I'm often asked that question, but many of those who ask it do not in their heart of hearts want an honest answer. People cling to life so, and most of us are mainly thinking of ourselves. But your friend really wanted the truth. I felt that he was wholly reconciled to death and that all that interested him was the timetable. Was it worth while to start a new book? I felt that he was detached from this world. The Prime Minister was impressed in much the same way. I wrote to Knox afterwards to tell him that the hour I spent with him was one of the most impressive experiences of my life."

Almost immediately afterwards Sir Horace Evans was raised to the peerage. Knox in his letter of congratulations remarked that one of them had left Downing Street with a patent of nobility in his pocket, the other with a death warrant. He died at Mells. On his last day Lady Eldon asked him whether he would like her to read

[12] New York, Sheed and Ward, 1958, pp. 99–100

to him from his translation of the New Testament. He answered "No" and then, after a pause, "Awfully jolly of you to suggest it, though." Those were his last words.

Insofar as Ronald Knox attached importance to posthumous fame, he probably based his hopes on his translation of the Bible, and perhaps rightly, but it is not improbable that his translation will continue to evoke very different reactions from those with some claim to be considered good judges of English prose. His most formidable critic was Father C. C. Martindale, S.J., a convert like Knox, and with a similar background, Father Martindale being an old Harrovian. I remember asking the late Arthur Pickard-Cambridge, who for many years had examined candidates for the University Classical scholarships, Hertford and Ireland, what he thought of Knox as a scholar. "A fine scholar, of course," he replied, "but of all those I examined there was one who was outstanding, in a class by himself—Martindale." Father Martindale took a First in Mods and Greats, the Hertford, Craven and Derby scholarships, the Chancellor's Greek verse and Gainsford Latin verse prize, and the Ellerton Theological Essay. Temperamentally the two men were very different. Knox was happiest with those of his own social wavelength, whereas Father Martindale is a mixer. When he came as chaplain on a Hellenic cruise he penetrated into the crew's quarters and heard confessions and on Sunday said a few words in Croat after his sermon, to the great amusement of those members of the crew who were present. When Father Knox was chaplain he made no contacts outside of the little group with whom he was travelling.

Father Martindale, a member of the committee to which Knox submitted his translations, hoped that Knox, who "had expressed different *kinds* of talk so well in *Let Dons Delight* . . . would make readers feel the real delicate differences between the naive Mark, the cultured Luke, the rather stiff Matthew." Knox replied that he was paying no attention to differences of style in the Evangelists, and he irritated Father Martindale by his claim that he would use "timeless English." It would be difficult to disagree with Father Martindale's comment, "as if ever there could be one."

Father Martindale was caught in Denmark by the Germans, a circumstance which brought his opposition to an end. In this controversy my sympathies were with Father Martindale, and this for many reasons, among others that the Knox translation never attains to the beauty of the Authorized Version at its best. Moreover, the note of Greek simplicity which is one of the great charms of the original is retained in the A.V. but often lost in the Knox translation. Thus: "Neither do I condemn thee: Go, and sin no more" (A.V. 10 words) seems to me nearer to the spirit of the original and better prose than Knox's "I will not condemn thee either. Go, and do not sin henceforward" (12 words). I gave other instances of similar contrasts in *And Yet So New*. None the less, the Knox translation has great merits. It is always lucid and never unintelligible, which cannot be said either of the Authorized or Douai Versions. It is, perhaps, in the Epistles that the Knox translation is clearly the best, for he makes sense of many verses which are all but unintelligible in the Douai.

Translation became the major interest of Knox's last years. He defended his methods in *Trials of a Translator,* and his last public appearance was to read his brilliant Romanes lecture on translation to an Oxford audience. The setback which caused the most pain was the rejection of his *Manual of Prayers,* which I have not seen; but I am not surprised that the clergy did not like it if the occasional sentences translated from the Missal in *The Mass in Slow Motion* are any guide. One of the most perfect examples of balance and poise in mediaeval Latin is the prayer beginning *Deus qui humanae substantiae.* The dignity and gravity of the stately Latin evaporate in "who was courteous enough to share our manhood."

The Church has paid heavily for Knox's preoccupation with translation in his later years, for the time which he devoted to translating the autobiography of St. Thérèse of Lisieux could have been employed to incomparably greater advantage in completing what would probably have proved to be the most important contribution to apologetics of this century. On January 1, 1956, he began a book of systematic apologetics written in the language of the modern world, but after writing three chapters turned aside to translate St. Thérèse. Many others could have produced an equally good translation. Nobody but Knox could have written a book the quality of which may be judged by the three chapters now issued as a pamphlet by *The Month*. Here is a key passage:

Our Catholic apologetic, nearly all of it, strikes the modern reader as inhuman. Just because it is worked out with mathematical precision, just because a suitable answer comes pat to every question, just because it always faces you with a dilemma from which there is no logical escape, it afflicts our contemporaries with a sense of *malaise*. . . . our answers seem too glib, too "slick"; there is something machine-made about them. They are clothed with an appearance of truth, but, if I may go back to my unphilosophic phrase—they do not smell of reality. What I am concerned with is our apologetics, and that great work of apologetic, some day to be written which shall suggest to the reader that in approaching Christian theology he is approaching something that is alive, not a series of diagrams.

It was *that* "great work of apologetic" which Knox could have written had he not turned aside to translate St. Thérèse.

"There is a kind of book," wrote Knox, "about which you may say, almost without exaggeration, that it is the whole of a man's literary life, the unique child of his thought."[13] Such a book was Knox's *Enthusiasm,* a study of those aberrations technically classified under the generic title of "Enthusiasm." The book contains some of his finest prose. It is not easy to make an analysis of Montanism, Jansenism, and modern Enthusiasts readable, but I have read few books on theology which were more successful in captur-

[13] Waugh, *op. cit.,* p. 313.

ing my attention. On a flight across the Atlantic I read *Enthusiasm* continuously from the early afternoon to dawn next morning. Knox, as he surveyed the arid record of past aberrations, may well have asked himself in the words of Ezekiel, "Son of man, can life return to these bones?" But as he wrote, "the breath of life came into them, so that they lived again: and all rose to their feet, host upon host of them." I am quoting from Knox's translation of the Old Testament, which I far prefer to his translation of the New.

Of all Knox's books, *Let Dons Delight* was the one which was most warmly welcomed by discriminating critics outside the Church. The setting is St. Simon Magnus College, Oxford, and the scenes are set at intervals of fifty years between the Armada and the Munich Agreement of 1938. In its particular genre the book has few rivals. The notes parodying contemporary sources prove, if proof were needed, that Knox's genius for parody had not suffered from the erosion of time. *Let Dons Delight* achieves on a large canvas what Knox in his youth had achieved on the smaller canvas of *Absolute and Abitofhell*. If the note of beauty seems lacking in Knox's translation of the *New Testament,* a passage in *Let Dons Delight* is convincing evidence of the fact that if Knox the translator gives priority to the homely and familiar, it is not because he is a stranger to beauty but because, for his own odd purposes, he sometimes elects deliberately to pass her by in this passage. Mr. Lee, the speaker, is leaving the snug security of St. Simon Magnus to join the recusants at Douai and to return to martyrdom.

All these last weeks, I know not why, that of the shepherd in Virgil hath been coming back into my mind continually; *At nos hinc alii sitientes ibimus Afros:* we are exiled from you now across the seas, and we shall be exiled yet longer from your thoughts and memories in England, and most in Oxford. Anyone that will be absolute over a point of doctrine shall find himself a stranger here. And we above all, that will stick to the old religion, shall have no part with you.[14]

[14] New York, Sheed and Ward, 1939, pp. 33–34.

Mutatis mutandis, this was Knox's farewell to Oxford when he resigned his Fellowship at Trinity.

It is difficult to predict which writings will escape the rust of time. There is, as Father Martindale felt, no such thing as "timeless English" and no writing which undoubtedly possesses a timeless appeal, but I am rash enough to believe that the best of Knox's sermons will be read many centuries hence.

If I wanted a book to make clear to a Protestant the difference between a saint such as St. Bernadette and a very good Christian such as Florence Nightingale, I would lend them either Father Martindale's *What are Saints?* or Knox's *Captive Flames,* a collection of sermons preached on famous saints and one uncanonized saint, Henry VI, the founder of Eton, included, as he remarked in his dedicatory letter to me, "in the hope that he would not arouse any Harrovian prejudice in you."

Knox was, perhaps, at his best in his addresses to priests and to school girls. He was never happier than in the company of priests. His own innate humility, which caused him to exaggerate the gap between the priestly ideal and his own practice as a priest, made him particularly sensitive to the special temptations of the priesthood and to the damage which can be done not only by a bad priest but also by a good priest who cannot control some disedifying fault, such as bad temper. "I wonder," he writes, "how much of the leakage we often hear talked about is due to the plain fact that the people are afraid of their clergy? The sons of Heli 'withdrew men from the sacrifice of the Lord'; what more terrible epitaph could there be on a priest than that?"[15]

He was in great demand as a giver of retreats, perhaps because he always gave, as was truly said of him, the impression that "he has seen the fault first in himself, only afterwards in his hearers. And always he saw the priesthood as the glory that it is." The edge of his wit had not blunted with the years. In *The Priestly Life* he conveys salutary truths with a touch of realistic irony:

[15] *The Priestly Life,* p. 42.

Part of the reason why God put you into the world was to exercise the patience of others by your defects; think of that sometimes when you are going to bed. It is a salutary thought. . . . Your bad temper, your excessive cheerfulness, your tiresomeness in conversation; he chose the right person, didn't he? Well, if other people are being so admirably exercised in patience by you, it seems a pity you shouldn't be exercised by them now and again in your turn; that's only fair. The offering of patience which you can make to God: the little things you have to put up with—and that offering is to be made in silence. How it spoils that offering if you make any comment on it, still more if you make any comment on it out loud, still more if you make any comment on it in the presence of other people! You must offer it to him like a casket of myrrh, not wasting the scent by opening the lid before it gets to him.[16]

Some of St. Francis Xavier's companions were faintly disedified by his readiness to consort with loose-living soldiers on the ship which was taking them to India. "I will go in by their door," he replied, "that they may go out by mine." Not everybody can make a success of the Xavier technique. I remember an Anglican bishop who gave an address in the Harrow School Speechroom, and who earned our disdain by the laborious fashion in which he worked in references to cricket. Young people are ready to resent any obvious attempt to play down to them. Superficially there might seem to be some resemblance between the bishop's references to cricket and the following passage from *The Mass in Slow Motion,* sermons addressed to the girls of Assumption College during their wartime residence in Aldenham: "The Mass is really a kind of religious dance . . . what *you* mean by a dance is the wireless in the hall playing revolting stuff and you lounging round in pairs and feeling all gooey."[17] Why, then, did we pull the bishop's address to pieces with ribald comments, whereas Knox's sermons to the girls "were so popular," Mr. Waugh tells us, "that one girl, who was being taken

16 *Ibid.,* pp. 66–67.
17 New York, Sheed and Ward, 1948, p. 3.

out for the day by her parents, insisted on returning for Benediction rather than go to the cinema"?[18] Perhaps it was because the young Harrovians felt that the bishop was chiefly interested in impressing *himself* on his congregation, persuading us that *he* could descend to our level, whereas every girl realized that Knox was passionately anxious to impress on their young minds the glory of the Church. Few priests were more conscious of the dangers which await the boy or girl in the secular and indeed anti-Christian climate of the modern world. Knox's determination to evoke in his young listeners a love for the Mass, that "medicine of immortality" which is the best inoculation against secularism, shines through what he described as "a highly specialized art-form, that of sermons to schoolgirls." The last sermon at Aldenham was preached just before the Actons, who brought Knox to Aldenham, left for South Africa, and I cannot better conclude this attempt to convey something of what Knox and his writings have meant in my life than to quote the moving passage in which he expresses in words of peculiar felicity the sorrow of those inevitable partings in this our mortal life.

When you have left Aldenham, there will be plenty of things to remind me of you: I shall still find myself walking warily through the passages for fear of cannoning into somebody, still keeping my window shut in case one of you should come along and exchange a few words with a friend in the dormitory upstairs; an inkstain here, a thumb-mark there, will recall the memory of your visit. But you won't find it so easy to remember me; you will grow into your new surroundings very soon, and they will be different surroundings. Only one thing is never different; the Holy Mass. Every now and then, perhaps, some gesture, some trick of manner about the priest who serves your chapel there, will bring back to you memories of Aldenham; you will find yourself saying, "Do you remember how old What's-his-name always used to blow his nose during the server's Confiteor?" And that will be something, if it helps to remind you that What's-his-name exists, or anyhow existed.

18 *Op. cit.*, p. 279.

I will leave you with the request which St. Monica made, just before she died, of her son St. Augustine: "I only ask you to remember me at the altar of the Lord." . . . The charmed circle is always being broken up; we are separated from the people we have grown accustomed to. But do let's get it clearly in our heads that there can be no real separation, in life or in death, so long as we stick to the Holy Mass. In Christ we are all one; the sacred Host is the focus in which all our rays meet, regardless of time and space. . . .[19]

[19] *The Mass in Slow Motion*, pp. 138–139.

9

Boris Pasternak

BY ROBERT PAYNE

ROBERT PAYNE *is an English-born writer and editor who was educated in South Africa and Europe. After teaching in China for some years, he came to the United States, where he now lives. A man of wide-ranging interests, he is the author of many books, among which are* Forever China, The Splendour of Persia, Dostoyevsky, *and* The Three Worlds of Boris Pasternak.

O where would I be now,
My Master and my Saviour,
If eternal life did not await me
Beside my table in the dark of night,
Like a new guest enticed
Into the net of my craft?

Il faut être libre souverainement, en roi![1]

I

Thirty years ago, when few people were able to obtain his works in Russia and only a handful of scholars, chiefly in England and France, were translating his rare and fragmentary poems and still more fragmentary short stories, Boris Pasternak was already a legend. Like Baudelaire, he had established his authority on the basis of a slender body of work which effectively changed the familiar course of a literature. He gave a new vision, a new excitement to Russian literature. When words passed through his mind, they assumed colors and shapes they had never possessed before, and his audacious images, however surprising at first, always succeeded in convincing the reader with their accuracy and inevita-

[1] "Magdalene" in *Doctor Zhivago*, by Boris Pasternak. This and the other excerpts from the same book which follow are reprinted by permission of Pantheon Books. Copyright © 1958 by Pantheon Books.

bility. He invented new rhythms which no one had heard before. He gave dignity to poetry, for no one could ever doubt that he regarded the making of poems as a heroic task to be performed with infinite devotion and dedication. He was the pure poet, exalted above other men by the possession of a rare gift of insight into the burning heart of things.

There was something about him, too, of the *vates,* the ancient seer-poet blessed with gifts of prophetic intelligence. He was one of the few men—Yeats, Rilke and Valéry were perhaps the only other ones among his contemporaries—who wrote as though the whole fate of mankind rested upon their devotions. He wore his singing robes like one accustomed to them, as though any other garment was unheard-of. For him poetry was not an avocation. Poetry was the song sung by the universe, and it was the poet's task to throw a net across the heavens and capture it. Wallace Stevens called poetry the necessary angel of earth, "Since, in my sight, you see the earth again." Pasternak would have answered that the heavens were also implicated, and all the skies, and all the universes.

Even thirty years ago people marvelled how he had survived, for he seemed to belong to another age entirely and there was something ironic in his presence in Soviet Russia, like a unicorn straying across a battlefield. Recently Ilya Ehrenburg has denied that Pasternak ever lived in Soviet Russia. He lived instead in his own world, which he was compelled to re-create every morning; and though sometimes he threw a bridge from his own island to the Communist mainland and walked unsteadily over it, he would walk back and draw up the bridge towards evening, having seen what he wanted to see and made a few errands. Though living in a Communist society, Pasternak maintained his remoteness from the partisan battles which were being fought all round him, and his very remoteness emphasized his authority, his gift of language, his sense of poetic dedication.

Very early in his career he became a legend, and this was due partly to his physical presence. Descended from a long line of Sephardic Jews, he looked a little like a Judean prince, courtly and dark-skinned, with deep-set, glowing eyes and thick lips and high cheekbones. The long, brooding, horse-like face was exceedingly mobile and sensitive, and he was proud of the beauty of his hands. He did not recite poetry; he chanted it in a deep and resonant voice throbbing with emotion, speaking slowly but somehow giving an impression of overwhelming urgency. Towards the end of his life his face and his voice changed. His features assumed an aspect of extraordinary nobility and power, while his voice lost something of its deep resonance, became lighter and gentler, but the words still rushed after one another in full spate. As a youth he possessed that ugliness which is almost beauty. In his old age he was truly beautiful with his shock of white hair and features which seemed carved out of granite.

It is too late now to separate the man from the legend. The man who lived and breathed and fought off singlehandedly the encroachments of the Communist system now belongs to history, which has its own way of preferring legends to the truth. But sometimes we can see him plain. The nakedness of many of his verses, the long autobiographical fragments embedded in his two short books of reminiscences, and the still longer autobiographical fragments in *Doctor Zhivago,* tell us what manner of man he was. Surprisingly his voice was rarely recorded, but there exists a recording made in the last months of his life which gives us an otherwise unhoped-for sense of closeness to him. On this recording he recites two long poems in Russian, discusses the contemporary literary situation in German, and finally reads a dedication in French to a young musician studying in Moscow. Speaking into the recording machine, Pasternak seems to have realized he was called upon to make an enduring statement of his ideas, to sum up in a few words everything he had ever thought and believed and experienced. He begins amusingly by saying he will paraphrase the words of Verlaine: *De la musique avant toute chose.* No, art is not primarily concerned with music, but something greater—with greatness itself. And so for the words of Verlaine he substitutes: *De la grandeur avant toute chose.*

What is *grandeur?* It is, he says, something which can only be known by those who have spent their whole lives with a sense of pity for women and children, with charity towards all. Those who devote themselves to others are already on the way to greatness. To give freely is to be blessed, and essentially life must be lived freely, and greatness can only emerge from the free person. *Il faut être libre souverainement, en roi, non par des autorités de son âge, des usages environs longs, mais de ses propres perfections acquises, franc de soi-même.* It is not good French, but the meaning is abundantly clear. One must live in sovereign freedom like a king, never surrendering to temporal authority or traditions however deeply rooted, but in the light of one's own acquired perfections in complete honesty with oneself. That is all, and it is enough. The poet becomes a moralist, but with what audacity he assaults the fortress of Communism. In seven unforgettable words he describes his vision of greatness: *Il faut être libre souverainement, en roi. . . .*

So in that last recording, speaking with uncommon urgency, Pasternak brings himself to a position not very far removed from that of Henri Bergson, who wrote on the last page of his last book that the universe is a machine for the making of gods. Characteristically Pasternak insisted that perfect freedom has its roots in charity, and without charity towards all living things no greatness is possible.

He was never a practicing Christian, rarely attended church services, and showed no interest in dogma. He came to Christianity through poetry, but it is important to realize that his concept of Christ was intensely personal and colored by ancient Russian legends of the Christ who forever wanders over the roads of Russia. He saw the world bathed in a light which is not of this earth, and in the end he came to know that the radiance came from Christ.

As far as we can tell from his writings, there was no struggle, no prolonged debate with himself, no wrestling with angels. Slowly and imperceptibly there came the flowering. The majestic poems at the conclusion of *Doctor Zhivago* are the fruit of quiet meditations, not of a sudden explosive conversion. That the greatest Christian poetry of our time should have come out of Soviet Russia is only one of the many ironies associated with his name.

II

At the core and center of Pasternak's being there was a heart of darkness and mystery. No one, perhaps least of all Pasternak himself, ever penetrated that darkness thoroughly, but he had the poet's gift of being able to throw momentary beams of blinding light across the darkness of the human soul, and in this light the mysteries revealed themselves. Like saints, or like old peasants, he will sometimes utter a phrase which seems to possess a divine relevance, a deep and heart-rending knowledge of the economy of God. The characters of *Doctor Zhivago* are more than life-size, and they act out their lives in a divine mystery in the flickering light of stormy skies. Sometimes there is a flash of lightning and we see them clearly. At such moments the redheaded doctor, Yury Zhivago, and Larissa, his quietly passionate mistress, become inextricably involved in our own lives: they become our consciences.

What is surprising, and to some extent inexplicable, is how quickly and easily men in the Western world took these characters of Pasternak's imagination to their hearts, for they are essentially Russian characters weighed down with the impedimenta of Russian tradition, with a purely Russian way of expressing themselves and with characteristic Russian intonations. Larissa is French—the last of many foreign heroines in his works—but she has lived so long in Russia that all her instincts have acquired a Russian form, and indeed in Yury Zhivago's eyes she comes to symbolize the Russian earth. Yury Zhivago himself descends from a long line of *yurodiviy,*

those wonder-working, saintly fools of God who were the despair
of mediaeval emperors and the delight of mediaeval storytellers.
"Yury" is the Russian equivalent of George and clearly hints at the
dragonslayer, while "Zhivago" just as clearly hints at rebirth and
resurrection. In the Russian Bible the angels greet the women at the
open tomb with the words: "Why seek ye the living (*zhivago*)
among the dead?"

Yury Zhivago's preoccupations are not those of the Western world.
His Christianity is closer to St. Gregory of Nyssa than to St. Augus-
tine, and is bathed in the oriental light of the Eastern Church, which
is little concerned with the redemption of sins and the agony of the
Crucifixion, but directs the worshipper's gaze relentlessly on the
majesty and universal power of Christ, seen in the light of setting
suns, in a blaze of glory. His most ardent aim is to warm himself in
God's holy fire, to be spiritually present in God, to be the sharer of
God's passionate espousal of mankind, for man, according to St.
Gregory Palamas, is "higher than the angels" and only a hair-
breadth separates him from the throne of God. Man, according to
the Eastern Church, is already divine, living in a world luminous
with divinity. Yury Zhivago's task is to reconcile divinity with the
facts of an appallingly bestial civil war and the anarchic mechanistic
social system imposed by Communism.

He does not, of course, ever reconcile the irreconcilable. He
does, however, discover a way in which men can live out their lives
on earth in the light of divinity. Angelic presences abound. He sum-
mons them, or perhaps they summon him. Through them—through
his strange half-brother Evgraf who appears at all critical moments
like an envoy from heaven, through Sima Tuntseva, the wise peas-
ant woman, and above all through the angelic presence of Larissa—
he is able to reach out to the other world, which is also our own
world seen in the divine light. There are many other angelic presences. There is the mysterious Prince Galiliev, who enters the stage
briefly, hinting at miraculous victories. There is the boy Vasya, sole
survivor of a massacre, who resembled "the painting of a royal page

or an angel of God." In nature, too, there are angelic presences. There are angels in the shadowy woodlands, in the rushing streams, and in a tree shining through the snow. The angels are everywhere if we had but eyes to see them, and they have left their footprints everywhere on earth, though their faces may be invisible.

Again and again Yury Zhivago declares the supremacy of man created in the image of God over all the horrors of the civil war and the sterile regimentations of dictatorship. "It is in the face of Heaven and in the holy light of its own uniqueness that everything takes place," says Sima Tuntseva; and since for Pasternak no other interpretation of human actions and behavior was possible, the story of *Doctor Zhivago* inevitably acquires something of the effect of a series of epiphanies. God is continually descending to earth, and the heavens are continually opening to reveal the Presence of God.

This shower of angels, this continual summoning of the angelic hosts, proceeds from a characteristically Russian imagination. The Eastern Church has always shown great respect and reverence for the angelic presences, for though men may be higher than the angels they are not like the angels in direct communion with God. Men see God in flashes, the angels see Him always. When Andrey Rublev, the greatest of Russian ikon painters, was asked to paint the Trinity, he simply painted three angels sitting beside the sacramental altar where the head of the Lamb was displayed on a golden chalice. He saw no impropriety in transforming God into angels blazing in blue and gold.

There is nothing essentially Christian in belief in angels, but Pasternak informs them with a quite extraordinary Christian feeling, and *Doctor Zhivago* is penetrated through and through with Christian concepts. There is a sense in which the whole book is a meditation on the Resurrection. Twice—once in the novel and then again in one of the poems at the end of the novel—Pasternak speaks of the Magdalene bathing the feet of Christ; but the vision of the

Magdalene is only a prelude to the vision of the open tomb, as she hurries through the ghostly dawn light on an errand of mercy, not for herself but for all who will come after her. That she should have bathed His feet just before the Crucifixion and that she should have been the first to greet Him when He rose from the dead—that this should happen—that it was the Magdalene and no other—filled Pasternak with an indescribable joy. "What familiarity, what equality between God and life, God and the individual, God and a woman!"

Haunted by the Magdalene, Pasternak returns again and again to her image as she kneels at Christ's feet in an ecstasy of gratitude, a gratitude which is shared by Yury Zhivago as he gazes spellbound, after a long night spent composing poetry, at the sleeping face of Larissa on a snow-white pillow. Seeing her, he utters words which are not very far removed from the words he puts in the mouth of the Magdalene:

"Lord! Lord!" he was ready to whisper. "And all this for me! Why hast Thou given me so much? Why hast Thou permitted me to enter Thy presence, why allowed me to enter Thy world which is altogether beyond price, under Thy stars, at the feet of this unlucky, reckless, uncomplaining, enchantingly beautiful one?"[2]

So he speaks after a night spent in the shuddering delights of composing poetry, in a storm of language, "the home and dwelling of beauty and meaning." But if language, with all the mysterious demands it makes on the poet, is indeed, as Yury Zhivago says, "the home and dwelling of beauty and meaning," then the face of Larissa is "the home and dwelling of divinity," infinitely more valuable than any poem, because it is beautiful in a far more immediate way and because it is touched with a divine mortality.

And so, at the very end of the novel, commenting on the death of Yury Zhivago as he lies in his coffin on the table where so many

---

[2] *Doctor Zhivago,* chapter 14, part 8.

of his poems were written, the coffin banked high with flowers which pour out their scent like a hymn of praise, Pasternak once more returns to contemplate the Magdalene in a brief sermon on the flowers of the graveyard, for are not the flowers the visible signs of the Resurrection?

Here, in the green of the earth, among the trees of the graveyard, among the flowerbeds with their springing shoots, are concentrated perhaps the secret transformations and mysteries of life which torment us. For a moment Mary Magdalene did not recognize Jesus risen from the grave, but took him for the gardener going about the graveyard. ("She, supposing him to be the gardener. . . .")[3]

At such moments, in the simple confrontation of the flowers and the gardener, Pasternak suggests a Christian feeling independent of all dogma, as free as Galilee, as precise as the shape of a flower opening. It is not our Christianity, but altogether simpler, more primitive, closer to the earth and to poetry, and perhaps closer still to the original Christianity as it was known when Christ walked and talked beside a shimmering lake: for Pasternak speaks as though Christianity were still fresh, with the dew still on it.

III

While *Doctor Zhivago*—that long meditation on the Resurrection and on the history of man—will always remain Pasternak's greatest achievement in prose, it is almost certain that future commentators will find his greatest achievement in poetry in the small album of poems collected together at the end of the novel. They are not there by accident, nor are they in any sense an appendix to the novel. These poems are as essential to the novel as the main characters and form a carefully wrought coda, a summing up of all that

[3] *Ibid.*, chapter 15, part 13.

has gone before. The themes of the novel here receive their most
complete and finished expression.

There are, altogether, twenty-six poems, of which eight deal directly with the Christian experience. There are two poems on the
Magdalene, and one each on Holy Week, Gethsemane, the Trans-
figuration, the Cursing of the Fig Tree, and the Star of the Nativity.
Finally there is a poem called "Evil Days," where Christ contem-
plates his whole past life with all its triumphs and agonies until the
moment when "He went down into the cellar by the light of a
candle, and suddenly the candle was snuffed out as the Risen One
rose to his feet."

It would seem that these eight poems are the fragments of a
cycle intended to deal with the entire life of Jesus. Many were
perhaps mislaid—there is an extraordinary discussion on the writing and losing of the poems in the novel—but many others may still
come to light. We are left then with only those poems which
Pasternak wanted to see in print, or those which had most relevance to the themes of the novel, and what is most remarkable
about them is their finality. Each of the Christian poems somehow
suggests a last lingering look at the figure of Christ. They are written from the heart, with a tremendous sense of urgency, with that
curious dancing excitement which we recognize in works written
at the end of an artist's life when he is no longer spurred by
thoughts of earthly fame, when he writes only according to the
dictates of the heart. These last poems are comparable in their
gaiety and quiet meditative beauty to the posthumous quartets of
Beethoven.

No doubt, in time, each of these poems will be provided with the
necessary commentary. The commentators will trace the source of
each image, and set each poem in perspective. But the time for
commentaries on these poems has not yet come. We need to know
more about Pasternak than we know. Much of his writing remains
unpublished, his letters have not yet been collected together, and we

know too little about the forces and influences which worked on him. So for a little while longer it is better just to read his poems.

Here is the longest of the Christian poems at the end of *Doctor Zhivago:*

STAR OF THE NATIVITY

It was wintertime.
The wind blew from the plain
And the infant was cold
In the cave on the slope of a knoll.

The breath of an ox served to warm Him.
The cattle were huddling
Within the cave.
Warmth hovered in a mist over the manger.

Up on a cliff shepherds shook from their sheepskins
The straws from their pallets
And stray grains of millet
And sleepily stared into the midnight distance.

Far off were fields covered over with snow,
And a graveyard, and gravestones and fences,
A cart with its shafts deep in a snowdrift
And, over the graveyard, a star-studded sky.

And seemingly near yet unseen until then,
Its light more timorous than that of a tallow-dip
Set in the window of some watchman's hut,
A star glimmered over the road to Bethlehem.

Now it looked like a hayrick blazing
Off to one side from heaven and God;
Like the reflection of an arsonous fire,
Like a farmstead in flames or a threshing floor burning.

It reared in the sky like a fiery stack
Of straw, of hay,
In the midst of a Creation startled, astounded
By this new Star.

An increasing redness that was like a portent
Was glowing above it.
And three stargazers heeded, and hasted
To answer the call of these unwonted lights.

Gift-laden camels plodded behind them,
And caparisoned asses, each one smaller and smaller,
Were daintily, cautiously descending a hill.

And all of the things that were to come after
Sprang up in the distance as a strange prevision:
All the thoughts of the ages, all the dreams, all the worlds,
All the future of galleries and of museums,
All the pranks of goblins, all the works of the workers of miracles,
All the yule trees on earth, all the dreams of small children,
All the warm glow of tremulous candles, all chains,
All the magnificence of brightly hued tinsel. . . .
(Ever more cruel, more raging, the wind blew from the plain.)
. . . All rosy-cheeked apples, all the blown-glass gold globes.

Part of the pond was screened by alders,
But, beyond rook nests among the treetops,
Part could be seen clearly from the brink of the cliff.
The shepherds could mark well the camels and asses
Threading their way at the edge of the milldam.
"Let us go with all others and worship the miracle,"
Said they, and muffled their sheepskins about them.

Plowing through snow made their bodies feel warm.
Tracks of bare feet, glinting like mica,
Led over the bright plain and beyond the inn's hut,

And the dogs sighting these tracks by the Star's light
Growled at them as if at a candle-end's flame.

The frosty night was like a fairy tale,
And some beings from the snow-crushed mountain ridge
Were mingling constantly, unseen, with all the others.
The dogs were wavering, looking back in terror,
And, in dire foreboding, cringed close to a young shepherd.

Through the same countryside, over the same highway
Some angels walked among the throng of mortals.
Their incorporeality made them invisible,
Yet each step they took left the print of a foot.

Day was breaking. The trunks of the cedars stood out.
A horde of men milled by the stone at the cave's mouth.
"Who are you?" Mary asked them.
"We are from a shepherd tribe, and envoys of heaven.
We have come to sing praises to both of you."
"You cannot all enter. Bide a while here."

In the gloom before dawn, gray as cold ashes,
The drovers and shepherds stamped to keep warm.
Those come on foot bickered with those who came mounted.
Near the hollowed-out log that served as a water trough
The camels bellowed, the gray asses kicked out.

Day was breaking. Dawn swept the last of the stars
Off heaven's vault as if they were ash motes.
And Mary, out of all the countless multitude, allowed
Only the Magi to enter the cleft in the crag.

He slept, all refulgent, in the manger of oakwood,
Like a moonbeam within a deep-hollowed tree.
In lieu of sheepskins His body was warmed
By the lips of an ass and the nostrils of an ox.

The Magi stood in shadow (the byre seemed in twilight);
They spoke in whispers, groping for words.
Suddenly one, in deeper shadow, touched another
To move him aside from the manger, a little to the left.
The other turned: like a guest about to enter,
The Star of the Nativity was gazing upon the Maid.

Such were the gifts—and there were many more—which Boris
Pasternak laid at the feet of Christ.

10

William Temple

BY ALBERT BAKER

ALBERT BAKER, *who died last year at the age of seventy-eight, was a Christian apologist of singular gifts. Not only was he deeply read in the natural sciences, morals, and theology, but he was a preacher of unusual power. He was a Canon of York, Proctor in the Northern Convocation, and author of more than a dozen books, including* William Temple and His Message.

William Temple was born in the Bishop's Palace at Truro in October 1881. His father, already a diocesan bishop, was within a month of his sixtieth birthday. To be an old man's son means either, as in the case of John the Baptist, an extreme contrast between father and son, or it means the opposite—the son is committed mind and heart to his father's purposes and methods. Frederick Temple was an outstandingly great and good man, and his son welcomed his influence gratefully, was always eager to learn from him. At his own enthronement at Canterbury, William, looking back to his father's enthronement (it scarcely needs to be said that never before has an Archbishop's son become Archbishop), said: "Of whom I say nothing except that he was, and is, among men the chief inspiration of my life."

In due course, William went to Rugby, where his father had been headmaster. He was always proud of Rugby, and extolled the virtues of the public school system, the system within which boys learn tolerance and responsibility by living together; but he was sensitive to the weaknesses and dangers of the system. And he inherited from his father a devotion to the cause of working-class education. William became, as is well known, the first president of the Workers' Education Association, and to the end showed a practical enthusiasm for it. It is not so usually known that his father, Frederick, had been for a short time the Principal of Kneller Hall, when it was a college for the preparation of people to teach in Charity Schools.

William went to Oxford with an exhibition to Balliol, where his

father had been Scholar and Fellow; he became President of the
Union, and took a first in Classical Moderation and Greats with
consummate ease. The presidency of the Union is, perhaps, significant. Twelve years later Hensley Henson, who certainly had a right
to an opinion, said that Temple was of the race of orators. The
Greats was important. It would be absurd, of course, to say that
William was a typical Greats man, but both negatively and positively, it left its mark on him. Greats is among the finest examina-
tions in the world—and I say this without bias, because I am not an
Oxford man. But it has no natural science, and William never quite
entered into the tremendous impression which has been made by
the theoretical and practical achievements of science, not only pro-
viding much of the content of our minds but also molding ines-
capably the minds themselves, our values, and ways of thinking.
What Greats sets out to do—William himself said it—is to encourage men to study philosophy historically and history philo-
sophically, a noble aim. Its effect on Temple was profound. This
dominance of the philosophical ideal was confirmed when he became Fellow of Queen's College, Oxford, in 1904, and taught Plato
there until 1910.

Always, his approach to theology started rather from the philosophy of religion than from dogma. He arrived at orthodoxy in
the end—for example, he has been among the most notable ex-
ponents in our time of the doctrine of the Incarnation, but he set off
not from authority but from reason, conscience, and insight. He
had never really doubted that God is, but it was by intelligence and
obedience that he found Him. A remark he once made about the
Bible is illuminating. He said that his father had taught him to read
the Bible, but to use his wits in reading it. Similarly, he said of the
Church that the notion of (himself) being *pained* at disagreeing
with the Church seemed so remote as to be ridiculous. He also said
the more united the Church becomes, the more necessary is it that
individual members should have and exercise freedom of criticism,
otherwise there will be no progress. But he also recognized that he

was commissioned to teach the whole faith of the Church—putting in the foreground inevitably those things which were proving their strength and virtue in his own life.

From Queen's he went to be headmaster of Repton, at twenty-nine years old, and stayed there four years, years noted for "buoyant sunshine" and "radiant vitality," for the lessons he gave to the Sixth Form, and for his sermons in the School Chapel. Every sermon in his first two years appeared in the volume *Repton School Sermons*. They are comparable to any volume of sermons published in this century: one or two of them rank among the masterpieces of English pulpit literature.

From Repton he went to St. James's, Piccadilly, and was in at the beginning of the Life and Liberty Movement; he went all over England campaigning for the self-government of the Church, if possible without Disestablishment. From that came the constitutional revolution in the English Church which produced the new order, familiar now for a generation; real authority in the parish for the Parochial Church Council, and for the laity in the Church Assembly, and the power of the Assembly to form the Church's laws in bills which become the law of the land *unless* they are overruled by Parliament. The initiative, that is, is with the Church, although the veto remains with the State. Then for two years he was Canon of Westminster. Always he was an outstandingly effective speaker, saying all that he meant, meaning all that he said, with no words wasted. His fault— if he had a fault—was that as he was a practiced writer *before* he was an experienced speaker, his paragraphs were somewhat too rightly phrased for the general audience to grasp at what he meant. As Ian Maclaren said of John Oman, he did not put enough water in the whiskey. But reading these sermons and addresses, with the opportunity occasionally to read a paragraph a second time, is an education in clear thinking on important subjects.

There are times when he reaches heights at which the ordinary man can but gaze and wonder. Not seldom these are seen in sudden flashes of insight when, in pregnant sentences, he propounds truths which, as someone has said, he may just have thought of for the first time, but which are possessions of abiding value and stimulus to those who read them. Sometimes, however, the sense of being in the company of a master of Christian thinking comes with an almost oppressive conviction during the progress of a long, connected piece of exposition. There is, for example, the great lecture on "Freedom and Determination" in *Nature, Man and God*. About halfway through my third reading of this, twenty years after it was published, I felt almost disheartened, not because the argument was long and involved, but at realizing that a man whom I loved—and who loved me, that really is the point—lived on such a height of Christian understanding, while I have been too content to remain on the mere foothills of faith. The meaning of that lecture is that freedom, being spiritual, as distinct from mechanical or organic determination—determination by what seems good and not by irresistible compulsion—finds its sufficient and only source in fellowship with the Spirit of the Whole, transcending any existing thing but not alien from it. "The human spirit will find here something which has for it the appeal as well as the claim of kinship, and will be drawn to make a response, which is at the same time a submission, to the Spirit of the Whole, and therein attain to the fulfilment of itself in the freedom which is also peace."[1]

Another memorable illustration of Temple's supreme achievement is his appendix in the *Readings in St. John's Gospel*, on the Lord's teaching on prayer. God has no need that we should tell Him of our wants or desires. He knows what is good for us better than we do ourselves, and it is always His will to give it. We must not in prayer have any thought of suggesting to God what was already in His mind—still less of changing His mind or purpose. But the worst of all diseases of the soul is detachment from God, whether by ignorance or by neglect. So the first requirement in prayer is that we trust to God for all blessings. But the next requirement is that we should persevere in prayer in spite of disappointment. God

[1] New York, St. Martin's Press, 1953, p. 243.

wishes to deepen our confidence, and to detach our faith in Him from all trust in our own judgment. And then when our wills are identified with the will of God, we are praying for what He desires to give and waits to give until we recognize Him as its source, so that our reception of it will strengthen our faith and not encourage our neglect of Him. The essential act of prayer is not the bending of God's will to ours—of course not—but the bending of our wills to His. The proper outline of a Christian's prayer is not "Please do for me what I want," but "Please do in me, with, and through me what You want."

In 1921 he became Bishop of Manchester, an opportunity and responsibility to which he rose with characteristic readiness and humility. He took an enthusiastic and characteristic part in the leadership of the Annual Mission on Blackpool Sands, addressing large audiences and giving careful answers to questions both at outdoor and indoor meetings. It was the beginning of the nineteen twenties, and his keen mind, his intellectual integrity, his confident trust in the God whom Jesus revealed, expressed in writings and addresses notably lucid and exact, but tolerant, began to make Christianity intellectually respected among people who were still hungry and unfed and a little weary after the long-drawn-out irrelevancies of the Forsyte, or Bertrand Russell's positivism, and the crackling thorns of Bernard Shaw. He had already gained the attention of the thoughtful by his considerable works: *Mens Creatrix* showed the various aspects of contemporary culture—science, the drama, education, and so on, given meaning and therefore units in a theistic pattern. And *Christus Veritas* had shown how a metaphysic which made value fundamental—and in many directions such a metaphysic was becoming fashionable many years ago—could hardly stop short of a theology of Incarnation, and that the Incarnation, in its turn, gives depth and richness to the spiritual life and aspirations both of the individual and society.

Temple was putting his hand to the tasks which Dr. Matthews summed up by saying that it is doubtful whether any other writer has done so much to convince the general public that the Christian faith has a claim to be seriously considered by rational men. Until well in his York period he conducted a series of missions to universities—the best known was that to Oxford—the addresses in which were afterwards published in a volume, often reprinted and still in print, called *Christian Faith and Life*. This volume deals with the great themes of the Faith, such as God, prayer, Christ, the Holy Spirit, the Church, the sacraments, and the Incarnation—in chapters at once simple and profound. And by these missions the lives of many men and women were given a new permanent seriousness and dedication. Not only so, but in 1932, the third year after he became Primate, he delivered the Gifford Lectures at Glasgow, published under the title *Nature, Man and God*. The lectures took the world as the fullest modern knowledge describes it, facing and including man's freedom and sin and redemption, and presented a comprehensive theology best summed up, perhaps, by saying that the title of this book might well have been "a sacramental universe." If there is a unity in any sense, the principle of its unity must be spirit. (Temple always thought that the positive sacraments of the historical Christian Church are to be understood, not as intrusions into reality, but as illustrations of universal principles which *run through* the universe at every level of experience.) The finite spirit of man, in every one of its activities, in the search for truth, in the appreciation of beauty, in the awed, inescapable acceptance of the obligation of goodness, enters into a relation which can only be interpreted as personal, mind finding Mind.

Temple's theology was Catholic, orthodox, and evangelical, but nonetheless personal, liberal, practical, and democratic. To him, the Church was far more than an organization, it was the organism of Christian fellowship. The sacraments are the means by which Christ gives Himself to be our life. Immortality is a gift of God in Christ. The Holy Spirit, by which Christians live, is the response of love in our lives to the love of the Father poured out on us in His Son.

And only as we grow in the costly human love which Christ shares do we grow up into Him.

Towards the end of these Gifford lectures, the Archbishop stated four "Principles of Christianity," which were to find increasing expression in his practical and theoretical involvement in the tasks and problems of Christian sociology. For just as the academic people thought he might be making Christianity intellectually respectable, so the journalist and the man in the street were convinced that he had put the Church on the map. These four "Principles of Christianity" were the sacredness of personality, membership in the brotherhood which is the family of God, man's obligation to serve God by serving his fellows, and, lastly, subordination of power to love, love exerting its power by self-sacrifice. The focus and pivot and dynamic source of all this is, of course, Jesus Christ.

His prophetic leadership and activity in the sphere of Christian social action made opportunities in many and varied ways. There were the great interdenominational conferences on Christian politics, economics, and citizenship (COPEC), of which he was an inspiring but very patient and understanding chairman (he had a great gift for chairmanship). There was the Malvern Conference of 1940, when he brought a weighty and representative group of Anglican clergy and laity to think out the responsibilities and opportunities of the Church and of Churchmen, for those whose minds and lives are ruled, indirectly or directly, by the conditions produced by science and machinery: industry, the mass mind, and international civilization. This culminated in the series of meetings addressed by Temple and Garbett to Edinburgh and back again, the addresses at which were published as *The Church Looks Forward*.

Much of his writing, and the picture of him in the mind of the common man, is shaped by his concern for the economic and political impact of Christianity and the Church; it is this which was implied, probably, by the remark of a writer in *Punch* that Temple was the non-churchman's idea of what an archbishop ought to be.

He wrote a wartime Penguin, called *Christianity and the Social Order,* the sale of which was enormous in America and in this country, and especially in the armed forces. And at the beginning of 1944, there was what was even for him an exceptionally weighty utterance in *What Christians Stand for in the Secular World,* in which he was working out his own Christian sociology in view of what Hitler and the war had forced the Church to face.

It was during the years that he was Archbishop of York that Temple came to be recognized as a world figure, a leader in the Christian movement for international peace, and the creative mind in the practical work of Christian reunion. It was no small thing at that moment, it would be no small thing at any moment, that there should be an Archbishop of Canterbury who interpreted the genius and tradition of Anglicanism as meaning that it is obliged to take, not steps, but strides to meet any Christian communion that seeks reunion; that we should pray for the guidance of the Holy Spirit, but not seek to dictate the road by which He shall lead us, still less insist that the reunited Church shall be the dear old Church of England, with the same coat and hat, unchanged except, perhaps, that it has adopted a new name.

In the insurmountable mercy of God this man who became Archbishop of Canterbury by Divine Providence, if ever man did, as Bishop Barry once said, occupied that exalted position for less than three years. But then, as always, he was greater than his office.

When Dr. Fisher was suddenly confronted with the heavy responsibility of carrying on Temple's work for the Church, he said, in a profoundly moving speech in the Church Assembly, that William Temple had set the lights to mark the channel for the Church of England and that he, Fisher, would keep the Church in the course Temple had marked out. What, then, was Temple's idea of the genius of the Church of England, of its vocation and destiny? There are two or three general notions, to begin with. First, he used to point out that, historically, the Church of England stands not for any particular doctrine (as the Baptists, for example, stand for adult baptism against the baptism of infants), but for the whole Catholic faith. Second, its claim is that it is a Church which *came through* the Reformation, not one which started in it. To be a loyal and understanding Anglican, therefore, a man should value those great elements of "historical" Christianity which are part of the Catholic tradition, and *also* those intuitions which are characteristic of the Reformation. It is true that both Catholics and Protestants have a rightful place in the Anglican Church, as children at home. But more than that, the Catholics must be Protestant Catholics and the Protestants must be Catholic Protestants. Men of each of the two traditions must be molded and inspired by the fellowship, in worship and thinking, with men of the other tradition. The Church of England, he said, has always bridged the gulf (or sat on the wall, if you like) that divides "Catholics" and "Protestants" from one another. Not only so, but the Anglican Church proclaims the authority of Holy Scripture and the duty of private judgment.

The Anglican Church has, from the Reformation settlement, proclaimed the duty of private judgment—not merely the right, but the duty. It means the freedom of individual inquiry, the lack of regimentation or dictation. This means a characteristic relation between clergy and laity. The scholar, the theologian, the preacher must never forget that they also are seekers for the truth of the Gospel, along with the laity whom they are called to help and serve. There must be no hint of dictation, of telling the laity *what* they are to believe, but rather a proclaiming of the *fact* of Jesus, making an appeal to spiritual values, trying to show men *how* to believe. Temple once said that man's conscience claims the right to judge God himself. When Abraham challenged God with the words, "Shall not the judge of all the earth be right!" he was doing that very thing. We must never forget that if an act or word or decision is bad, it does not become good merely because it is in the Bible. And it is also true that ordination to the priesthood, or consecration to the episcopate, does not make a man an authority on a subject he has not studied.

In a sermon at Cambridge in 1925 he expounded the foundations of his doctrine of the Incarnation. He took two texts. The first was Genesis 1,3: "God said, Let there be light, and there was light." Creation is so easy: the utterance of the command effects its fulfillment. The other text (unexpectedly) was Matthew 27, 46: "Jesus said with a loud voice, My God, My God, why hast thou forsaken me?" Redemption is infinitely hard. Creation coincides naturally with the popular notion of omnipotence; redemption belongs to a thought of God which considers Him as almighty only by His own self-sacrifice.

God as supreme over the whole of mere existence is Creator, but as supreme over good and evil is Redeemer. No one who has thought of God as Creator has conceived Him as putting forth effort to create; the physical universe is to the Almighty a very little thing. But not everything is even to Him a little thing. The fashioning of a child's soul—that self-willed souls should be won to love Him, and thus make love, not self, the center of their living—that costs what is represented by Gethsemane and Calvary, a task to ask from Incarnate God, the Bloody Sweat and the Cry of Desolation.

More than once—when he is dealing with Calvary or with man's self-worship and how he is to be won from it—he shows that it is only in His love, and in love revealed in sacrifice, that God is ultimately almighty. If God's power is of the nature of infinite horsepower, there is no evidence that God exists. But we have the picture of a man in a garden. He said, "Let this cup pass from me." And *nothing happened.* He is the God who is silent, who will not strive nor cry, nor cause his voice to be heard in the street. He makes His sun to shine on the evil as well as on the good. That undiscriminating generosity is what it means to say, God is Love. The God whom Jesus revealed is the God of things as they are, the God who has no power but love.

We must go to Jesus, and get our ideas of God from Him, *not* keep our ideas of God, such as they are, and get such light as we can on them from Jesus. If Jesus is the revelation of God, God's knowledge is more of the nature of *insight* than foresight, not the knowledge of an infinite Einstein, but the wisdom of the Galilean; only so can we rationalize the reality of history. God is love in an ultimate and fundamental sense in which it is not true that He is justice or force. And His holiness also must be interpreted in terms of His love. His love makes demands of us that justice has no right to make: He will never be satisfied until we all become children of God: "Be ye perfect as your Father in heaven is perfect." Until men give Him their hearts, He cannot do anything about it. But this holiness is just that the Creator, the Sinless One, became more terrifyingly awful in the breath-taking gift by which He takes the initiative to bridge the gulf between Himself and us.

The story of the universe, culminating in man, is a progress from *chaos* to *order,* the history not of *force,* but of *reason,* of the personal quality which is love. And if it be true that the omnipotence of God is love, and His wisdom is humility, the possibility of sin is explained. Love is the Divine ground of real human freedom, not the freedom of a bird in a cage, but a land of far distances. Evolution is inexplicable if God is infinite force, but what if it means the infinite patience of God, the age-long agony of a humble love working itself out through the mistaken choices and false starts and blind alleys of the animal world, and at last in and through man's freedom and self-will? If God is love, creation is the revelation and self-expression of God, not His self-limitation, and the Incarnation is not God's self-emptying, as some have fondly imagined, but His self-giving and self-manifestation. God is Love, and in Him is no coercion at all. The central, fundamental affirmation of the Christian religion is that Jesus of Nazareth is the unique, final revelation of God. The task of theology—not yet adequately fulfilled—is to give back value to the words, "He that hath seen me hath seen the Father."

Temple's personality was at once uniquely unified and richly comprehensive. He was intensely interested in the arts, always a great reader of poetry, with a prodigious memory, very knowledgeable on painting, a provocative writer on the method and meaning of tragedy; and he had competent appreciation of music—he was one of the few high ecclesiastical dignitaries who could sing the priest's part in the Eucharist with confidence. All this implies, of course, that he had an eye and mind for the concrete and particular, and this was reflected also in his voracious reading of history and of biographies—particularly, perhaps, political biography. But it was balanced by his mastery of metaphysics, from Plato and his predecessors to Whitehead and his interpreters; and he understood the *principles* of natural science, if his ignorance of its methods was, as he once said, so complete as to be distinguished. He had very little parochial experience, but he was a first-class chairman, a very good listener, with a ready laugh which put most people who met him quickly at their ease. He was a Church reformer in the sense that he wanted every member to have a responsible share in guiding its policy, and he had a sensitive interest in, and understanding of, the needs and thoughts of people of all classes and nations and denominations.

But all this richness of thought and experience was focused and held together and its meaning was deepened by his devotion to Christ and His Kingdom. "He loved the Lord like blazes," as Von Hügel said of St. John. He once said Christ is, of course, all humanity, and he took for granted that every human concern is a part of Christianity. He taught us that God is interested in many other things besides religion, and said that it is easy to be too religious. But he gave explicit and self-conscious expression to his own religious experience. He had given his heart to Jesus, and every interest and purpose of his life was dominated by that affection.

11

John LaFarge

BY GEORGE N. SHUSTER

GEORGE NAUMAN SHUSTER, *formerly President of Hunter College, is an educator of national stature. The author, co-author, and translator of numerous books, including,* Cultural Co-operation and the Peace, Religion Behind the Iron Curtain, Education and Moral Wisdom, *he is a long-time student of Church history and affairs, on which he speaks with acknowledged authority. He is a member of the Board of the Encyclopedia Britannica.*

When you think of Father LaFarge, you remember first of all that he is a Jesuit priest. If his account of the matter is to be credited, and there is no reason at all why it should not be, he decided to become one without a spasm of emotion or any sense that he was sacrificing even a part of himself on the altar of the Lord. After mature reflection, he simply responded to the call. One cannot imagine that he could at any time have written something like *Tintern Abbey* or *Queen Mab*. Perhaps this was so because he lived as a boy with a father who doubtless managed the equivalent in painting or stained glass from the days of his youth until old age. But I think the bent of his character and genius was rooted in the heritage of the France which is disciplined and down-to-earth. Certainly among the saints, and it must hastily be added that this essay is in no sense a prelude to canonization proceedings, the one who most resembles him is Francis de Sales.

The life of the great Bishop of Annecy is like a hypothetical musical composition in which a strict canon by Bach has somehow been fused with the melodic line of Palestrina. On the one hand, he was a master of the Catholic way of bringing order into the business of the soul; and on the other, he shunned no association with men of other faiths which offered some hope of spiritual profit. When human nature was ready to dare much, he joined in every risk it wished to take, as was the case with Jane de Chantal. Otherwise the "manner" with him, too, was "ordinary." The biographer relates that when he was on his deathbed and the barbarous medicos of the time were branding his neck with a red-hot iron in order to keep him from lapsing into unconsciousness, his only comment to his dreadful tormentors was that they were to do "whatever they thought fit." Here was a man rooted in a France different from that which produced either Bossuet or Claudel; and one fancies that somehow a few square yards of soil from it were brought to this country so that John LaFarge could come to be.

At any rate, New York and Newport, Harvard and Innsbruck, provided intellectual and cultural background. From every point of view these were grist for the making of a gentleman, but in this instance it was one from whom every trace of condescension would always be absent. He, too, would never inflict pain, as Newman had stipulated, but that would be with him a habit and not a prescription. It was as natural for him to possess good breeding as it is for a star to be coated with celestial gold, and yet he perennially seemed in the presence of others not to have the slightest notion of being a star. This accounts in part for his extraordinary influence with those who are spiritually or socially downtrodden. He learned to speak with the Negroes of Maryland in their own language, even as he could converse with Boston intellectuals in theirs. There are precious maxims of St. Ignatius which commend such prudence to his followers. But I believe that even if Father LaFarge had never read them he would nevertheless have known how to put them to work in the world.

Father LaFarge's first major obedience, after a spate of chores in New York's hospitals and prisons, was working among the people of southern Maryland, site of the oldest mission of the Jesuits in the United States. By most people the area would have promptly and vigorously been denominated the "sticks," but for John LaFarge it was Arcady, in spite of a lack of intellectual companionship. And of course in many ways it was Arcadian. The faithful had no comely churches, nor anything which the imagination could call "liturgical art," stretch itself to the point of infinity though it might. But these people had festivals once brought from England. They danced,

staged mock tournaments, had "sociables." The new assistant to
the pastor of Leonardstown had soon mapped the parish terrain as
skilfully as Marshal Vauban did the fortress of Luxemburg. And
gradually he came to know the Negro as he then was in the rural
environment of the near South. All this meant coming to grips with
unfamiliar social problems, whether the society was that of the
Church or of the nation.

Then came a memorable date in the history of American Catholicism during this period. It is referred to laconically in Father La-
Farge's memoirs as follows: "A year later, on July 22, 1926, I received word that I was appointed to the staff of *America,* and departed for New York on August 16." This assignment was to make
evident his great gifts and to yield the fruit of his wide experience.
Being an editor of stature and consequence now demands a versatility of outlook and interests scarcely any longer possible in any
other profession. The professor and scholar has one mine which he
digs deeper and deeper. And so on. But if an editor serves an intelligent public he must be interested, not passively but actively and
creatively, in the whole spectrum of the opinion of that public.
Father LaFarge's versatility has been of a quite special kind. So far
as one can tell, his Catholic outlook on life had little room for
reflection in depth on those problems, queries, and doubts of an
intellectual character which loom so large in the lives of some other
modern men. The Church for him is like a storehouse of gold from
which one can borrow prodigally without worrying about whether
there is a hole somewhere in the vault or whether the number of
carats could diminish. When he visited Baron von Hügel, for example, he was frankly irritated by that great scholar's criticism of
the Roman outlook and by his high estimate of the writings of Père
Loisy. The Baron was of course a specialist and a very distinguished
one who unfortunately did not live to see the day when Catholic
Bible criticism would come of age.

Father LaFarge's attitude has, I think, been this: there is a vast
amount of treasure in the Catholic storehouse which is lying idle

and ought to be put to good use. Since it has not been so put, a great many undesirable things have been happening or developing in the world, among them Communism, rabid nationalism, and the deepening of racial prejudice. He did not confront these things, as a number of his co-religionists were in the habit of doing, with a book of rules and the easy statement that if everybody would only do what was said in this book the world would recover. Life was for him not that simple. The things in the rule book are good, just as is the motto Be sure to keep a sound mind in a sound body. Alas, mind and body may not be sound, and the task then is to diagnose the ailment and if possible effect a cure.

America was already a weekly of quality when he joined the staff; and at least two of its editors were or had been men who could see both trees and forest. But as yet no one had hung out patiently the sign of cordial welcome to all who are of good will which has since then become the journal's notable characteristic. It was, even as its counterpart the *Commonweal,* still somewhat cribbed and confined. Conscious of being not a few knots this side of the Gulf Stream down which the great tide of Catholic opinion was moving in more or less blissful contemplation of its virtues, it was sometimes frightened by its isolation and upon occasion also prone to tossing a stick of dynamite into that tide more or less to see what noise it would make. There was no large audience. The generations which would soon begin to move out of greatly improved Catholic colleges or from secular universities were still in the offing. More often than not the clergy had got so bogged down in collecting the pew rent and exercising the normal pastoral care that they had neither time nor inclination to "go highbrow." Generally they were content with recalling something said in the seminary, and frequently recalling it badly.

It was just like Father LaFarge to begin, shortly after his arrival in the vast, strange, restless city in which he had never really cared to live, with cultivating "a closer acquaintance with the new and dynamic Catholic Rural Life Movement." Nothing could indicate more effectively what were to be the dimensions of his intellectual outlook henceforth. It would proceed from the American farm to the movements and problems which were rapidly changing the nature of human society. And in each case the objective he sought was not merely study of a situation for the sake of studying it, but rather profound and reasoned inquiry into what could in practice be done to put into effect, in some measure at least, Christian principles of social thought and action.

The task was primarily an educational one. Catholics themselves had to be persuaded to take the social teachings of the Church seriously, and then to see that these teachings were not "answers" to every query put by an unsettled and groping age, but principles in the light of which something might be attempted to bring about improvement. There were far too many who simply wanted to be "told" what was right. That in the realm of social methodology one might not know what the right course was unless one had slowly and painstakingly experimented was novel doctrine. But the non-Catholic world required education, too. Groups which possessed almost unlimited good will and also considerable knowledge of events, situations, and their causes were so ignorant of the mind of the Church that they often viewed with antipathy and even hostility a power of the spirit which might have proved a strong ally.

One cannot say that in order to perform this educational mission Father LaFarge became what is called a joiner, though certainly few men have associated themselves with so many worthy causes. Were it drawn up, the list would be a sort of catalogue of the ships which the ethical intellect of our time has tried to steer through stormy waters. It must suffice to indicate that it extends from Dr. Louis Finkelstein's Institute for Religious and Social Studies to Mrs. Lecomte du Noüy's efforts to explore the relations between science and religion. And the remarkable thing about the matter is that Father LaFarge not merely associated himself with all these but left the imprint of his personality on every one. Observing him do so has been for many a very rewarding experience. He has not, as some of us (including the present writer) unfortunately often do, tried to have the course of the discussion move as he would wish it to move. Now and then he builds a wisely conceived little dam which keeps the waters from rushing pellmell in the wrong direction. He does not seem to be aware of exercising any great amount of tact in doing so. The wisely conceived little dam persuades one of its own rightness.

This it does, it seems to me, because Father LaFarge became deeply aware, as few men do, of the many, many groups of people seeking the Good in America and thus, it may be, slowly undermining a hard and crusty surface, like so many conscious or unconscious earthworms of God. Perhaps he alone has sensed the possibilities which may lie in their potential confluence. Just as a truly great university may look, when viewed in the drab light of day, like a restless crowd bent on grabbing credits if they be students or promotions if they be members of the faculty, and nevertheless be in essence a series of hard-working, serious, relatively amiable men and women each reverently grappling with truth in his own way, so American society, looked at in the mass, may appear to be merely people out to grab as much as they can get while being culturally conditioned by opinion makers and the great media of information, and yet actually consist of numerous groups concerned each in its individual fashion with the Light by which men truly live. It requires a great gift of God's grace to see that this is so and to have a picture of what might happen if all these rivulets finally came together in a mighty stream. But there is need also for the philosophic temper, patience and a knowledge of what happens in many hearts when a Voice speaks, speaks indistinctly it may be and yet speaks, so that afterward a man cannot forget that he has heard.

But it is of course in the movements he himself initiated that Father LaFarge's own views and hopes are most clearly reflected. He has not been a man of one movement because of his awareness of the many aspects of the needed reformation of society. To repeat, in this he seems like St. Francis de Sales rather than like St.

Vincent de Paul. And yet I suppose that there are two or three with which his memory will be particularly associated for a long time to come.

No doubt the first is the Catholic Interracial Movement. It required great courage and practical idealism to believe some years ago either that Negroes would often turn from the Pentecostal religions which had been their fare since slavery or that they and white men would set much store by communing one with another. As for the American Church itself, there was enough trouble attempting to get various immigrant minorities working together in some sort of amity. Why cross the color line? Catholic whites were not in general living by a racial code of their own. They subscribed in this respect also to the custom of the nation. The Negro who worked for you was more frequently than not a pleasant person to have around, provided he or she stayed in the kitchen, the basement, or the yard and did not drop in for cocktails. In the great cities the color line was like the place along the river to which the flood water came. It changed the character of neighborhoods, engulfed churches, eroded parishes. Somewhere in the huge resulting ghettos there were Catholics, to be sure. Many of them came from the West Indies, South America, or even Africa. Priests and religious had to be provided for them, of course, but they were needed also in Paraguay and Borneo. Indeed, it was felt that the Black Belt was probably a worse place to which to be assigned than any of the far countries. One could pray for such missioners and if need be drop something in the collection box in their behalf, but one simply did not join them, not even in thought.

Father LaFarge's Interracial Council was naturally a missionary activity, but of a quite new kind. It buttonholed the faithful and not those *in partibus infidelium*. This it did first of all for the reason that Catholic Negroes had a claim on the Communion of Saints, not because they had sought it out or struggled for it, as the NAACP had fought for equal rights, but because the Lord and Master had given that claim to them as their spiritual birthright. They were no longer to be strangers but members of the family. But the other things which shall be given were there too—the possibility of joint action to face up to the corrosion of urban morals, to the steady obsolescence of the neighborhoods into which Negroes had come, and—worse still, perhaps—the loss of belief that this world could sometime foreshadow the Kingdom of God.

Today the idea which was implicit in the Councils from the beginning has caught fire in many places. It is not yet a successful or triumphant idea. But there is a light on the horizon. Toward it more and more people are groping their way. More and more feel that warmth is there. And who can doubt that as time continues and progress is made, not a few will remember that a man from New York and Newport, become a Jesuit, had brought back from Maryland insights into the "Negro question" which he was persuaded were equally applicable to city life? Father LaFarge did not deliver harangues about them. There were no picket lines, no angry shouts. The plan was to do something simple, human, reasonable, and just. Perhaps I may recall the first time that I accepted an invitation to address one of the groups he managed to get together somewhere in Harlem. It was as a matter of fact an assembly as a congregation, and yet strangely novel also, a coming together not for *a* purpose but for *the* purpose, Christian and American alike, because it was cut according to the pattern of both.

I do not know whether in the long run Father LaFarge's approach to the Negro will prove to be the one his countrymen will take. But two other of his pioneer endeavors have come to a fruition, however indirectly, which in the early period no one could have predicted. The first was his service to the Liturgy. Although to my knowledge he never formulated a theory about the matter, few men have realized more fully that the life of a religion is a community life. All the great faiths build communions of men by some law which is implicit in the following of religious leadership. Where two or three are gathered in His name, Christ is present also. Religious cultures express the meaning of this being together in language and art. In terms of aspiration to holiness these two are given form in the Liturgy, which is the community worshipping as the individual cannot. But what was known as the Liturgical Movement at first too often resembled a group of art critics less interested in the substance than the form. It was very necessary to be simple about this too, purposeful, aware of the people who were after all the worshippers.

Beyond any doubt one of the most astonishing things which has happened in America is that the liturgical idea has been so widely accepted as natural and normal, not merely inside Father LaFarge's own Church but outside it as well. There is no Christian communion which is not different because of it from what it was some decades ago. Man in general no longer worships apart from his fellows but with them. Meanwhile the Liturgists as a group have moved far ahead in terms of both scholarship and art. But one may perhaps venture the surmise that as they have progressed they have become less recondite for the sake of erudition. It is after all what the people do that counts, rather than what is written about what they might do. And so, one thinks, Father LaFarge can look back with satisfaction. The liturgical fledgling has grown far taller and stronger than it was when the great Jesuit all but took it in off the street.

The second endeavor found corporate expression in the Catholic Association for International Peace, but was far broader in scope and import. For a long time it was difficult to persuade the average American—and in this respect Christians were hardly above the average—that peace was something more than not getting into a war or getting out of it. How could one educate him to realize that in the modern time social forces have supplanted dynastic powers, and that war or peace will depend upon whether those forces are controlled? It was necessary to begin with a patient analysis. Was it economic rivalry which in the first instance bred armed conflict? Or was it perhaps emotional nationalism? Or could one find the key in the lack of a law binding on the nations and somehow enforceable?

Yet the patient analysis was not enough. One needed foresight, too, in the sense that storms moving into the sky, as Stalin, Mussolini, and Hitler moved, must be recognized before their fury broke. In no other respect was the work done by *America* and its editor more genuinely a pioneer effort. At one time even the assertion that since Catholics, wherever they might be, were in one Church and that accordingly their association in an international peace effort for the good of the human family was more imperative even than it was for other men, was unpalatable doctrine. In the long run, alas, the eyes of many were opened not because of what was written so that they might read, but because the darkness descended and death was among them.

These are some of the things which came to pass because a man once young vowed to give his life for the service of his Master. He did not attach undue importance to the offering, but it was all he had. The Jesuit lives according to a strict rule, and the environment in which he is placed seems always to suggest that when he moves out of it not much will be left behind. Benedictine abbeys bring together beauty for the House of God even as bees amass honey. The single monk in his spare cell has none of it, but he moves during the day and the night to the church where the glory of the Lord is present by analogy. Jesuits live with Grand Rapids furniture of the bargain store variety. When they move there is little to transport except themselves. And yet the Jesuit too goes out into the glory of the Lord. This is what he sees in the souls of men everywhere, in the streets, in rich men's houses, in the shacks of the poor, among Negroes and aristocrats. For the image of Christ is in each one, and the Jesuit bows low so that he may lift up. It is perhaps this one ought to see when one thinks of John LaFarge. But who shall malign us if we discern also the image of Man as he might some time generally be if he made of his mind and heart gardens in which no weed was suffered to grow?

12

Billy Graham

BY JOHN SUTHERLAND BONNELL

JOHN SUTHERLAND BONNELL *is a Presbyterian divine who, for nearly three decades, exercised a notable ministry in New York City. By his fervor for evangelism and the skilled counselling of a variety of people he became a powerful force in American Protestantism, and his pulpit eloquence early established him as a national figure. His many articles on religion and related subjects in well-known magazines have brought him frequently before the general public. Among his books are included,* What Are You Living For?, I Believe in Immortality, Heaven and Hell, No Escape from Life.

In almost any company it requires nothing more than a mention of the name Billy Graham to provoke a sharp discussion. "What do you think of him?" "Is he sincere?" "If he is genuine, why are people, including some of the clergy, critical of him?"

Whatever his traducers say concerning him, the fact remains that William Franklin Graham continues to be one of the most dynamic spiritual personalities of our generation. One cannot dismiss with a few words of biting criticism or contempt a man who has, in person, preached the Christian gospel to more people than anyone since the birth of Christ; who has visited every continent of the world, leaving behind him thousands of lives changed for the better; and whose devoted followers are numbered in the millions.

Only the twentieth century could have produced a religious phenomenon like Billy Graham. It required the combined resources of radio, television, the press, and electronic amplification for outdoor audiences to enable him to reach the multitudes who have heard his voice. In the past Christian people have often marveled at the unprecedented ministries of evangelists George Whitefield and John Wesley. These celebrated clergymen preached in the open fields to congregations, in eighteenth-century England, that numbered 1,000 to 20,000 persons. But in our time Billy Graham has preached to 100,000 in New York, 116,000 in Chicago, 125,000 in Sydney, Australia, and 140,000 in Melbourne. It would seem reasonably certain that a speaker facing such vast audiences as these would appear to persons farthest from the platform a diminutive figure. In the case of Dr. Graham, however, this is not true. The impact of the evangelist's personality is almost as powerful on those seated on remote benches as on that part of his congregation directly before the rostrum. Certainly, so far as physical stamina and magnetic personality go, he is superbly equipped for his chosen life work. His spiritual qualifications will be the subject of later discussion.

Billy Graham was born on a North Carolina farm on November 7, 1918, in the closing days of the First World War. His father, William Franklin Graham, after whom Billy was named, was a successful dairy farmer. His mother, Morrow Coffey, came from an old Southern family that pre-dated the Revolutionary War.

He would have been a remarkable prophet who could have foreseen in the youthful Billy Graham a potential evangelist with worldwide renown. His passion for speedy driving, his bent toward mischievous conduct, and especially, his all-absorbing interest in baseball, indicated almost any type of career other than that of the Christian ministry. At the age of seventeen, this tall, lanky youth was toughened and disciplined by rising at 3 A.M. each day to milk his quota of more than three score cows. Two years earlier he had been allotted his own milk route in Charlotte.

Always foremost among his avocations was baseball. Doubtless he often daydreamed of becoming a famous star of the baseball diamond, like his hero, Babe Ruth, and not without reason, for in his middle teens he was already receiving fifteen dollars per game when he was called upon to play at first base. On one unforgettable occasion when the New York Yankees stopped off for a few hours at Charlotte, the great Babe himself watched Billy playing and then predicted, "Someday you may be in the Yankee Stadium." The famous batter's words were destined to be fulfilled in ways of which Babe Ruth never even dreamed. Billy Graham did appear in the Yankee Stadium, going to bat not for any big league baseball team, but in the service of his Master, Christ. On that occasion he drew more people together than ever assembled to watch a baseball game in the history of that celebrated playing field.

One aspect of Billy's early training might have given a clue to his future: the discipline of family devotions. Each morning after breakfast, the Graham family met around the table to read, in turn, from the Bible. The children were all expected to memorize one verse of Scripture daily. Twice on Sunday, morning and evening, they attended public worship in a neighborhood Presbyterian church. During these impressionable years, Billy Graham was storing up in his mind and heart passages of the Bible on which he would draw when his native gifts had come to fruition and he faced great congregations or answered the questions of some who sought to embarrass or confound him.

It was while he was still in his teens and attending school that the most momentous day in the life of Billy Graham dawned. It was a period when itinerant evangelists often appeared in the community to hold services for a week or ten days and sometimes even for a month. On this occasion the visiting preacher was Mordecai Ham, famous for his denunciation of sin and of sinners. He possessed to an unusual degree the ability to arouse powerful emotions in his hearers. He warned them of the inescapable judgment of God on unrepentant sinners doomed to suffer for all eternity in the flames of Hell. As Evangelist Ham's voice rose steadily in fiery exhortation to "flee from the wrath to come," some of his listeners, stricken by a guilty conscience and frantic fear, would cry aloud or fall prostrate to the ground, writhing and praying for God's mercy and forgiveness. Among those who walked to the front and knelt in prayer was the youthful Graham. The impulse that sent him down the aisle with bowed head and prayerful heart was not so much the fear of impending judgment or an overwhelming sense of sin, as the sudden awareness that he had never yielded himself unreservedly to Christ, or sought God's will for his life. With this decisive act came shortly the realization that he was destined for the Christian ministry. This momentous decision of their son was heartily approved by Frank Graham and his wife. For years Billy's mother had prayed that if it were God's will, her son might be led to become a minister of Christ's gospel. She now viewed his decision in this matter as an evident sign of the divine leading and an answer to her prayers.

It was quite in keeping with Billy's conversion at Mordecai Ham's meeting that he should now go to Bob Jones College to train for a career in evangelism. This college was much more noted for fervent evangelism than for solid Christian scholarship. It was not long until young Graham felt himself somewhat inhibited at Bob Jones College, and he transferred to a Baptist institution, the Florida Bible Institute. Here the atmosphere was much more congenial to the expanding mind of the maturing youth. While absorbing all that this institution had to offer, Graham, with his lifelong friend, Grady Wilson, was paying his way by caddying on a Tampa golf course, washing dishes and shining shoes, and above all selling, most successfully, Fuller brushes.

It was while attending the Florida Bible Institute that Billy began in earnest to study the sermons of notable preachers and to practice preaching on his own. Despite the crudities that inexperience led him into at times, it soon became apparent that here was a young man of excellent promise. Before long, whenever he was announced as the preacher, a larger than usual congregation would invariably assemble. Billy Graham was on his way. By the age of twenty-one, Billy had graduated from the Florida Bible Institute with a Bachelor of Divinity degree, had transferred his allegiance to the Baptist denomination, and had been ordained a minister of a Baptist Association of northern Florida.

Once again Graham felt the need of more education, and it is altogether in keeping with the circumstances of his conversion and early college training that he should now go to another institution that was fundamentally conservative in theological outlook—Wheaton College in Illinois. Consequently, when Billy Graham chose as his major at Wheaton the subject of anthropology, we may be sure that the emphasis of his course would be quite different from that of such universities as Princeton, Harvard or Yale, or indeed of many smaller, yet fully accredited institutions.

It was during this period that another epochal experience befell Billy Graham, second only to his conversion. This was his meeting at Wheaton College with Ruth Bell, the daughter of medical missionaries in China, Dr. and Mrs. L. Nelson Bell. It may not have been love at first sight between Billy and Ruth, but, if not, it was interest at first sight and a deepening affection. Two months after graduation they were married, in August 1943. During almost two decades of married life, Ruth Graham, attractive, intellectually alert and deeply dedicated to the service of Christ, has been a tower of strength to her husband and a devoted mother to their five lovely children.

No one is more ready nowadays than is Billy himself to admit that his lack of training in Christian theology has been a handicap to his ministry. The pronouncedly conservative atmosphere of his college association has conditioned his thinking and has at times antagonized people who are basically favorable to him. In his earlier preaching and writing he was also led to make assertions that hurt the cause he was endeavoring to uphold, and to this day have estranged not a few persons who are unaware of the broadening of his theological outlook. Few ministers of this generation have striven more zealously than Billy Graham to overcome mistakes of the past and to learn wider and deeper interpretations of the Christian gospel. As a consequence of the maturing of his theological viewpoint and the growth of his ecumenical understanding, Billy numbers among his genuine friends and well-wishers today denominational officials, ministers, and lay people who are considerably more liberal in their theological expressions than he.

A powerful factor in the fashioning of Billy's career as an evangelist was his teaming up with Torrey Johnson in the Youth for Christ Movement. This organization sought to provide servicemen with a constructive program that would relieve their boredom, especially on Saturday nights, and give them inspiration and contact with Christian youth. The movement began in the Chicago area but soon spread across the United States and Canada. With the end of the war it was broadened to include in its meetings and membership girls as well as boys. When the Movement became international, Graham travelled to many countries of the world as well as to practically every state of the union, sometimes addressing audiences of from ten to twenty thousand persons. During these speaking assignments his latent powers of speech and forensic abilities were further developed. At this time, too, he began to build the team that has supported his efforts and prepared the way for his crusades.

The turning point in Billy Graham's evangelistic career came in Los Angeles, where he had rented a six-thousand-seat tent for a three weeks' crusade. The attendance did not come up to expectations and Billy's hopes began to sag. At this critical juncture two powerful public relations personalities came quite unexpectedly to his assistance. They were William Randolph Hearst and Henry Luce. Each of these independently sent word out to their respective publishing empires to "build up" Graham. Within twenty-four hours the press section of his tent was overcrowded and a series of action pictures began to appear in the newspapers. The result was crowded meetings and an extension of two weeks in the crusade.

About this time, also, the conversion at Billy's meetings of three well-known public figures—Jim Vaus, Jr., who had associations with the notorious Mickey Cohen gang, Stewart Hamlin, who owned a string of prize race horses, and Harvey Fritz, a popular TV entertainer—was played up in the national press with stories and pictures. Added to this came the beginning of Graham's national and international radio network program, The Hour of Decision. It made him increasingly a religious figure of world-wide significance.

For half a decade following the beginning at Los Angeles, Billy Graham continued to organize crusades across the United States and Canada with uniform success. Now a further question came to the fore, Could he carry through in other countries of the world the undoubtedly successful crusades he had conducted on the North American continent? The answer would shortly be known. In 1954 Graham and his team arrived in London, England, to which he had been invited by more than a thousand ministers. He had been asked to conduct a mission lasting three months in the Harringay Arena with its twelve-thousand-seat capacity. For the first time in his career he found himself facing a press that was almost universally hostile. For some months in Britain there had been an increase in anti-American feeling and now, so far as the press at least was concerned, the growing animosity was fastened on Graham. Reporters and special writers in the press vied with each other in ridiculing what they called a "gospel circus" and in lampooning Billy, whose beliefs, they declared, were completely outmoded. One responsible newspaper said that they were "five hundred years out of date."

From the first night, however, when a capacity crowd overflowed the Harringay Arena, to the closing meetings when the people began to assemble hours before the opening of the services, the success of the crusade was overwhelming. Night after night bishops and other clergy of the Church of England, including the Archbishop of Canterbury, were present, as well as many well-known leaders of the nonconformist churches. The one major topic of conversation in London was Billy Graham and his crusade. Churchmen from many parts of England began to report increase in attendance at their services and a general upsurge in religious interest and church membership.

One year later the All-Scotland crusade opened in Glasgow. In contrast with his London experience, at the outset the crusade began in Glasgow with more interest and a greatly decreased opposition from the press. Despite a nightly downpour of rain, the people began to assemble long before the doors were open. The meetings were relayed by telephone, radio, and television to distant parts of the British Isles. In Glasgow itself, Britain was now being introduced to a sight that had not been seen within her borders for many a decade: thousands of men and women queued up patiently in a steadily falling, soaking rain, waiting for the commencement of a religious service.

The climax of Billy's career, insofar as world-wide attention was concerned, came with the New York crusade in 1957. This was destined to be the longest series of meetings in Billy Graham's colorful career. This time the press was favorable, but once again, the bulk of the opposition from the public in general came from the clergy. Many of these had grave misgivings lest Billy's conservative theology should aid and abet a militant fundamentalism which would create new problems for hard-pressed churches in this great metropolitan area. While Madison Square Garden was not completely filled every night of the crusade, on many occasions it was not only crowded to the doors, but there was also a large overflow in the street. Graham drew the biggest throng that Times Square had ever witnessed, not excluding V-J Day and New Year's Eve celebrations, and packed more than a hundred thousand persons into the Yankee Stadium. In a very real sense Billy Graham's success in New York was his greatest achievement because he had demonstrated his ability to overcome the enormous difficulties presented by a largely secularized city.

As of the present time Billy Graham is at the apex of his career. He has held crusades on every continent of the world with a large measure of popular response. Even the fact that he has been compelled to speak through an interpreter in such lands as Africa, India, Japan, and Korea seems to have interfered but little with the effectiveness of his message. His most recent crusade in Chicago, where, at the climax meeting in Soldier Field, June 17, 1962, officials estimated the turn-out of people at 116,000, demonstrated that he has lost none of his drawing power. This, incidentally, was the largest audience Billy had brought together in the Western Hemisphere. How long his immense popularity as a religious spokesman will last no one can tell. Will the public taste turn away from vast concourses of people who listen avidly to a speaker? Will Billy Graham's own tremendous physical and emotional resources continue to withstand the strain? These are questions that only the future can reveal.

How shall we evaluate these crusades? What happens to the vast number who have "decided for Christ" in them? Do the results justify the vast expenditure of energy, time, and money? What have the critics to say in answer to these questions? One has only to read the "explanations" of Billy Graham's success offered by some of these to see how frequently they cancel each other out. In England some of the severest strictures have come from *The New Statesman and Nation.* Approximately a year after his London campaign, William Salter, in this weekly, says that people who normally would scorn such "emotional religion" now take it for granted that he is a good thing. He added, "I think he is a bad thing." Salter finds Billy's success due to the fact that he is a "superb performer with a keen eye to stage management."

J. B. Priestley, writing in the same periodical, not having been present at any of the services, but having seen Billy Graham on TV in a Good Friday service, pays tribute to Billy's evident sincerity. He declares that he did not find him "personally disagreeable." Priestley offers three reasons for Graham's success: first, support by the churches; second, his jet-engine public relations; third, his arrival in England at the right time when there was a vacuum in British public life. People, he suggests, wanted a show, and Billy provided it. He concludes that no great harm was done and no great good. These reflections pretty well summarize the attitude of un-churched critics in Britain.

Some liberal churchmen in America took much the same ground, declaring that the success of the crusade was due to "Madison Avenue" techniques and that his sermons were inspired by old-line fundamentalism. Among the critics in Britain who were offended by Billy's fundamentalism was the Bishop of Durham, now Arch-bishop of Canterbury. On the other hand, warm support was tendered to Billy Graham by Dr. Fisher, at that time Archbishop of Canterbury.

While I was in London in August 1962, I discussed the subject of the British crusades with the well-known and very popular liberal preacher, Dr. Leslie D. Weatherhead, Minister Emeritus of the City Temple. Dr. Weatherhead concludes that a residue of real good was accomplished in Britain, though he discounts the value of inflated statistics of "Decisions." This phase of the crusade drew strong criticism from other members of the British clergy. Billy's success, he feels, was due primarily to his complete and sincere dedication to Christ. Here was a man who knew what he believed, whose faith was firmly grounded and whose heart was therefore at peace. This trumpet-like note of conviction and certainty sounding in all Billy's sermons made an immense appeal to a multitude of Britons who were floundering amid disillusionment, uncertainties, and doubts.

Further on the positive side, the Rev. J. C. Pollock, editor of *The Churchman,* a quarterly journal of Anglican theology, said that as a result of the Graham crusade there were many thousands of Christians in England who were not there four years earlier and that the Christian minority was no longer on the defensive. In the two-year period following 1954, the British Scripture Union for the daily reading of the Bible increased its membership by 120,000 persons.

In America, Billy Graham's liberal critics concentrated their attack on both his fundamentalism and his alleged lack of social emphasis. Sometimes his critics have been highly publicized theologians who attacked Billy's beliefs with pronounced harshness. Yet, at the same time, other well-known liberal theologians warmly defended him and upheld his right to be heard. Prior to the crusade in New York when a number of church courts of different denominations faced the issue of whether or not they would support this evangelistic effort, minority groups of liberal and extreme fundamentalist leanings fought any such approval to the last ditch, though it proved in most cases to be a losing battle. The liberals predicted that much harm would be done to the churches by what they regarded as a reactionary theology. The militant fundamentalists declared that Billy had "gone over" to the modernists. It may be of interest at this point to note that several ministers whose church members attended the crusade by the hundreds have not found a single instance where their people became unsettled by Billy Graham's essential conservatism. In certain American cities, and New York was not an exception, some so-called liberals manifested a spirit of intolerance that we had come to ascribe exclusively to militant fundamentalists. While Graham has unquestionably abandoned extremist viewpoints, he is still fundamentalist in theology, though his attitude toward Christians of a more liberal viewpoint is a long day's journey from that of some who boast of their conservatism.

A fact overlooked by many who are still opposed to the evangelist is that he has been growing steadily in intellectual and spiritual maturity. Also, his crusades, especially in large cosmopolitan centers, have become a factor in the growth of ecumenicity. Christian pastors and laymen from a score of denominations have learned to work together, centering their attention and loyalty upon the great Christian verities we hold in common—the central, abiding affirmations of our faith. In London, for instance, Church of England rectors worked harmoniously with Plymouth Brethren. Billy Graham is himself most effective when dealing with universal Christian truths, rather than when he takes an occasional journey into areas where there are quite understandably sharp differences in theological opinion and interpretation.

It must be remembered that it is not the task of the evangelist to teach theology to great masses of people assembled for a crusade. Rather, the purpose of the sermon is to bring them face to face with the inescapable responsibility of making a decision for the Christian life. The one persistent criticism, even of Graham's best friends among the clergy, is that at times he lays overmuch emphasis on the moment of Christian decision. Dr. Weatherhead met this contention in part at least when he said, "Let Billy Graham get people into the churches. It is our responsibility to give them a solid theology."

The Apostle Paul was keenly aware of the varied fields of labor and different areas of responsibility in the Church of Christ. He wrote to the church in Ephesus:

And he gave some to be apostles; and some, prophets; and some, evangelists; and some, pastors and teachers; for the perfecting of the saints, for the work of the ministry, for the edifying of the body of Christ: till we all come in the unity of the faith, and of the knowledge of the Son of God unto a perfect man unto the measure of the stature of the fulness of Christ (Ephesians 4: 11–13).

This variety of tasks is the answer to those who declare that Billy Graham does not provide an adequate theology for converts at his crusades. Likewise, as I have listened to discussions on the subject of Graham's unawareness of social responsibilities, I have often wondered how many of his critics have accomplished even a fraction of what he has achieved in the matter of better race relations. His witness has been clear and unequivocal on this effort. Similarly, on vexed problems of broken homes, delinquency, divorce, the misuse of sex, and economic injustices, he has undeniably made his influence felt. In the field of juvenile delinquency, for instance, a notable piece of service is being carried on by Jim Vaus, Jr., himself once allied with gangsters, in the Hell's Kitchen area of New York City. With his associates in Youth Development, Inc., he is transforming the lives of formerly lawless youth. This organization is now strongly backed by well-known New York business executives. These young people are finding a new way of life in Christ as Jim Vaus did in one of Billy Graham's earliest crusades.

Graham is of course a controversial personality. So will any man be who undertakes a ministry to tens of thousands of his fellow men, or, indeed, any really worthwhile public service. He has his limitations and has made his mistakes. No one is more ready to admit this than is the evangelist himself. Even his severest critics, if they are just, will agree that he is a sincerely humble man despite widespread adulation. He possesses extraordinary powers of personal magnetism and forth-going friendliness, and oftentimes turns bitter antagonists into steadfast friends. He can face a great audience of college students and professors in such universities as Edinburgh, Cambridge, or Yale and successfully challenge them with the claims of Christ. He can stand before a hundred thousand persons and stir individual consciences with the appeal of the gospel. It is yet too early to arrive to a final verdict with respect to Billy Graham's spiritual contribution to our age. This must await the perspective of history. But even now we can say that this dynamic personality possesses the remarkable gift of being able to touch the hearts and inspire the lives of millions of his fellow men, and in doing this, he has become one of the greatest religious forces of our generation.

13

Dorothy Day

BY DWIGHT MACDONALD

DWIGHT MACDONALD is well known for his writings on American politics and for his many articles and sketches on many sides of life in this country. For some years an editor of the Partisan Review *and later the editor of the lively journal of opinion* Politics, *he is the author of several books, including* The Ford Foundation: The Men and the Millions *and* Memoirs of a Revolutionist.

Many people think that Dorothy Day is a saint and that she will someday be canonized. In 1933, with the late Peter Maurin, a French-born itinerant preacher who has been affectionately described as "an apostle on the bum" and who advocated "a Utopian Christian communism," she founded the Catholic Worker movement, and, despite her best efforts to the contrary, she still dominates it. She is a rangy woman of sixty-five whose thick gray hair is braided tightly around her small, well-shaped head. High cheekbones and slanting eyes give her a Slavic look, although her ancestry is Scotch-Irish. Her face—patient, gentle, and understanding—might suggest a passive temperament were it not for her wide, mobile mouth and the expression of her eyes, which is at times dreamily remote, at times as naïvely expectant as a young girl's, but always alive. She smiles a good deal when she talks, and she often makes little jokes about herself and her movement. "We Catholics talk about the saints and martyrs, but I've heard it said that the Catholic Workers are made up of the saints, and the martyrs who are willing to live with the saints," she said once. Her own patron saint, after whom she named her only child, is the gay and impetuous Teresa of Avila, who used to pray, "May God deliver me from surly saints." In her sensible shoes and drab, well-worn clothes, Miss Day looks like an elderly schoolteacher or librarian; she has the typical air of mild authority and of being no longer surprised at anything children or book-borrowers may do. She also looks like a grandmother, which she is.

Upon first meeting her, most people who are familiar with her career are surprised to find that, far from being dynamic, she is quiet and almost diffident. Although she has been speaking in public for years, her platform manner is retiring and hesitant, and she makes not even a stab at rhetorical effect. She has no "presence" at all, but in spite of that, or perhaps because of it, she is impressive to meet or hear, communicating a moral force compounded of openness, sincerity, earnestness, and a deprecatory humor. She has lived with intellectuals all her adult life, from the time when, at the age of nineteen, she established herself in Greenwich Village society as a writer for radical publications, but she is not one herself. She is more a feeler and a doer than a thinker. Not that she does not constantly deal with ideas, and often most fruitfully, but her mind works by free association rather than logic, and her writings and public talks—"speeches" would hardly be the right word—are as haphazardly put together as her clothes. Her temperament combines mystical feeling and practicality in a way not common in the everyday world but not uncommon in the annals of hagiography.

Early in 1933 when, at the age of thirty-five, Dorothy Day joined hands with the late Peter Maurin to launch the Catholic Worker movement, the Roman Catholic Church in this country was still deeply uninterested in liberal social causes. Abroad, especially in France, "social Catholicism" had already become strong, but in the United States the hierarchy felt it wiser not to meddle in such matters. To be sure, the Church here had its eminent liberals, like Father John LaFarge, who subsequently became editor of the Jesuit magazine *America,* and the late Msgr. John A. Ryan, of the National Catholic Welfare Council, but they were few in number, they were priests, and they "worked through committees," a fact that gave them a rather forbidding aura of respectability. Miss Day, who had long been a radical and who had joined the Church only five years previously, and Maurin, a French-born religious zealot who had spent most of his fifty-six years tramping about America, living like a hobo and expounding his doctrine to all who would listen, felt that the Church as a whole should concern itself more with the problems faced by ordinary men and women in adjusting themselves to the economic pressures of an industrial capitalist society. Inspired by Maurin's idealism and Miss Day's intensity and drive, the Catholic Workers became agitators among the people; they foreshadowed that renaissance of the "lay apostolate" that has since arisen in the Church. The *Catholic Worker,* the organization's monthly paper, to which Miss Day and Maurin contributed voluminously and which later on in the thirties reached a peak circulation of a hundred and fifty thousand, gave the Workers a vastly larger audience than is enjoyed by most comparable strivers to make a better world. "There were never any committees around the *Catholic Worker* office," a veteran of the paper's early days recalls. "We just went out and *did* things. We didn't form a Committee to Promote Improved Interracial Relations. We took Negroes into our homes and lived with them. We didn't get up big-name letterheads to raise funds for strikers. We went out on the picket lines ourselves."

This direct-action approach, coupled with the fact that 1933 was the bottom year of the Depression, gave the Workers a crusading appeal that struck fire in certain Catholic circles, especially among young priests, students in theological seminaries, and some of the more enlightened members of the laity. Catholic Worker groups started up all over the place—often by spontaneous combustion, without any help from headquarters. A curious social paradox was involved. Heretofore, American Catholicism had been a lower-class affair, its followers consisting mostly of post-1840 immigrants from Catholic countries like Ireland, Poland, Italy, and Austria-Hungary; the upper classes—rated as such simply by virtue of having got here earlier—were solidly Protestant. But by 1930 the immigrants had begun to rise socially and economically, their children and even their grandchildren were going to college, and Catholicism began to produce middle-class intellectuals as full of reforming zeal as their Protestant counterparts had been for a century or more. As long as the majority of Catholics were proletarians, the hierarchy could, if it liked, deal with them in an authoritarian way and dragoon them into a conservative social pattern, but as the laity became richer and better-educated, there was an increasing ferment of liberalism in the old bottles of the Church. Today, the hierarchy is still largely conservative—Cardinal Spellman of New York, probably being more typical than Bishop Sheil, of Chicago—but the lower clergy and the laity have produced such Catholic phenomena as the inter-racial Friendship Houses; the St. Francis Xavier Labor College, in New York; the Chicago Catholic pro-labor monthly, *Work;* and a whole crop of so-called "labor priests," like Father John M. Corridan, who played an important part in the insurgent longshoremen's strike in New York a decade ago.

Many of the individuals who are now working in such strange Catholic vineyards were given their first impulse and their training by the Catholic Worker movement. As Father Dennis Geaney, a Catholic educator, once wrote of Miss Day in *Work,* "It was a Christian revolution she was starting. She was opening the minds of bishops, priests, seminarians, and lay people to the fact that Christianity was not a stuffy sacristy affair. She was a trumpet calling for all of us to find Christ in the bread lines, the jails, as a tenant farmer, migratory worker, or Negro. We think of Church history as being made by popes and bishops. Here is a woman who has placed her stamp on American Catholicism. The seed she sowed in the thirties is bearing fruit a hundred-fold in the fifties."

The *Catholic Worker* was started, as the name suggests, as a competitor of the Communist *Daily Worker,* and it was no accident that most of its first issue, in 1933, was distributed in Union Square on May Day. In their maiden editorial, which asked, in effect, "Why should the Devil have all the good tunes?," Maurin and Miss Day wrote, "It's time there was a Catholic paper printed for the un-employed. The fundamental aim of most radical sheets is conversion of its readers to radicalism and atheism. Is it not possible to be radical and not atheist?" The Church's social program up to that time was contained largely in two papal encyclical letters—the *Rerum novarum,* of Leo XIII (1891), and the *Quadragesimo anno,* of Pius XI (1931). These rebuke the greed of unrestrained capitalism, encourage labor unions, and in general put the interests of the worker above the interest of private property. "Our job is to make the encyclicals click," Maurin once said.

In the thirties, the Catholic Workers were in the thick of events and Miss Day, despite a solid Republican and Episcopalian family background, was in the thickest of them. Whenever she could spare the time, she was out in the streets selling copies of the *Catholic Worker.* "Selling the paper in front of Macy's . . . made one indeed look the fool," she later noted in her autobiography, *The Long Loneliness.*[1] (Looking the fool has never bothered Miss Day, one of whose favorite quotations is Saint Paul's pronouncement: "The foolish things of the world hath God chosen, that He may confound the wise.") In a single year—1936—she travelled to Detroit to report on and help along the sitdown strikes out of which came the United Automobile Workers; to Lowell, Massachusetts, where there was a textile strike (the Catholic Workers fed the pickets and supported the strike so enthusiastically that the mayor of Lowell phoned the Chancery in Boston to check up on this crowd of Catholics who were making a noise like Communists; the Chancery reassured him—firmly, if with resignation—that they were Catholics all right); to Pittsburgh, where the C.I.O. was beginning to organize steel (she and Mary Heaton Vorse, the labor journalist, took a hotel room for a dollar and a half a day and visited every liberal priest in the district, including old Father Adalbert Kazincy, who had been almost alone among the Catholic clergy in backing the 1919 steel strike but now had many priests to keep him company); to Akron where the rubber workers were striking; to Birmingham, where more steel workers were organizing; and to the Gulf Coast,

---

[1] New York, Harper, 1952. This and the quotations which follow from the same book are reprinted with the permission of Harper & Row, Publishers, Inc.

where there was "trouble" in the shrimp fisheries. That year, the Catholic Workers in New York City spent thousands of dollars feeding and lodging pickets during the seamen's strike that led to the establishing of the National Maritime Union; the fact that Joseph Curran, who became the head of the union, and most of the other leaders were then enjoying active support from the Communists didn't bother them at all. In March, 1937, the Association of Catholic Trade Unionists was formed around a kitchen table in one of the Workers' early headquarters, a house on Mott Street.

In some ways, the Catholic Workers do not see eye to eye with their ecclesiastical leaders, a fact that has led to much curious speculation among sideline observers. "How do they stay in the Church?" is the question most often asked about the organization, the runner-up being "What does Cardinal Spellman think of them?" The latter question, at least, cannot be authoritatively answered, for the Cardinal has maintained a discreet silence on the subject. Like his predecessor, the late Cardinal Hayes, he has endorsed their works of mercy, but he will not be drawn further. Some time ago, at a reception, Miss Day tried. She asked him outright how he felt about the Workers. "You'll find that many of the bishops are on your side," the Cardinal answered, with a diplomatic smile. He could not have been pleased when the *Catholic Worker* attacked him in 1949 for breaking a gravediggers' strike in a local Catholic cemetery, and added injury to insult by raising funds to meet the rent and grocery bills of the strikers, who were, incidentally, pious Catholics themselves. On most secular issues, from pacifism to psychoanalysis, the Cardinal and the Workers disagree. However, he has stayed his hand, whether from conscience or from expediency or because the Church is a house of more mansions than are dreamed of in Paul Blanshard's philosophy. They believe that he did not stay his hand, however, on the issue of the Spanish Civil War—the *Worker*, like the liberal Catholic weekly, the *Commonweal*, did not support Franco—and that the Chancery's influence was a factor in the removal of the *Worker* from sale in many of the city's Catholic churches during that period. Later on, in 1948, the *Catholic Worker* editorially advised young men not to register for the draft. Although this was clearly illegal, the editors didn't hear from the F.B.I., but they did hear from Monsignor Gaffney, then one of Cardinal Spellman's diocesan Vicars-General, who summoned Miss Day and "corrected" her—that is, ordered her to cease and desist, which she did.

For all her brushes with authority, however, Miss Day is a Catholic first and a radical second. "The hierarchy permits a priest to say Mass in our chapel," she remarked to a friend. "They have given us the most precious thing of all—the Blessed Sacrament. If the Chancery ordered me to stop publishing the *Catholic Worker* tomorrow, I would."

Politically, the Catholic Workers are hard to classify. They are for the poor and against the rich, so the capitalists call them Communists; they believe in private property and don't believe in class struggle, so the Communists call them capitalists; and they are hostile to war and to the State, so both capitalists and Communists consider them crackpots. They are often taken for some kind of Communist front inside the Catholic Church, but actually the *Catholic Worker* and the Communist *Worker* have little similarity beyond their names. Being as a general rule pacifists, most Catholic Workers refuse to serve in the Army, to work in war industries, and to pay federal income taxes (since most of the budget goes for war purposes), even on those rare occasions when they have enough income to pay taxes on. Despite the extreme position it takes on such issues, the organization has never had any trouble with the authorities, and Miss Day rather resents this tolerance, as a slur on its political effectiveness, just as she dislikes the protection its name gives them against local constabularies. During the strike of Ohrbach store employees in 1934, the police regularly hauled off to jail all the pickets except the Catholic Workers. "I'd as soon arrest the Holy Father himself!" exclaimed one uniformed co-religionist.

The varied and strenuous activities Miss Day engaged in at that time were not of a kind likely to give comfort to the other members of her family, but then few of her activities ever have been. In the eyes of her father, she was a black sheep almost from the start. She was born in Brooklyn Heights in 1897, the daughter of John I. Day, a peripatetic sportswriter, who later became racing editor of the *Morning Telegraph* and who was instrumental in establishing the Hialeah race track in Florida. Essentially a conservative, Mr. Day contrived to combine respectability with journalism, as have his three sons; one of them was managing editor of the New York *Journal-American,* another publicity director of the Thoroughbred Racing Association, and the third was, for many years, Riga correspondent for the Chicago *Tribune.* There were also two daughters, one of whom early settled down to married life in Rye. The other found the family pattern unsatisfying. "There was never any kissing in our family, and never a close embrace," Miss Day says in her autobiography. "There was only a firm and austere kiss from my mother every night . . . we were like most Anglo-Saxons. We could never be free with others, never put our arms around them casually. We were never handholders. We were always withdrawn and alone, unlike Italians, Poles, Jews." Unable to embrace her parents, Miss Day embraced the poor and oppressed. As a young girl in Chicago, where her father was then sports editor of *Inter Ocean,* she began reading radical literature. "Kropotkin especially brought to my mind the plight of the poor, of the workers . . . and made me feel that . . . my life was to be linked to theirs," she writes. "I had received a call, a vocation, a direction to my life. I felt, even at fifteen, that God meant man to be happy." In 1914, shortly before her seventeenth birthday, Miss Day entered the University of Illinois on a scholarship, which she supplemented by caring for children and doing housework. There she joined the Socialist Party—"I was in love with the masses," she says—and made a close friend of a classmate and fellow-rebel, the wealthy and brilliant Rayna Prohme, who later became a Communist, worked with Michael Borodin in China in the middle twenties, died at the age of thirty-three in Moscow, and ended up as the romantic heroine of Vincent Sheean's *Personal History*. In 1916, after two years at the university, Miss Day moved with her family to New York, where her father had taken the job on the *Telegraph*. Soon after they arrived, she went to work as a reporter and columnist on the Socialist *Call*. Her father, who disapproved of career women and was definitely not in love with the masses, tried without success to persuade the editor to fire her. She rented a room on Cherry Street, in the slums of the lower East Side, and never again lived with her family.

On her own at nineteen, Miss Day spent the next ten years in the tumult of Greenwich Village life, which in those days, under the newly ascendant stars of Marx and Freud, was often very tumultuous indeed. The job on the *Call* was followed by one with the Anti-Conscription League; the United States was at war with Germany by then, and she was assigned the enjoyable task of pasting "peace" stickers on the venerable façade of the Union League Club. Presently, she joined the Industrial Workers of the World, because she liked its anarchistic verve and shared its members' distrust of Marx. In the summer of 1917, she became Floyd Dell's assistant on the *Masses,* a lively radical monthly that he and Max Eastman were editing. Her job ended that fall, when the magazine was suppressed and Eastman indicted under the Espionage Act. She was one of about sixty women who in 1917 picketed the White House in protest against the treatment of some suffragettes who had been imprisoned in Washington after staging a demonstration; a batch of the pickets, Miss Day among them, were arrested and sentenced to terms of up to six months in a women's workhouse, where they were manhandled until they staged a hunger strike. Her next job was on the *Liberator,* which Max Eastman's sister Crystal was running as a successor to the *Masses*. Miss Day liked it there well enough but says she found it "more fun to hang around the Provincetown Playhouse, on Macdougal Street, where Eugene O'Neill and others of my friends had plays in rehearsal." The crowd also hung around a Village saloon called the Golden Swan. ("It was a

crowd that did a lot of sitting around," according to Miss Day.) In
the back room, O'Neill could easily be persuaded to recite "The
Hound of Heaven" to the assemblage, which often included the
Hudson Dusters, a local gang of mildly sinister repute.

Miss Day spent 1918 as a probationary nurse at Kings County
Hospital. ("I hate being Utopian and trying to escape from reality,"
she wrote to a friend at the time. "Now that we are in the thick of
the war and there is so much to be done, I might as well try to do it
instead of sitting around playing at writing. And what is my writing
now but book reviews, editing, toying with a novel of social significance?") When the war ended, she returned to her Village haunts,
throwing herself into the life there with the adventurous ardor that
has always been characteristic of her, and without which she almost
surely would not have had the courage to start so thankless an
enterprise as the Catholic Worker movement. "We made friends
with the world," she says, recalling how she and her companions
used to pick up interesting-looking strangers in Washington Square
and take them home to dinner. "Dorothy did some foolish things,
but she was always protected by the armor of innocence," one of
her acquaintances of that period said. Floyd Dell once described
her as "somewhat elfin—that is, not quite human—and very
friendly, with a sort of pre-adolescent charm. She was an awkward
and charming young enthusiast, tall and slim, with beautiful slanting
eyes." A young poet wrote about her eyes in the *Masses,* and the
sitters-around thought she looked like the famous bust of the Egyp-
tian queen Nefretete. Her admirers included Donn Byrne, who later
became a novelist, and Mike Gold, a dedicated Communist, to
whom she was engaged for several years. They never got married,
because Gold, whose ideas on family life were completely bour-
geois, thought she was too flighty to make a good mother and
housewife.

In the early twenties, Miss Day divided her time between New
York and Chicago, working as a reporter, a proofreader, a librarian,
and, during one interlude, a clerk at Montgomery Ward's. She also

underwent one of the most painful experiences of her life when, the victim of a ghastly series of coincidences, she was arrested in Chicago on a charge of prostitution. This occurred one night when she went to stay with a woman friend who, down on her luck, had been exhibiting suicidal tendencies and had taken refuge in a local I.W.W. lodging house ordinarily reserved for visiting male members of the organization. Unfortunately, as Miss Day discovered later, the woman had a police record as a prostitute, and, even more unfortunately, some of United States Attorney General A. Mitchell Palmer's "Red raiders" stormed the wobblies' headquarters that night. Finding two women there, the police decided that prostitution would prove to be a tougher rap than revolution, and booked them accordingly. After four days in a cell with a number of real and quite unrevolutionary prostitutes, whom she came to like, if not admire, Miss Day got out on bail, and the case was subsequently dropped. The episode intensified her lifelong sympathy for the underdog.

While holding down her various jobs, Miss Day was writing on the side, and in 1923 A. & C. Boni published her first novel. It was about Village life (the hero and heroine lived in a loft they made habitable by painting everything orange and black), and it was neither a popular nor a critical success. But the Bonis had titled it *The Eleventh Virgin,* and they sold it to Hollywood on the strength of the name. When the movie people got around to reading it, they found the sex—or pay dirt—was all in the title, so they had a completely new story written; then they changed the title. However, the author got twenty-five hundred dollars out of it, which she used to buy a cottage on the shore of Raritan Bay, at Huguenot, Staten Island, where there was a colony that included, as residents or regular visitors, the Kenneth Burkes, the Malcolm Cowleys, Hart Crane, and Mike Gold. Miss Day had just met and fallen in love with a young biology instructor named Forster Batterham, and in 1925 they began living together, in a common-law marriage, in her cottage. The following year, she finished a second novel, about two sisters who were in love with the same man, which was bought by the Bell Syndicate people for newspaper serialization under their title, "What Price Love?"

In March, 1927, Miss Day had a baby, whom she named Teresa. In her autobiography she tells how the birth of her child led her—indeed, compelled her—to become a Catholic. "Forster had made the physical world come alive for me and had awakened in my heart a flood of gratitude," she writes. "The final object of this love and gratitude was God. No human creature could receive or contain so vast a flood of love and joy as I felt after the birth of my child. With this came the need to worship, to adore. I had heard many say they wanted to worship God in their own way and did not need a Church in which to praise Him. . . . But my very experience as a radical, my whole make-up, led me to want to associate myself with others, with the masses, in praising and adoring God. Without even looking into the claims of the Catholic Church, I was willing to admit that for me she was the one true Church."

Batterham felt differently. He was deeply irreligious, his temperament being as naturalistic as hers was spiritual. He shared her sympathy for the oppressed, just as she had come to share his passion for observing and studying nature, but his morality, unlike hers, was firmly grounded on this earth; he felt no need to justify or explain the natural world in terms of religion. Since, as a principled atheist, he would have nothing to do with marriage, she had to choose between leaving him and living in mortal sin. "To become a Catholic meant for me to give up a mate with whom I was much in love," she writes. "It was a simple question of whether I chose God or man. I had known enough of love to know that a good healthy family life was as near to Heaven as one could get. . . . It was not because I was tired of sex, satiated, disillusioned, that I turned toward God. Radical friends used to insinuate this. It was because through a whole love, both physical and spiritual, I came to know God."

On December 28, 1927, Miss Day was baptized a Catholic in the

Church of Our Lady, Help of Christians, in Tottenville, Staten Island. A year later, she was confirmed and after the ceremony she was invited to tea in the rectory parlor, where an earnest nun with whom she had struck up a friendship was one of the guests. Presently, Miss Day told her friend that she must be getting home to her baby. "Oh, I didn't know you were married!" exclaimed the nun. "I'm not," Miss Day said. The nun hurriedly poured herself another cup of tea.

This momentous step of Miss Day's came as a surprise to most of her friends—there was not a Catholic among them—although a few had been conscious of a streak of piety in her. All through her Village days, she had occasionally gone to Mass, and she had chosen the Bible as her reading during the hunger strike in prison that followed the Washington picketing. Malcolm Cowley remembers that once she suddenly pulled him into a Catholic church in the Village while Vespers was going on, and that at one point during the service he saw tears running down her face. "Many a time, after sitting in taverns all night, or coming at dawn from a ball at Webster Hall, I went to an early-morning Mass at St. Joseph's Church, on Sixth Avenue," Miss Day herself recalls.

Miss Day's conversion made little immediate change in her external life—aside, of course, from her break with Batterham. She worked with the Anti-Imperialist League, and in 1929 she wrote a play dealing with the conflict between Communism and Christianity. An agent sold it to Pathé Films, and, with her daughter, Miss Day spent three months in Hollywood at a hundred and twenty-five dollars a week. In accordance with the local custom, she was given nothing to do; not in accordance with the local custom, she went to no parties, lived cheaply in the Los Angeles slums, and drove around in a second-hand Model T Ford. When her contract was not renewed, she took her baby and a thousand dollars she had saved from her salary and went to Mexico, where she lived for six months, writing a few pieces for the *Commonweal* but mostly getting accustomed to her new life as a mother and a Catholic. In the summer of 1930, she returned with Teresa to her cottage in Staten Island, where she earned a little money by interviewing garden owners for the Staten Island *Advance*. She also tried, fruitlessly, to sell short stories to slick-paper magazines. In the fall of 1932, she and Teresa moved into an East Side tenement. There, on the evening of December 10, 1932, Maurin, a stocky, unkempt man, came to call on her with a letter of introduction from a friend of hers.

Intellectually, Miss Day and Maurin hit it off right from the start. Maurin had a program—"a Utopian Christian communism"—all thought out; Miss Day had the journalistic experience, the practical approach, and the talent for leadership needed to give reality to his vision. It is possible that without that vision, she would never have been stimulated to put her energies behind the Catholic Worker movement; it is certain that without her practical turn of mind, Maurin would have remained an ineffectual eccentric. And it is unlikely that without her journalistic experience, his message would ever have reached many people. One of Maurin's dreams was the setting up of houses of Hospitality in cities all over the country, in which the needy could be fed, clothed, and lodged without regard to race or creed.

Today, the Catholic Workers maintain such a house at 175 Chrystie Street in New York City, and keep a benevolent eye on the autonomous operations of seven similar houses in Oakland, Cal.; Washington, D.C.; Detroit; Rochester; Salt Lake City and Chicago. Maurin also advocated a back-to-the-land movement, and over the years, since 1933, the Workers have had approximately twenty farms in various parts of the country where indigent wayfarers were given shelter and city dwellers, down on their luck, were sent for rehabilitation. Still in existence today, and serving the same purposes, is the twenty-three-acre Peter Maurin Farm in Pleasant Plains, Staten Island.

Neither of these objectives, rural or urban, would ever have materialized had it not been for Miss Day's gifts as an organizer and her ability to get on with people; it is she who, through the years, has recruited the staffs of young Catholic volunteers who run the houses and farms, living in common poverty with the people they help, and it is she who has raised the funds that keep the Workers going.

Under Miss Day's guidance, the Catholic Workers have devised an inexpensive and effective technique of fund-raising: they pray to Saint Joseph, their patron saint. "We appealed to him for help last month," the editors wrote in the second issue of the *Catholic Worker*, "and within two weeks not only our current printing bill was paid but money was there for the February bill, also." Their creditors pray, too. "The printer called us up this morning wanting to know, affably, when we were going to pay our bill," another editorial reads. "We told him he'd better get busy and pray for it hard." Later, the *Worker* reported, "Enough money has come in to pay $300 to our very forbearing printer, and he says he is still praying." Things get behind sometimes—their grocery bill for the Chrystie Street house has run as high as six thousand dollars, and once they discovered that they owed two thousand dollars for flour alone—but sooner or later Saint Joseph is always good for the money. Their credit is solid, and their business relations—with their printer, their butcher, and their grocer—are friendly to the point of sentimentality; the fact that the first two are Jewish firms doesn't seem to make any difference to Saint Joseph. At the very mention of money, Miss Day grows impatient. "That is all in the hands of Saint Joseph," she once wrote in the *Catholic Worker*, apropos of a particularly huge avalanche of debts that was threatening to engulf the organization. "He is our patron and it is up to him. I haven't any doubt about it. I've seen him perform daily miracles around here."

Some of the miracles are chronic. Twice a year, the Workers print an appeal in their paper, and twice a year they get enough donations, all in small sums, to cover their ordinary running expenses. Others are special, as when the Workers wanted to buy a farm in Newburgh. "Miraculously, we were given ten thousand dollars by friends, all the money coming in within a month from half a dozen of our readers," Miss Day recalls. Again, when they were wondering whether they could afford to buy the Staten Island farm, Miss Day asked the Lord for a sign by eleven o'clock one morning, and, sure enough, at ten-thirty someone phoned in offering to lend them three thousand dollars. There was also the time in 1950 when, after months of unsuccessful searching for a new headquarters, they sat down and undertook a novena (a kind of prayer marathon), which led them right to Chrystie Street. Sometimes prayer doesn't get results, but then the remedy is clear. "When things go wrong, we know we are not praying enough," Miss Day says. And sometimes Heaven doesn't respond as expected, or, indeed, as wished—a common failing of supernatural agencies, as Macbeth, for one, discovered. Once, needing a thousand dollars in a hurry, Miss Day prayed for it, and got it when her Staten Island cottage, insured for precisely that amount, promptly burned down. Her gratitude was tempered by her affection for the place, and by the fact that it was worth a lot more than a thousand dollars. "Sometimes I wish God weren't quite so literal," she said later.

Owing in part to the vast changes that have come over the social scene in the last few years, the Catholic Workers are no longer quite as active in public affairs as they once were, and the circulation of their paper has shown a corresponding slump. It is nevertheless still fairly high—seventy thousand, which is more than the combined circulations of the *Nation* and the *New Republic*. It is true that the *Catholic Worker* costs only one cent a copy (and twenty-five cents a year, which gives it the perhaps unique distinction of costing more than twice as much to subscribe to as to buy on the newsstands), and it is also true that "bundle orders," which often end up as throwaways, account for many of the copies, and that the business department is dilatory about culling out lapsed subscriptions. But even if only half the copies get into the hands of interested readers, this is quite an achievement for an uncompro-

misingly high-brow and extremist paper. It has another distinction
that is almost unique among crusading periodicals: It just about
breaks even.

The *Catholic Worker* is an eight-page tabloid. Typical front-
page banner headlines have included "CHRIST THE KING CAN
ALONE RECONSTRUCT THE WORLD," "THE PROBLEM
OF WAR AND THE OLD TESTAMENT," "THE COMING
COLLAPSE OF MODERN INDUSTRIALISM," "THE NA-
TURE OF MAN" and (in an especially gnomic mood) "SEA-
MEN GO EVERYWHERE." In its coverage of world events, the
paper's forte is clearly not spot news, except possibly when it gets
hold of something like the Holy Father's Christmas Message. The
Worker's staff is unpaid and unprofessional. (Maurin once got talking with three enthusiastic young men on Columbus Circle, and
brought them down to the Chrystie Street house. One became the
paper's bookkeeper, another became its circulation manager, and
the third married the assistant editor.)

The *Worker's* contents are schizoid, accurately reflecting the two
aspects of the movement—works of mercy and a concern with ultimate philosophical questions. Miss Day's column, called "On Pilgrimage," is easily the paper's most popular feature—an odd com-
posite of Pascal's "Pensées" and Eleanor Roosevelt's "My Day." A
good hostess on the printed page as well as off, Miss Day in "On
Pilgrimage" is constantly introducing the sublime if not to the
ridiculous at least to the commonplace. In one installment, after
quoting at length from Newman and Saint Teresa of Avila, she
continued, "Every time I am making what I consider a thorough
confession—that is, telling tendencies that I wish I could overcome,
like eating between meals, indulging in the nibbling that women do
around a kitchen—and mention it as a venial sin not only in regard
to myself but also to my neighbor who is starving all over the world,
the confessor makes no attempt to understand but speaks of scru-
ples. . . . These are tendencies to gluttony, and gluttony is one of
the seven deadly sins." Only a person who is deeply thoughtful

about religion would be likely to see a connection between nibbling in the kitchen and the seven deadly sins, and it is one of Miss Day's outstanding achievements that she has revived the linking of the serious and the trivial that saints and prophets once did so effectively but that long ago went out of fashion. The union of the everyday and the ultimate is the essence of the Catholic Worker movement; even the paper's routine announcements express it, as in this item: "Saturday Work Days and Discussions at Peter Maurin Farm. April 14: Build up low corner of ploughed field and dig cesspool drainage ditch. Discussion: 'No one ever stayed on the land when he could have gone to the city, without a supernatural motive.' "

Back in the days when the Catholic Workers were playing a conspicuous part in the labor movement, the fight for racial justice, and in the political struggle with the Communists, their paper was full of news and opinion about such matters. Today, when the Workers are less active in these fields, the paper reflects the change. "Many a priest who became famous for his interest in labor," Miss Day says in her autobiography, "felt we had deserted the cause of the union man . . . had departed from our original intention and undertaken work in the philosophical and theological fields that might have been better left to the clergy. . . . Labor leaders felt that in our judgment of war, we judged them also for working in the gigantic armaments race, as indeed we did. Ours is, indeed, an unpopular front." Miss Day might have gone on to point out that, strictly speaking, the Workers did not desert the union man so much as the union man deserted them, partly because he no longer needed their help, partly because in a period of war and disillusionment their radical purity at best bored and at worst shocked him. Their pacifism, for example, was no embarrassment in the thirties, when liberals and Leftists thought in terms of "merchants of death," but in the decades after Pearl Harbor, when "arsenals of democracy" became a more popular phrase, the *Catholic Worker's* circulation declined slowly but steadily from a hundred thousand in 1939 to its present seventy thousand. The number of Houses of

Hospitality has also dwindled, from thirty in 1940 to seven today, largely because with the full employment that is the consequence of a chronic state of war, the need for them has become less acute.

Such has been the general trend—a trend with economic overtones. The decline in the popularity of the *Catholic Worker* began, however, with a head-on clash between expediency and principle, in which the Workers, as they always do, clung to principle. The conflict arose over their stand on the Spanish civil war. From the beginning of that war, the entire Catholic clergy and the Catholic laity supported Franco, as the champion of religion against infidel Communism and anarchism. The only Catholic publications in New York that refused to support him were the *Worker* and the *Commonweal,* both of which took a neutral position. "There is much right and much wrong on both sides," the *Catholic Worker* editorialized in September, 1936. "Our main concern is that 'the members of Christ tear one another.' This is not a condemnation. It is a cry of anguish, the sob of one who sees his brother in agony." Three months later, the Workers devoted the whole front page of their paper to a translation of an article, written by a Spanish Catholic, which had appeared in *Esprit,* a French radical Catholic magazine, and condemned both sides in the civil war. The Workers' was, indeed, an unpopular front.

Popular or unpopular, the work goes on, and Miss Day goes on with it. "In the last two months, I have visited twenty-seven cities, from Fall River, Mass., to Fargo, North Dakota," she wrote in the *Catholic Worker* once. "I have been bone-tired and mind-tired. I have slept on buses and trains, on boards and beds, in rooms with babies, in dormitories, in solitary splendor. I have eaten in homes where elegance is the rule and at Houses of Hospitality with men from skid row." The only real vacation she has taken since the organization of the Workers was during parts of 1943 and 1944, when she felt that after ten years of uninterrupted work it was spiritually necessary for her to renew acquaintance with herself and with God by meditation. She spent six months in a convent and another six months living quietly in the country with her daughter, who by that time had married and set up housekeeping on a farm in Virginia. A priest told Miss Day that once having put her hand to the plow, she had no right to withdraw it, but she knew better; she felt that she was not the "indispensable leader," or that if she was, it was high time the movement learned to dispense with her. Since her cross-country trip in 1951, she has confined her travels to the East and has pretty much let the Chrystie Street house run itself, spending only a night or so a week in the tiny hall bedroom that is reserved for her there. Most of her time has been divided between Peter Maurin Farm and her daughter's present home, a mile down the road; Teresa now has five children of her own, and Miss Day helps with them and with the housework.

"Where there is no love, put in love and you will take out love," wrote Saint John of the Cross. The Catholic Workers quote this and believe it. Usually it works, but when it doesn't, they are not resentful, since they consider love an end and not a means. Some years ago, they rented an apartment in Cleveland to shelter single women; a homeless married couple was temporarily admitted; once in, they wouldn't move out or let anyone else in. The Workers, although they had paid the rent in advance, sighed and looked for another apartment. Perhaps the saddest experience they have had was with their first communal farm, near Easton, Pennsylvania, which, as the years passed, was more and more taken over by down-and-out families, who came to consider the place theirs and to resent the Workers' using it at all. At last, the Workers sold half the farm and gave the rest to the familes who had preempted it.

The Workers' abhorrence of coercion extends even to proselytizing. They never ask the religion of the people they help, and the men on the bread line don't have to pray or sing psalms to get fed, nor do their boarders (whose favorite paper is the *Daily News,* not the *Catholic Worker*) have to attend the two brief daily services held in the Chrystie Street house. Any discipline makes Miss Day uneasy. John Cort, a former disciple of the Workers and later a

C.I.O. official and labor columnist, once lived with ten other men on the top floor of the old Mott Street house. "Some of them slept late, left their beds in a mess, and shirked their turn to sweep up," he has since recalled. "Finally, I typed out three rules and posted them: 'One, everybody out of bed by 9 A.M. Two, each man is expected to make up his own bed. Three, each man is expected to take turns sweeping up.' One of the fellows there felt these rules were a violation of personalism, a doctrine of inner discipline that Dorothy and Peter were strong for. We took it to Dorothy—the Abbess, as some of us called her—and she agreed with him. The rules came down. I think it possible that she really agreed with me but ruled for this other guy because he was excited about it and she felt his faith in the movement was more brittle than mine. She herself was personal all the way, and she often decided things on a personal basis."

Some of the Workers have at times found freedom oppressive. One of the most energetic toilers on the Easton farm once went on strike because he didn't have a boss. Sitting down under a tree, he announced, "I won't work until someone asks me to and tells me what to do." No one did, and after a time he gave up and grumpily picked up his hoe again. Maurin used to do a lot of heavy work, like breaking rocks for making roads; sometimes he went so far as to leave mauls lying around in conspicuous places, but if no one took the hint, he just swung all the harder. More practical and less principled than Maurin, Miss Day admits that when she gets "really desperate," she actually asks members of her staff to do this or that. If they refuse, however, there is no penalty. "I could stay in my room all day reading or just sitting and no one would say anything," one of her present crop of Workers said not long ago. "After a month, they might act a little cold toward me, of course."

As Cort's story indicates, Miss Day does have a certain authority, but it is an authority that is yielded to her voluntarily, out of love and respect—all too voluntarily, from her point of view, for she is a leader whose chief worry is that her followers have too great a tendency to follow. "Low in mind all day, full of tears," she wrote one evening in 1936 in a journal she has kept since she was a girl. "What with Easton, New York, Boston, Ottawa, Toronto, and Missouri groups all discouraged, all looking for organization, all weary of the idea of freedom and personal responsibility—I feel bitterly oppressed. I am in the position of a dictator trying to legislate himself out of existence. They all complain that there is no boss. Today I happened to read Dostoevski's "Grand Inquisitor," most apropos. Freedom—how men hate it and chafe under it, how unhappy they are with it!"

In the old days, Miss Day used to look at Maurin in moments of discouragement and, with a groan, say, "Why did you have to start all this anyway?" In a gloomy passage in her journal, she remarks, "Sometimes you get discouraged, there's so little change in people. Those who drank go on drinking, those who were ornery go on being ornery." But faith and hope always rise again in her, no matter how great the despair of the moment, and a few pages farther on she is writing, "The goodness of people makes my heart expand in happiness."

Biographical Notes
BY MELVILLE HARCOURT

TUBBY CLAYTON

Philip Thomas Byard Clayton must be one of the few men of renown for whom a schoolboy nickname was transformed into a title of honor. Over the years he has known intimately the great and near-great, he has walked with kings and commoners, presidents and bellboys; but by the high and low of two generations he has been hailed and loved under a single sobriquet—Tubby! To some, no doubt, the name accurately evokes the image of a scholar-poet built, perchance, on ample lines, but the majority see him as a clerical dynamo who audaciously regards the globe as his personal stamping ground. It was the fields of Flanders and the little town of Poperinghe, Belgium, in the First World War that brought to fine flowering his particular genius; but his spirit had been disciplined at St. Paul's School, London, and Exeter College, Oxford, where he took a brilliant First. He left the staff of the largest parish in England, St. Mary's, Portsea, to join the British Expeditionary Force as a chaplain in 1915, and within a matter of months found himself in charge of a tall white house on the Rue de l'Hôpital, Poperinghe. By cantrips solemn and gay, and a devotion that recognized neither time nor strain, Tubby Clayton made Talbot House—for so it was called—a haven of laughter and hope amid the sorry shambles of war. After the war he took the spirit of Talbot House (Toc H in the Morse code) and determined to perpetuate it; thus was born the world movement of Toc H. The ancient parish Church

of All Hallow's, Barking-by-the-Tower, London, to which he was
appointed by the Archbishop of Canterbury in 1922, became the
Guild Church of the Movement and from its boundaries he has
exercised an international ministry. Now seventy-seven years old,
Tubby has been honored by Church and State, written some of the
best prose in the language, and been responsible for over two-
thousand men taking Orders in the Anglican Communion.

DOROTHY DAY

Dorothy Day is a woman whose mild manner conceals a character
of unusual strength. She is among the rare Christians of our time
who have deliberately paid for their principles with minor martyr-
doms—poverty, loneliness, imprisonment—all of which have failed
to deter her obsessive interest in the poor and outcast of every race
and creed. She has known pain, but its rigors have enlarged, not
narrowed and embittered, the spirit. Her career has been bizarre, to
say the least—lost causes, left-wing journalism, common-law marriage, suffragette marches—but the beginnings were conventional
enough. She was born in 1897 in Brooklyn Heights, New York, an
eminently respectable neighborhood flavored with Episcopalianism,
but the family early moved to California, and later to Chicago. It
was at the University of Chicago that her youthful Episcopalianism
began to wilt before the repulsive spectacle of urban poverty: "The
ugliness of life in a world which professed to be Christian appalled
me," she wrote in her autobiography, *The Long Loneliness*. "I felt
my faith had nothing in common with that of Christians around
me." Thus began the long, circuitous trek from Socialism to Catholicism, with fervid activity on radical journals—*The Masses,
The Liberator, The New Masses*—until her conversion in 1927.
Her meeting with Peter Maurin in 1932 was unquestionably the
turning point of her life. He was a French-born Roman Catholic
layman who for years had wandered the States peddling a kind of

"nature" philosophy, a curious amalgam of reality and fantasy that probably owed more to the English Distributists and Peter Kropotkin than to practical common sense. It was the virtue of Miss Day to discern its positive qualities and use them. Together they launched the *Catholic Worker,* a provocative periodical expressing Christian views on unpopular subjects; as its circulation increased, so did the mendicants hammering at the door of Miss Day's tenement apartment in lower Manhattan. The first of the famous Houses of Hospitality was born to meet their needs, and gradually, in town and country, they became havens of refuge for the embattled and poverty-stricken. Her own books tell the story movingly but omit to add, in the words of a noted cleric, that Dorothy Day is a woman who has placed her stamp on American Catholicism.

T. S. ELIOT

Thomas Stearns Eliot is a remote man whose fastidious personality has dominated the world of poetry for well-nigh a generation. His modesty may be contrived when he writes:

> How unpleasant to meet Mr. Eliot!
> With his features of clerical cut,
> And his brow so grim
> And his mouth so prim. . . .[1]

But in point of fact few people have had the opportunity to appraise his own assessment; those that have declare him to be charming and urbane. Eliot's work may not be the key to his personal character, but it has been a progression from awareness of the horror and boredom of contemporary living—"shape without form, shade without color, paralyzed force, gesture without motion"—to the certitude of faith articulated most perfectly in his poem *Ash Wed-*

[1] From *The Complete Poems and Plays of T. S. Eliot.*

nesday. His birthplace, St. Louis, Missouri (the year was 1888), seems an unlikely nursery for the middle-aged declaration that he was "Anglo-Catholic in religion, royalist in politics, and classicist in literature," but residence at Harvard, the Sorbonne, and Merton College, Oxford, possibly confirmed a bias that was instinctively conservative. Oddly, his early poems were anything but conservative; he became the "apostle of disillusionment" and his major work of this period, *The Waste Land,* was hailed as "genius" or execrated as "gibberish" according to the age of the critic. He became a naturalized British citizen in 1927, and has received both the Order of Merit and the Nobel Prize for his contributions to literature.

BILLY GRAHAM

The real wonder of William Franklin Graham is that such a phenomenon exists at all in the twentieth century. And yet, not only does he exist, but in a world notoriously indifferent to religion he has preached more words to more people in more places on the unpopular subject of "sin and salvation" than almost any man in the history of the Christian evangel. Apart from the skillful use of radio and television—which has expanded his audiences enormously—he has attracted crowds up to a hundred thousand in many parts of the world, and there is little doubt that the machine-gun delivery and stabbing finger of Billy Graham have been a climacteric experience in the lives of thousands of newly converted, from Sydney, Australia, to Madison Square Garden in New York. There are those who compare him to Billy Sunday, but the similarity between the hell-fire revivalist of a former generation and the quiet-mannered Graham is slight; the forty-four-year-old Graham is a gentler man, with an elusive charm that instantly communicates itself to people of every type and station. A native of North Carolina, he was converted at the age of seventeen and left his parents' farm to study for the Baptist ministry at the Florida Bible Institute in Tampa, later (after ordination) taking a degree from Wheaton College, near Chicago. It was his interest in Youth for Christ, an organization designed to bring young people to God, that started him on his travels with George Shea and Cliff Barrows, a youthful trombonist who was to become his platform manager. He was appointed President of Northwestern Schools, an evangelical college, in 1948, but the mounting pressure of speaking engagements eventually forced him to resign from both the college and Youth for Christ. Thenceforth Billy was on his own, with one room and two hired secretaries in Minneapolis. That was in 1950—five years later the Billy Graham Evangelistic Association, Inc., was a vast organization with an annual budget in excess of $2,000,000. But if the figures are many and big, Billy has proved that quantity and quality are not always ill-matched, and there are numberless people in the unlikeliest places who thank God in their prayers for evangelist Billy Graham, the man who says with engaging modesty, "I'm not an intellectual or a theologian. It's not me who draws the crowds. It's God."

TREVOR HUDDLESTON

For twelve years Trevor Huddleston lived amid human misery and walked in the shadow of a people's despair. "Hell," he wrote in his book *Naught for Your Comfort,* "is not a bad description of South Africa, nor a very great exaggeration. . . . When you are in hell you see good but you can never reach it: you know that you are made for God, but between yourself and Him 'there is a great gulf fixed.' It is not a bad description of the ultimate meaning of 'apartheid.' " But Huddleston, seeing the good, tried to reach it and lead his native South African parishioners to it with all the tender passion of Christian love. It was not easy. He lived with his people, he shared and suffered with them, and they came to love the spare, dedicated Englishman with the same intensity that South African officialdom hated him. He showed the native African, despite the evidence of his sufferings, that love is a universal coinage, and it is a man's heart that matters, not his skin. His training, though apparently conventional, had well fitted him for his task. Born in 1913, the son of Captain Sir Ernest and Lady Huddleston, he was educated at Lancing, Christ Church, Oxford, and Wells Theological College before being priested in the Anglican Communion in 1935. He joined the Community of the Resurrection, Mirfield, and was professed in 1941: henceforth he was a priest to the world and not merely an English locality. He was assigned in 1943 to be priest-in-charge of the Sophiatown and Orlando Anglican Mission, Diocese of Johannesburg. The appointment was conventional, but not the personality appointed. He had a burning, and from the official point of view, highly inconvenient belief in the Incarnation, and the power of its applied doctrine to heal the fissions of society. His singular identification with the pains and needs of his African flock were never more movingly expressed than when he wrote, "Whenever I hear old Martha's confession, I am near to tears, I only want to kneel and wash those old and weary feet." He was recalled to England by his Order in 1955, became Prior of its London house in 1958, and returned to Africa in 1960 to become Bishop of Masasi, Tanganyika.

MARTIN LUTHER KING

Martin Luther King is a great leader of men. His singularity however lies in the deftness with which he has matched his moral genius with the crisis of the hour. In a time of racial turmoil he speaks not merely for the colored people of the American South but, by implication, for degraded minorities everywhere: he pleads for the recognition of human rights and opens the door to action with the words, "only when people themselves begin to act are the rights on paper given life blood." This statement is a key to the character of the man who at thirty-five is regarded as the leader of the Negro cause in the United States and who, drawing "the spirit of passive resistance from the teachings of Jesus, and the techniques of execution from Gandhi," has suffered assault and imprisonment in his steady witness for racial integration. A Southerner by birth, he raced through the Negro schools of his native Atlanta, marked up an extraordinary record at the predominantly white Crozer Theological Seminary, and took a Doctorate in Philosophy from Boston University. His ambition was to serve, as did his father, in a Baptist pastorate in his native state, but the sight of the squalid misery of his people, and the white man's contemptuous denial of the Negro's basic rights, forced him to step beyond the accepted limits of parish life into the frenetic world of civil agitation. He was relatively unknown when he was elected president of the Montgomery Improvement Association, but within a few months his name was on every lip; his masterful handling of the year-long boycott of the Montgomery transit system revealed the mind of a born strategist whose most potent weapon was "action through non-violence." He achieved his immediate goal—Negroes and whites in Montgomery ride side by side on integrated buses for the first time in history—and, indirectly, created an image of himself (and, by the same token, the "ideal Negro") that, depending on the person, is feared or revered throughout the South. Much remains to be done, and Martin Luther King will endure much in doing it, but his words have the timeless and imperial tone of the prophet—"Love or perish! Christian love can bring brotherhood on earth. There is an element of God in every man—the strong man is the man who can stand up for his rights and not hit back."

RONALD KNOX

The world of Ronald Arbuthnott Knox was instinct with humor and wit. They gave to his learning a kind of astringent grace but brought with them, too, the derivative virtues of tolerance and understanding. "Humor," he once wrote, "is nothing less than a fresh window of the soul," and whatever he penned or thought was done with sparkle and originality. His *Essays in Satire,* which are unique in the language, scarcely prepare one for the disciplined erudition evident in his brilliant translation of the Bible. Perhaps his diversified talents owed as much to environment as to inborn genius. The youngest of four sons and two daughters in the rigidly evangelical household of Edmund A. Knox, sometime Lord Bishop of Manchester, he was more expansively nurtured at Eton and Balliol College, Oxford, among a coterie of rare spirits that included Julian Grenfell, Patrick Shaw-Stewart, and Charles Lister. He was already a spokesman for the Anglo-Catholic party when ordained to the priesthood of the Church of England and the same year, 1912, he became the Chaplain of Trinity, Oxford, of which he was a Fellow and Lecturer. Two years after his reception into the Roman Communion in 1917, he was priested "on his own patrimony" (this gave him complete freedom of movement), and in 1926 he was appointed to the Catholic Chaplaincy of his old University. Ronald Knox left Oxford finally in 1939. The remaining years were spent in the country houses of his many friends, and it was there that he did much of his most important writing. He died in Somerset at the age of sixty-nine in 1957, leaving behind at least one imperishable legacy—the Ronald Knox translation of the Bible.

JOHN LaFARGE

John LaFarge comes from a family that has carved deep furrows into the social and cultural life of North America. The family, it is true, may have inherited more than a fair share of the protean genius of a formidable ancestor, Benjamin Franklin: but for several generations it has produced a succession of highly articulate pedagogues, writers, and scholars to observe and interpret the changing facets of American life. The intellectual assurance of John LaFarge is probably largely the result of this heritage, but the tolerance of his civilized being is wholly personal, for he firmly believes, with Sir Thomas Browne, that "the most amiable man is your truly devout man." The son of a noted American writer and mural painter, he was born on February 13, 1880, at Newport, Rhode Island, and left Harvard in 1901 to study for the Roman Catholic priesthood at the University of Innsbruck, Austria: after his ordination to the priesthood in 1905 he entered the Maryland-New York Province of the Society of Jesus. He was a born teacher, with a gift for popular exposition that inevitably took him beyond the classroom into the arena of national affairs; his editorship of *America,* the great Catholic weekly, was memorable for its impartiality and balanced perspicacity. A steady stream of books—among them *Jesuits in Modern Times, Inter-Racial Justice, The Race Question and the Negro, The Manner Is Ordinary*—and articles in periodicals all over the world, revealed a mind at once spacious and inquiring, one to whom God and justice were synonymous. His championship of the Negro is legendary. Life, he admits, is illogical, but if a man's skin can become dark from an excess of light, no soul has yet been blackened by an excess of love. His interests are greatly diversified, and have extended far beyond racial problems. A list of the learned societies with which he is associated testifies to an unwavering devotion to the world of scholarship. He is a Fellow of the American Academy of Arts and Sciences, and one of his proudest distinctions is the World Brotherhood Award.

BORIS PASTERNAK

The rock-hewn face of Boris Pasternak, with its compassionate mouth and brooding eyes, has become so familiar with the reading public that it is forgotten that until the late 1950s he was almost unknown in the Western world, apart from an informed group of the literati. His genius burst upon us with the effulgence of a new sun, and *Dr. Zhivago* introduced men to the immensities and tortures of the Russian soul, to a strange, ambivalent world of disillusionment and faith in the human spirit. It was not for nothing that its author had written,

> In everything I strive to reach
> The very kernel:
> In work and in exploring ways,
> In pangs of heart.[2]

Born of gifted Jewish parents—his father was a well-known painter, his mother a concert pianist—in Moscow, 1890, he embraced the Orthodox Faith years after his formal schooling at Moscow and Marburg (Germany) Universities; and his faith often illumines an individualism that is rare indeed in modern Russia. As a youth he lived in a home thronged with the literary and artistic great. His first love was music, inspired by the blazing genius of Scriabin— "Lord, what music it was! . . . as new as the forest, breathing life and freshness, playfully elemental, and free like a fallen angel." But literature soon took first place and the image of Tolstoy, he wrote, "stalked me through life." Despite the enormous popularity of the novel *Dr. Zhivago,* Pasternak is regarded by his compatriots, and most exiled Russian critics, as the greatest lyrical poet in the U.S.S.R.: sadly enough, much of his creativity was stanched by official opposition. His acceptance of the Nobel Prize for Literature and his subsequent refusal of it is a dark story whose details are not fully known, but something of the agony of this man's soul— he died in 1961—comes through to us when he cries,

> I am lost like a beast tracked down,
> Somewhere men live in freedom and light.[3]

[2] From *The Poetry of Boris Pasternak,* trans. by George Reavey (New York, G. P. Putnam's Sons, 1959). Reprinted with the permission of G. Putnam's Sons.
[3] *Ibid.*

POPE PIUS XII

For the greater part of his life Eugenio Maria Giuseppe Giovanni Pacelli was a man whose prime concern was the peace of the world. When Albert Camus, the French-Algerian writer, stated in 1948, before the Dominican Monastery of Latour-Marbourg, in reference to the Second World War: "I waited for a great voice to speak up in Rome. I, an unbeliever? Precisely. For I knew that the spirit would be lost if it did not utter a cry of condemnation when faced with force. It seems that that voice did speak up. But I assure you that millions of men like me did not hear it . . . ," he, and those for whom he spoke, must have been distracted indeed, because the voice of Eugenio Pacelli, Pope Pius XII, had rung out with brilliant clarity in addresses, encyclicals, and countless audiences to denounce war and the calculated cruelties of godless men. Few men of our time have spoken with such empirical insight into the disruptive forces that have so tragically smashed a whole way of life, and few have been more admirably equipped to suggest the means of restoration within the context of Christianity. Born in Rome in 1876, he was early marked for his exceptional gifts. Two years after his ordination to the priesthood in 1899 he entered the service of the Papal Secretariat of State and by the age of forty-one he was Apostolic Nuncio to Bavaria and Titular Archbishop of Sardia: twelve years later he was appointed to the Sacred College of Cardinals, and in 1930 he took office as Papal Secretary of State. It was while he was serving in this post that he visited South America and took cognizance of its serious educational problems. His visit to the United States in 1936 was notable for the friendship he formed with President Franklin D. Roosevelt, who in 1940 sent a personal representative to the Vatican. The elevation of Cardinal Pacelli to the Papal See in 1939 was regarded as the logical sequence to a remarkable career, although he was the first Papal Secretary of State to be elected in centuries and the first Roman pope since 1730. His

Pontificate, the twelfth longest in the history of the Papacy, witnessed, among many official acts, the creation of over a score of non-Italian cardinals from twenty-one nations and the establishment of four pontifical universities in South America, besides vigorous pronouncements in the field of social reform. He died in October 1958 at Castel Gandolfo.

ALBERT SCHWEITZER

Few men of our time are more variously gifted than Albert Schweitzer, who has been called, not unjustifiably, "the Leonardo da Vinci of the twentieth century." Theologian, philosopher, musicologist, surgeon and physician, his mind has a staggering circumference that is matched by a humanitarianism which, like St. Francis of Assisi's, embraces not only man but Brer Fox and Brother Dandelion. Born in Günsbach, Alsace, eighty-six years ago, he was an inheritor of both French and German cultures although, he once confessed, "I dream in German." A brilliant academic career brought him a theological professorship at the age of twenty-one; before he was thirty he had published a treatise on the religious philosophy of Kant and was recognized as one of the world's foremost authorities on Bach. Turning his back upon the enviable prizes of European scholarship, he qualified as a doctor of medicine and in 1913 opened his first hospital at Lambaréné, using an old fowl-house as his consulting room. Gradually the news of his struggle against the deadliest enemies of the West African native—leprosy and sleeping sickness—reached the ears of Europe, whose admiration turned to wonder at the reinforcement of his genius by a steady flow of books on Africa, theology, philosophy and music. He paid for his work by periodic visits to Europe, where he lectured and gave organ recitals. In 1954 he received the Nobel Prize for Peace. He is, it has been said, one of the few truly great men in a century that too frequently adulates the near-great.

WILLIAM TEMPLE

William Temple has been described as a man of "magnificent intellectual gestures," and certainly the adjective "Olympian" is the most applicable to his personality. "Had he lived," wrote Cyril Garbett, the former Archbishop of York, "he would have been the greatest figure ever to occupy the See of Canterbury," and there is no doubt that for nearly a quarter of a century his influence extended far beyond his own country and communion. His father, Frederick Temple, a celebrated headmaster and prelate, was the only Archbishop of Canterbury in England's long history whose son became an even more distinguished occupant of the See. By heritage and training he was destined for statesmanship, but, through native genius, he was perhaps more fitted than most men of his time to interpret the restless spirit of the twentieth century. Born in 1881 at the Palace, Exeter, during his father's tenure of the diocese, and educated at Rugby and Balliol, he was successively a philosophy don at Queen's College, Oxford, headmaster of Repton, Rector of St. James's, Piccadilly, Canon of Westminster, Bishop of Manchester and Archbishop of York, where he labored for thirteen years before being translated to Canterbury. "To a man of my generation," wrote George Bernard Shaw, "an Archbishop of Temple's enlightenment was a realized impossibility," and it was no mischance, but genuine humanity, that led him to join the British Labor Party shortly after becoming Bishop of Manchester or to remain President of the Workers' Education Association for sixteen years. During those busy and exacting years he found time to publish, among other things, *Readings in St. John's Gospel* which, in the words of one critic, "will take a high and honored place among the best devotional literature which the greatest of the Gospels has inspired"; and his Gifford Lectures published under the title *Nature, Man and God* have long been regarded as an outstanding contribution to modern theological thought. He died in October 1944, at the age of sixty-four, two years after his enthronement at Canterbury.

PAUL TILLICH

There is a gothic grandeur about the thought of Paul Tillich that has sometimes mystified scholars and, not infrequently, brought consolation and hope to lesser people. Born in Germany—a country peculiarly productive of philosophers and theologians—in 1887, he "encountered the conception of the Infinite" at the age of eight and, from then on, the greater part of his life has been spent in the search for truth, or "ultimate concern" as he calls it. There are those, among them Karl Barth, who distrust his interpretations, and the theologian Nels Ferré has called him "the most dangerous theological leader alive": dangerous or not, he has attempted to resolve the classic antilogy of faith and doubt, and in the "dialectical conversation" of his more popular books—*The Protestant Era, The New Being, The Courage To Be,* and others—he has confronted the "state of anxiety" in man's existence. No doubt, the Teutonic depth and thoroughness of his thinking was derived more from his home atmosphere (his father was a prominent Lutheran minister) than from the national tradition; but by the time he had left the University of Halle and was a Lutheran pastor in Berlin, it appeared that the intellectual life had all the answers: "It still seemed possible then to sit in the center of the world and to be able to understand everything." The First World War shattered the illusion, and his army chaplaincy brought him into touch with human misery in its acutest form: "Much of my German classical philosophy broke down," he wrote, ". . . the traditional concept of God was dead." After teaching appointments at various universities —he was dismissed from Frankfurt University by the Hitler Government—he came to the United States in 1933. His voice was soon heard in the land, and today he is widely regarded as America's foremost Protestant thinker, who has given unified meaning to Protestant theology. His three-volume *Systematic Theology* is one of the intellectual achievements of our time.